CTEL California Teachers of English Learners
Teacher Certification Exam

By: Sharon Wynne, M.S.

XAMonline, INC.
Boston

To obtain permission(s) to use the material from this work for any purpose including workshops or seminars, please submit a written request to

XAMonline, Inc.
25 First Street, Suite 106
Cambridge, MA 02141
Toll Free 1-800-509-4128
Email: info@xamonline.com
Web: www.xamonline.com
Fax: 1-617-583-5552

Library of Congress Cataloging-in-Publication Data
Wynne, Sharon A.

CTEL California Teachers of English Learners Teacher Certification / Sharon A. Wynne.
    ISBN: 978-1-60787-025-8, 1st edition
1.CTEL: California Teachers of English Learners 2. Study Guides. 3. CTEL
4. Teachers' Certification & Licensure. 5. Careers

Disclaimer:
The opinions expressed in this publication are the sole works of XAMonline and were created independently from the National Education Association (NES), Educational Testing Service (ETS), or any State Department of Education, National Evaluation Systems or other testing affiliates. Between the time of publication and printing, state specific standards as well as testing formats and website information may change that are not included in part or in whole within this product. XAMonline develops sample test questions, and they reflect similar content as on real tests; however, they are not former tests. XAMonline assembles content that aligns with state standards but makes no claims nor guarantees teacher candidates a passing score. Numerical scores are determined by testing companies such as NES or ETS and then are compared with individual state standards. A passing score varies from state to state.

Printed in the United States of America   œ-1

CTEL: California Teachers of English Learners
ISBN: 978-1-60787-025-8

TABLE OF CONTENTS

SUBAREA III.   CULTURE AND INCLUSION

**DOMAIN VI.   CULTURE AND CULTURAL DIVERSITY AND THEIR
RELATIONSHIP TO ACADEMIC ACHIEVEMENT**

SUBAREA   I   LANGUAGE AND LANGUAGE DEVELOPMENT

DOMAIN I   LANGUAGE STRUCTURE AND USE

COMPETENCY 1.0   Phonology and Morphology

Skill 1.1   Demonstrate knowledge of features of English phonology (e.g., phonemes, intonation patterns, pitch, modulation), with a focus on features that may inhibit communication for different language groups.

Phonology can be defined as "the way in which speech sounds form patterns" (Diaz-Rico and Weed, 1995).   Phonology is a subset of linguistics, which studies the organization and systems of sound within a particular language. Phonology is based on the theory that every native speaker unconsciously retains the sound structure of that language and is more concerned with the sounds than with the physical process of creating those sounds.

When babies babble or make what we call "baby sounds," they are actually experimenting with all of the sounds represented in all languages. As they learn a specific language, they become more proficient in the sounds of that language and forget how to make sounds that they don't need or use.

PHONEMES, PITCH, AND STRESS

Phonemes, pitch, and stress are all components of phonology. Because they all affect the meaning of communications, they are variables that English Language Learners (ELLs) must recognize and learn.

Phonology analyzes the sound structure of the given language by:

- determining which phonetic sounds have the most significance
- explaining how these sounds influence a native speaker of the language

For example, the Russian alphabet has a consonant, which, when pronounced, sounds like the word *rouge* in French. English speakers typically have difficulty pronouncing this sound pattern, because inherently they know this is not a typical English sound (Díaz-Rico and Weed, 1995).

Mastering a sound that does not occur in the learner's first language requires ongoing repetition, both hearing the sound and attempting to say it. The older the learner, the more difficult this process is, especially if the learner has only spoken one language before reaching puberty. Correct pronunciation may literally require years of practice because initially the learner may not hear the sound correctly. Expecting an ELL to master a foreign pronunciation quickly leads to frustration for both the teacher and the learner. With enough focused repetition, however, the learner may eventually hear the difference and then be able to imitate it. Inadequate listening and speaking practice will result in a persistent heavy accent.

Phonemes are the smallest units of sound that affect meaning, i.e., that distinguish two words. In English, there are approximately forty-four speech sounds but only twenty-six letters, so the sounds, when combined, become words. For this reason, English is not considered a phonetic language—a language in which there is a one-to-one correspondence between letters and sounds. Consider the two words, *pin* and *bin*. The only difference is the first consonant: the *p* in *pin* and the *b* in *bin*. This makes the sounds *p* and *b* phonemes in English, because the difference in sound creates a difference in meaning.

Focusing on phonemes to provide pronunciation practice allows students to have fun while they learn to recognize and say sounds. Pairs or groups of words that have a set pattern make learning easier. For example, students can practice saying or thinking of words that rhyme but begin with a different phoneme, such as *tan*, *man*, *fan*, and *ran*. Other groups of words might start with the same phoneme followed by different vowel sounds, such as *ten*, *ton*, *tan*, and *tin*. This kind of alliteration can be expanded into tongue twisters that students find challenging and entertaining.

Vowels and consonants should be introduced in a deliberate order to allow combinations that form real words, although "made-up" words that have no real meaning in English can also be encouraged when introducing new sounds.

Pitch determines the context or meaning of words or series of words. A string of words can communicate more than one meaning, for example, depending on whether it is presented as a question or statement. The phrase "I can't go" is a statement if the pitch or intonation falls. However, the same phrase becomes the question "I can't go?" if the pitch or intonation rises for the word *go*.

Stress can occur at a word or sentence level. At the word level, stresses on different syllables can actually modify a word's meaning. Consider the word *conflict*. To pronounce it as a noun, one would stress the first syllable, as in *CONflict*. However, to use it as a verb, one would stress the second syllable, as in *conFLICT*.

In different dialects the same word is sometimes pronounced differently, even though both pronunciations have the same meaning. In some parts of the United States the word *insurance* is pronounced by stressing the second syllable, while in other parts of the country the first syllable is stressed.

At the sentence level, stress can also be used to vary meaning. In the following questions, notice how the meaning changes according to the stressed words:

>**He** did that? (Emphasis is on the person)
>He **did** that? (Emphasis is on the action)
>He did **that**? (Emphasis is on the object of the action)

This type of meaning differentiation is not easy for most ELL students to grasp, and requires innovative teaching, such as acting out the three different meanings. Still, since pitch and stress can change the meaning of a sentence completely, students must learn to recognize these differences. Not recognizing sarcasm or anger can cause students considerable problems in their academic and everyday endeavors.

Unlike languages such as Spanish or French, English has multiple pronunciations of vowels and consonants which contribute to making it a difficult language to learn. Phonetic rules are critical in learning to read and write, in spite of their numerous exceptions, but they do little to assist in the development of listening and speaking skills.

PHONOGRAPHEMICS

Phonographemics refers to the study of letters and letter combinations. Unlike most languages, in English one symbol can represent many phonemes. While some phonetic rules apply, English has numerous exceptions, which make it a complex language for nonnative speakers to learn.

In teaching English to speakers of other languages, the wide variation of phonemes represented by a single symbol must be taught and *drilled*. If it is difficult for native speakers to learn the English spelling system, it's a great leap for nonnative speakers. Graphemes should be introduced long after spoken English. Students must first begin to be able to speak and hear the language before they can be taught to spell it.

The phonology of English is an important component of an English for Speakers of Other Languages (ESOL) program.

Phonographemic differences between words of English are a common source of confusion and thus need to be taught explicitly with plenty of learning activities to enable learners to acquire them sufficiently. Some areas of focus for the ESOL classroom include:

- **Homonyms:** Word forms that have two or more meanings, e.g.,, *can* (to be able) / *can* (a container)
- **Homographs:** Two or more words that have the same spelling or pronunciation but different meanings, e.g.,, *stalk* (part of a plant) / *stalk* (follow)

- **Homophones:** Two or more words that have the same pronunciation but different meanings and spelling, e.g.,, *wood/would*, *cite/sight*, *to/too/two*
- **Heteronyms:** Two or more words that have the same spelling but a different pronunciation and meaning, e.g.,, *Polish/polish*

Some useful activities for instruction would be to identify misspelled words, to recognize multiple meanings of words and sentences, to spell words correctly in a given context, and to match words with their meanings.

Skill 1.2   Analyze how English Learners' aural comprehension and pronunciation may be affected when English words contain phonemes that are unfamiliar to them or that do not transfer positively from the primary language (e.g., digraphs; diphthongs; schwa; initial, medial, and final consonant clusters) and identify strategies for supporting positive transfer from the primary language and for promoting English Learners' auditory discrimination and production of English phonemes (i.e., ability to distinguish, identify, and manipulate phonemes and phonological patterns). Apply knowledge of basic sound patterns in English reading and writing with a focus on helping English Learners avoid interference from their primary language due to nontransferable features.

English Learners' aural comprehension and pronunciation may be affected by unfamiliar phonemes or those that do not transfer positively from their primary language. Some of the problematic phonemes are digraphs, diphthongs, and the schwa sound.

A **digraph** is any two letters that form a single sound, such as /ph/ in phone or /ea/ in read. For example, the two distinct /th/ digraphs found in *the*, *there*, and *they* or in *three* and *threshold* do not occur in many languages, such as Spanish. Mispronouncing words with this digraph is common. For example, pronouncing *tree* when the speaker intended to say *three* causes misunderstandings.

A **diphthong** occurs when two vowels combine to form a sound that slides from one to the other, such as /oy/ in *boy* or /ou/ in *house*. The most common diphthongs in English are /ai/, /aw/, and /oi/. These sounds cause difficulties in both pronunciation and comprehension. It is common for English Learners to substitute a sound that is found in the first language for the more difficult diphthong.

The **schwa** sound is made by every vowel in English: /a/ as in *about*, /e/ as in *the*, /i/ as in *pencil*, /o/ as in *onion*, /u/ as in *but*. Since the schwa sound does not occur in Spanish, as in several other languages, it is common for speakers to substitute more familiar vowel sounds, often with a loss of accuracy in pronunciation or comprehension by the listener.

When the mouth is trying for the first time to form sounds that are new to the speaker, it requires effort and concentration to achieve accuracy, and errors in pronunciation and aural comprehension often persist into the most advanced levels of English acquisition. This factor affects the teaching of literacy. In teaching beginning reading to a native speaker, it is common to begin with the short vowel sounds: /a/ is for *apple*, /e/ is for *elephant*, etc. Since it is an extremely difficult task for a student whose first language is Spanish to hear the differences among, for example, *pat, pet, pit, pot,* and *put*, it creates frustration for both the teacher and the student to insist upon perfect pronunciation or aural comprehension in the beginning or even intermediate stages of literacy.

For ELLs learning a new language, it is vital for native speakers to model the language. There are also specific issues that ELLs need to address in order to improve their language skills. To improve their pronunciation, ELLs need to work on:

- **Pronunciation:** To work on pronunciation, ELLs can find a dictionary and study its phonetic alphabet. Once they are familiar with it, they can choose ten to twelve words from a book and try to transcribe them and then pronounce them.
- **Intonation:** Some researchers doubt whether this can be taught (Barnes, 1988). However, it is important because one's message may be misconstrued if the speaker uses an incorrect intonation pattern. One exercise is for ELLs to listen to a passage and mark the intonation pattern using forward slashes or backward slashes over the syllables or words to indicate a rising or falling pattern. Curved lines can also be used to indicate the appropriate rising and falling of the voice.
- **Stress:** Stress means accent. To teach ELLs how to accent words, dictionary assignments can be used. For sentences or longer texts, ELLs can mark the stress on words or syllables as the teacher dictates a short passage.

Skill 1.3   Demonstrate knowledge of features of English morphology and principles of English word formation (e.g., morphemes, combining a root and affix, recognizing common roots derived from Greek and Latin that have English cognates, combining two lexical morphemes to create a compound, using inflectional endings), with a focus on English morphemes that may inhibit communication for different language groups.

Morphology refers to the process of how the words of a language are formed to create meaningful messages. Awareness of the principles of morphology in English allows teachers to provide meaningful activities that will help ELLs in the process of language acquisition.

Morphemic analysis requires breaking a word down into its component parts to determine its meaning. It shows the relationship between the root or base word and the prefix and/or suffix to determine the word's meaning.

A **morpheme** is the smallest unit of a language system that has meaning. These units are more commonly known as the root word, the prefix, and the suffix. They cannot be broken down into smaller units.

- **The root word or base word** is the key to understanding a word, because this is where the actual meaning is determined.
- **A prefix** acts as a syllable, which appears in front of the root or base word and can alter the meaning of the root or base word.
- **A suffix** is a letter or letters, which are added to the end of the word and can alter the original tense or meaning of the root or base word.

Skill 1.4   Apply knowledge of morphology in order to identify strategies, including word analysis, for promoting relevant aspects of English Learners' language development (e.g., vocabulary, spelling, fluency).

The following is an example of how morphemic analysis can be applied to a word:

- Choose a root or base word, such as *kind*.
- Create as many new words as possible by changing the prefix and suffix.
- New words would include *unkind*, *kindness*, *mankind*, and *kindly*.

Learning common roots, prefixes, and suffixes greatly helps ELLs to decode unfamiliar words. This can make a big difference in how well a student understands written language. Students who can decode unfamiliar words become less frustrated when reading in English and, as a result, are likely to read more. They have greater comprehension and their language skills improve more quickly. Having the tools to decode unfamiliar words enables ELL students to perform better on standardized tests because they are more likely to understand the question and answer choices.

Guessing at the meaning of words should be encouraged. Too often students become dependent on translating dictionaries, and do not develop morphemic analysis skills. Practice should include identifying roots, prefixes, and suffixes, as well as using morphemic knowledge to form new words.

ESOL learners need to understand the structure of words in English, and how words can be created and altered. Some underlying principles of the morphology of English include:

1. Morphemes can be free and able to stand by themselves (e.g.,, *chair*, *bag*) or they can be bound or derivational, needing other morphemes to create meaning (e.g.,, *read-able*, *en-able*).
2. Knowledge of the meanings of derivational morphemes such as prefixes and suffixes enables students to decode word meanings and create words in the language through word analysis, (e.g.,, *un-happy* means not happy).

3. Some morphemes in English provide grammatical rather than semantic information to words and sentences (e.g.,, *of*, *the*, and).
4. Words can be combined in English to create new compound words (e.g.,, *key* + *chain* = *keychain*).

Some principles of morphology from the native language can be transferred to English and may promote or interfere with the process of learning the second language.

Skill 1.5   Demonstrate knowledge of phonological and morphological skills that promote fluent reading and writing (e.g., organized, systematic, explicit phonics; decoding skills; application of spelling patterns and sound-symbol codes [orthography]; structural analysis; application of students' prior knowledge of the primary language to promote English language development in reading and writing).

Phonological decoding skills are closely related to prereading. Other phonological knowledge useful to students includes recognizing and creating rhymes, learning how to syllabicate, and phonemics. Only by explicitly and systematically teaching these skills can English Language Development (ELD) be achieved. ELD is also augmented by consistent spelling instruction. Words related to content need to be taught in an organized fashion. Structural analysis would include morphological analysis of the base word, prefixes, and suffixes. Students whose language is based on the Roman alphabet and has the same Latin basis as many English words may benefit from using their primary language to expand on the concepts being delivered in the English language classroom.

Skill 1.6   Apply strategies for identifying and addressing English Learners' difficulties related to phonology and morphology (e.g., applying principles of contrastive analysis to determine differences between the primary language and English, utilizing contrastive analysis resources in California State-adopted Reading/Language Arts/English Language Development [RLA/ELD] programs, using students' prior knowledge of the primary language to promote English language development, applying vocabulary strategies such as context clues, word structure, and apposition to determine the meaning of unknown words).

Contrastive analysis involves comparing and contrasting the linguistic features of students' primary language and English. By explaining to students how features of their native language compare with the English language, students can acquire a technique to support their ELD without necessarily having to rely on others. For example, the Spanish infinitives end in *-ar*, *-er* and *-ir*. These translate to the infinitive form in English: *to* + a verb. Another example from Spanish is the *-cion* (*transportacion*) word ending which is translated usually to *-tion'*(*transportation*) in English, but sometimes it may be

-cion (*suspicion*). Contrastive analysis increases students' awareness of language differences and improves vocabulary.

Other techniques for improving vocabulary are emphasis of context clues (What are the people/characters doing in the picture? What kind of weather are they having? Where is this taking place—in the city, in a park, on a beach? etc.), analysis of the word structure (What is the root/base word? What does the prefix mean? the suffix? How does this change the base word?), and apposition (What is the appositive in the first paragraph? Who is the teacher? Who is Mr. Brown?).

Skill 1.7   Demonstrate the ability to evaluate English Language Development (ELD) programs for adequate attention to the areas of phonology and morphology.

There are several important issues to consider in the evaluation of programs concerning adequate development of phonology and morphology. Both the National Reading Panel (2000) and the International Reading Association (1996-1997) have endorsed the teaching of phonics as a key component in the teaching of reading. However, several questions need to be addressed in evaluating programs: Which type of phonics (synthetic, analytic, linguistic, or a combination), how much time, and what kind of activities?

Alderson (1992) set forth several key questions to be answered when evaluating programs:

- What is the purpose of the activity?
- Who is the activity for: all students or only those students who have not mastered the skill?
- Who is going to evaluate the activity: the teacher, the student, or the class?
- What kind of content is being taught?
- What methodology will be used: visual, aural, or a combination of both?
- When will the lesson be taught: before reading/spelling instruction, during the instruction, or after the instruction?

Garinger (2002) proposed a composite evaluation checklist when considering materials for classroom use:

A. Practical Considerations
- Value/Availability
  - Is it available locally?
  - Where can it be purchased (obtained)?
  - Cost-effectiveness?
- Layout/Physical Characteristics
  - Interesting? Attractive? Appropriate mixture of graphics and text?
  - Clear? Well organized? Effective use of headings?

- Cultural Component
    - o Target culture content? Accurate reflection of target culture?
    - o Free of stereotypes?
    - o Inclusive of all cultures? Sensitive?

B. Language-Related Considerations
- Skills (language and cognitive)
    - o Does it integrate the skills well? Does it offer a good balance? Does it focus on the one(s) it claims to?
- Language
    - o Authentic language?
    - o Variety?
    - o Recycling?
    - o Grading/sequencing?
- Exercises
    - o Is there a balance between free and controlled exercises?
    - o Promote communication?
    - o Meaningful?
    - o Allow for negotiation?
- User Definition
    - o Is it well defined?
    - o Does the text content accurately reflect this definition?
    - o Are there exact descriptions of what the students should be able to [do] once they have completed the texts (e.g.,, benchmark level)?

Texts and programs should take into consideration the students' different skill levels. As with all skills, students will need varying amounts of phonics instruction. Some will be able to read with little or no phonics instruction and other will need more intensive and direct teaching (Schumm, 2006). Assessment and differentiated instruction are very important when teaching phonology and morphology.

COMPETENCY 2.0   SYNTAX AND SEMANTICS

Skill 2.1   Demonstrate knowledge of syntactic classes (e.g., noun, verb, adjective, preposition), syntactic rules in English (e.g., verb tense, subject-verb agreement), and English sentence patterns.

Syntax involves the order in which words are arranged to create meaning. Different languages use different patterns for sentence structure. Syntax also refers to the rules for creating correct sentence patterns. English, like many other languages, is a subject-verb-object language, i.e., in most sentences the subject precedes the verb, and the object follows the verb. ELLs whose native language follows a subject-verb-object pattern will find it easier to master English syntax.

LANGUAGE ACQUISITION

The process of second-language acquisition includes forming generalizations about the new language and internalizing its rules. During the silent period, before learners are willing to attempt verbal communication, they are engaged in the process of building a set of syntactic rules for creating grammatically correct sentences in the second language. We don't yet fully understand the nature of this process, but we do know that learners must go through this process of observing, drawing conclusions about language constructs, and testing the validity of their conclusions. This is why learners benefit more from intense language immersion than from corrections.

Language acquisition is a gradual, hierarchical, and cumulative process. Learners must go through and master each stage in sequence, much like the stages Piaget theorized for learning in general. In terms of syntax, learners must master specific grammatical structures, first recognizing the difference between subject and predicate; putting subject before predicate; and learning more complex variations, such as questions, negatives, and relative clauses.

While all learners must pass through each stage to acquire the necessary language skills, learners use different approaches to mastering these skills. Some use cognitive processing procedures, thus their learning takes place more through thought processes. Other learners use psycholinguistic procedures, which employ speech practice as the principal means of learning.

Experts disagree on the exact definition of the stages, but a set of six general stages would include:

Stage of Development	Examples
1. Single words	I; throw; ball
2. S-V-O structure	I throw the ball.
3. *Wh-* fronting	Where are you?
Do fronting	Do you like me?
Adverb fronting	Today I go to school.
Negative + verb	She is not nice.
4. Y/N inversion	Do you know him? Yes, I know him.
Copula (linking v) inversion	Is he at school?
Particle shift	Take your hat off.
5. *Do* second	Why did she leave?
Auxiliary second	Where has he gone?
Negative *do* second	She does not live here.
6. Cancel inversion	I asked what she was doing.

Each progressive step requires the learner to use knowledge from the previous step, as well as new knowledge of the language. As ELLs progress to more advanced stages of syntax, they may react differently, depending on their ability to acquire the new knowledge needed for mastery. A learner who successfully integrates the new knowledge is a "standardizer"; he/she makes generalizations, eliminates erroneous conclusions, and increasingly uses syntactical rules correctly. However, for some learners, the next step may be more difficult than he/she can manage. These learners become "simplifiers"; they revert to syntactical rules learned at easier stages and fail to integrate the new knowledge. When patterns of errors reflect lower-level stages, the teacher must re-teach the new syntactical stage. If simplifiers are allowed to repeatedly use incorrect syntax, learning correct syntax becomes much more difficult.

Skill 2.2   Apply knowledge of syntactic rules and sentence patterns to provide accurate modeling of English syntax and to promote English Learners' communicative competence.

ELL students need to be exposed to authentic, natural English in the classroom setting as well as outside the classroom. To achieve this goal, the ESOL teacher should be a good language model. Foreigners frequently complain that English speakers swallow their words or sound as if they have mashed potatoes in their mouths. The teacher needs to be aware of this and speak slowly and distinctly, especially when communicating new information. This will help the ELLs become acquainted with the rhythm patterns of English.

Yet, teachers should not be afraid to expose students to nonnative speakers of English. Today, the number of nonnative speakers of English is far greater than the number of native English speakers! Teachers can provide students with opportunities to hear a variety of speakers through listening exercises using taped stories and music, CDs, videos, field trips, and classroom visitors. A wide range of experiences will maintain high motivation and promote language learning.

Skill 2.3 **Apply strategies for identifying and addressing English Learners' difficulties related to syntax (e.g., locating and using texts to learn about the syntax of English and students' home languages, applying principles of contrastive analysis, utilizing contrastive analysis resources in California State-adopted RLA/ELD programs; using students' prior knowledge of their primary language to promote English language development).**

Barring physical disabilities or isolation from other humans, language is universal. Developing language is a lifelong process in one's native language, and similar processes must be gone through to thoroughly acquire or learn a foreign language. Many studies have found that cognitive and academic development in the first language has an extremely important and positive effect on second-language learning (Bialystok, 1991; Collier, 1989, 1992; Garcia, 1994; Genesee, 1987, 1994; Thomas and Collier, 1995). It is, therefore, important that language learners continue to develop their first-language skills because the most gifted five-year-old is approximately halfway through the process of first-language development. From the ages of six to twelve, the child continues to acquire subtle phonological distinctions, vocabulary, semantics, syntax, formal discourse patterns, and the complexities of pragmatics in the oral system of his/her first language (Berko Gleason, 1993).

These skills can be transferred to learning a second language. When ELLs already know how to read and write in their first language, they can transfer many of their primary language skills to the target language. They have already learned the relationship between reading print and spoken language, that print can be used for many different things, and that writing conveys messages from its author. Grellet (1981) has stated that the "knowledge one brings to the text is often more important than what one finds in it." Thus, teachers can build on this previous knowledge and address specifics in English as they arise.

Collier emphasizes that students who do not reach a threshold of knowledge in their first language, including literacy, may experience cognitive difficulties in their second language (Collier, 1987; Collier and Thomas, 1989, Cummins, 1981, 1991; Thomas and Collier, 1995). Uninterrupted cognitive development is key. It is a disservice to parents and children to encourage the use of the second language instead of the first language at home, because both parents and students are working at a level below their actual cognitive maturity level when using the second language. While nonnative speakers in kindergarten through second or third grade may do well if schooled in English part or all of the day, from fourth grade through high school, students with little or no academic or cognitive development in their first language do less and less well as they move into the upper grades where academic and cognitive demands are greater (Collier, 1995).

Skill 2.4   Analyze English words, phrases, and sentences with respect to meaning (semantics).

Semantics encompasses the meanings of individual words as well as combinations of words. Native speakers have used their language to function in their daily lives at all levels. Through experience, they know the effects of intonation, connotation, and synonyms. This is not true of foreign speakers. In an ESOL class, ELD focuses on teaching what the native speaker already knows as quickly as possible. Beginning ESOL lesson plans should deliberately build a foundation that will enable students to meet more advanced objectives.

Teaching within a specific context helps students to understand the meaning of words and sentences. When students can remember the context in which they learn words and recall how the words were used, they retain that knowledge and can use it when different applications of the same words are introduced.

Using words in a variety of contexts helps students reach deeper understanding of the words. They can then guess at new meanings that are introduced in different contexts. For example, the word *conduct* can be taught in the context of conducting a meeting or an investigation. Later the word *conductor* can be used in various contexts that demonstrate some similarity but have distinctly different uses, such as a conductor of electricity, the conductor of a train, or the conductor of an orchestra.

Second-language learners must learn to translate words and sentences that they already understand in their primary language into the language they wish to acquire. This can be a daunting task because of the many ways meaning is created in English. Voice inflection, variations of meaning, variations of usage, and emphasis are among the factors that affect meaning. The lexicon of language includes the stored meaning, contextual meaning from word association, knowledge of pronunciation and grammar, and morphemes.

Skill 2.5   Apply strategies for identifying and addressing difficulties English Learners have with words, phrases, and sentences with respect to semantics (e.g., words with multiple meanings, false cognates, idioms).

Students can benefit from reinforcing the meaning of different semantic items in multiple ways by using the following techniques: semantic feature analysis, mapping, rehearsing, summarizing, and writing.

Words with multiple meanings should be studied in context, and it should be pointed out that words do have multiple meanings. One glance at the word *get* in an unabridged dictionary will illustrate the numerous ways this word can be used. A good way to illustrate this point would be to show students the many uses of different words and their function in sentences. Demonstrating how words are used in different ways in a sentence (e.g., as a noun or a verb) is another way to illustrate the point. "I need a *record* <noun> of my *recording* <gerund> sales," and "I *record* <verb> the data for my science project in my notebook" are examples of how to use record in different ways.

False cognates can be addressed as they come up by pointing out that not all apparent cognates really are cognates. Teachers who are fluent in the minority language may wish to keep a list of false cognates (with examples of their use in both languages) available for handouts or consultation.

Idioms, particularly those that cannot be translated literally, present a particular challenge to ELLs. Here again, creating contexts facilitates learning. Grouping idioms according to types of language use helps. Some idioms rely on synonyms, some on hyperbole, others on metaphor. Having students translate idioms from their native language into English strengthens their ability to appreciate the meaning of idioms. Also, creating their own original idioms increases understanding.

The way idioms are taught greatly affects how well they are remembered and the level of frustration the ELL experiences. Visual representations of idioms make meaning easier to understand and provide a memory cue to prompt recall. Using commercially produced illustrations or having students draw their own representations of the meaning makes learning idioms easier and more fun. Students can also write stories or perform skits to illustrate the meaning of idioms.

Skill 2.6 Demonstrate understanding of how to apply knowledge of syntactic and semantic context clues to help determine meaning and resolve language ambiguities.

Native speakers automatically use syntactic and semantic contextual clues to determine meaning and resolve ambiguities. For example, an unknown word such as *gniscious* does not give the reader much help in decoding its meaning. If encountered in a sentence such as, "Thanks for the *gniscious* breakfast," or "Walking through the woods, he was horrified to encounter a *gniscious* beast," the task becomes easier. When a word appears before a noun in English it is likely to be an adjective, describing the word that follows. Logic tells us that if someone is thankful for a *gnisious* meal, the word *gnisious* probably is similar to *delicious*, and the identical suffixes strengthen that hypothesis. On the other hand, if a walker is horrified to encounter a *gniscious* beast, the word might mean something similar to *vicious*.

English learners have no such advantage. In many languages, such as Spanish, adjectives normally follow nouns rather than precede them. If the students' vocabulary bank does not include *delicious* or vicious, there are no similarities upon which to draw. For this reason, the use of syntactic and semantic context clues must be directly taught.

GAMES TO HELP TEACH SYNTAX

Students often respond to games or game-like activities much more than to dry classroom lectures. The following games help learners derive meaning from working with syntax:

- **Cuisiniere rods:** Cuisiniere rods can be used to replace the words in sentences. Start students out with a blue rod to represent nouns and a white rod to represent verbs—the two main components of the English sentence. Give examples. Next, add in other components of the sentence, such as auxiliary verbs represented by a green rod, negative words represented by a black rod, and adjectives represented by a pink rod. As each new rod is introduced—over a period of days or weeks—give the students worksheets with the new sentence structures and ask them to point to the correct rod as they study the syntax. By manipulating the rods, students are able to visualize the correct word order of the sentence (McKay, 1987).

- **Shunting words:** After students read a text and find it difficult, the teacher types the text into a computer, removing all punctuation and spacing. Seat up to three students at a computer. Have them read, punctuate, and space the text. Circulate to help groups of students with sections they cannot figure out and with unknown vocabulary. This exercise works on word segmentation; practices seeing or hearing clauses; focuses on syntax, punctuation, and meaning; gives reading practice; and creates interaction with texts (Rinvolucri and Davis, 1995).

- **Expanded Sentences:** Have a student draw a simple picture on the board, such as a sports car with a girl and a boy in it. The teacher writes a short sentence such as, "Sports cars are expensive." A student volunteer adds one word where the teacher indicates with a caret (^): "Sports cars are ^ expensive." The game continues until no more words can be added to the sentence (Rinvolucri, 1984).

Skill 2.7   Demonstrate the ability to evaluate ELD programs for adequate attention to the areas of syntax and semantics.

Teachers should be able to evaluate ELD programs to ensure that the programs address at least the following elements of syntax and semantics:

- **Syntax:** the order in which words are arranged to create meaning
- **Semantics:** the meanings of individual words, as well as combinations of words
- **Idioms**: figures of speech where the literal meaning is not the intended meaning

- **Perfunctory speech,** or **"empty language,":** has little meaning but is important in social exchanges

COMPETENCY 3.0   LANGUAGE FUNCTIONS AND VARIATION

Skill 3.1   Demonstrate knowledge of the different social functions of language (e.g., to inform, amuse, control, persuade).

Halliday classified language into the following **functional categories** (1985):

- **Instrumental:** language as a means of satisfying needs or acquiring things, e.g., asking the teacher for supplies in art class, requesting a book from the librarian
- **Regulatory:** used to control the behavior, feelings, or attitudes of others, e.g., creating role-plays with others, organizing tasks in project work
- **Interactional:** social interaction, working with others, e.g., cooperative group work on diverse classroom projects and activities
- **Personal:** expressions of individuality, pride, and awareness of self, e.g., sharing and telling about oneself and personal experiences
- **Heuristic:** asking and seeking knowledge, e.g., asking how something works, explaining ideas in a story, or retelling a story
- **Imaginative:** making up stories and poems, creating new worlds, e.g., using wordless books or pictures to create stories, using dramatics to act out an original story
- **Informative:** sharing information, descriptions, or ideas, e.g., sharing ideas about what to include in a project, explaining what happened the night before or in a movie
- **Divertive:** jokes, puns, riddles, language play, e.g., telling jokes to others

Skill 3.2   Demonstrate knowledge of language structures appropriate to specific academic language functions (e.g., describing, defining, explaining, comparing, contrasting, making predictions, persuading) across the content areas.

Certain words, phrases, and structures are used in academic language to express ideas in ways that others can understand. Teachers can share vocabulary or structure lists with students so they are aware of the variety of language available to them and what is expected from them when writing or speaking academic language.

Some of these are listed below:

Describing	• The ... has all the colors of the rainbow. • It was as boxy as .... • It is taller/shorter/fatter/heavier than...
Defining	• This word means... • History defines ...as... • It really means...
Explaining	• One way to interpret her words is... • His actions mean that...
Comparing	• This is similar to an event... • That part was like when I ...
Contrasting	• This is different from... because... • Today, this could mean that...
Making predictions	• We have seen many new ..., but I foresee... • I think that...
Persuading	• I know what you mean, but I believe that... • There is a lot of evidence that..., but the crux of the matter is...

Skill 3.3   Identify different types of variation that occur in a language (e.g., dialects, historical variation, social versus academic language) and demonstrate knowledge of why language variation evolves (e.g., reasons involving geographic, political, cultural, social, and vocational issues).

Sociolinguistics is the study of how social conditions influence the use of language. Social factors such as ethnicity, religion, gender, status, age, and education all play a role in how individuals use language. Dialects differ depending on these and other factors. Sociolinguistics tries to understand the relationship between language and social elements. Different **dialects**, or how language is spoken, are frequently referred to today as **varieties** of a language. Varieties of a language may be considered separate languages if there is a strong literary, religious, or other tradition.

Historical variation may occur in the sound system, the grammar, or the lexicon. It may be a gradual change in the pronunciation of a word, or it may be abrupt, as in the case of pidginization of the language when contact with a new culture occurs. It is beyond anyone's control, but language is constantly changing. In the words of H. L. Mencken, "A living language is like a man suffering incessantly from small haemorrhages, and what it needs above all else is constant transactions of new blood from other tongues. The day the gates go up, that day it begins to die."

France is a prime example of a country that has tried to keep its language "pure." In spite of tremendous efforts, the French language has evolved. It has acquired new terms for twentieth- and twenty-first-century technology and experiences. It has been modified by immigrants who have moved to France. Living languages are simply not static.

Social language is different from **academic language.** The languages are used in different contexts and for different purposes. Their vocabularies are distinct. Structures and grammar may also be distinct. Social language is generally used with peers, in relaxed and informal contexts. Academic language is often used to convey scholarly concepts with concern for accuracy, objectivity, and dispassionate comment.

The United States has experienced disparate social influences, which accounts for the substantial differences between American and other varieties of English, even British English from which American English originated. Ralph Waldo Emerson said, "The English language is the sea which receives tributaries from every region under heaven." Most obvious of these tributaries has been the continuous flow of immigrants who have brought their customs and languages to the united States. Each culture contributes new words, and new immigrants continue to change the language today.

Language is influenced by the **geography** of the land in which it is spoken. Imagine the different words needed to describe the geographical features of the snowy, icy northern countries and the words needed to describe the lands of the harsh, barren deserts. Nomadic peoples in these areas use different vocabularies with words not easily translated because the people living in other regions have no concepts upon which to base the words.

Wars have also added words to our language. During World War II, people began to use words and phrases such as *flak, blitz, R & R, black market, pin-up, mushroom cloud,* and *fallout.* During the Korean War, *chopper* and *brainwashing* came into use. During the Vietnam era, *napalm, friendly fire, search-and-destroy mission,* and *the domino theory* entered the language. The Iraq War has added *the green zone, al-Qaeda,* and *weapons of mass destruction.* Wars also give new meanings to old words, such as *embedded,* which in the context of Iraq means journalists who join army units.

Contemporary culture changes language significantly. Advertisers have such great success that brand names come to represent entire categories of products, such as *Kleenex* for tissue, *Xerox* for photocopy, *Hoover* for vacuum cleaner, and *Coke* for cola. People pick up and use phrases from popular TV shows: *Yabadabadoo; like, cool, man; and D'oh!* Other cultural trends, such as the drug culture, sports, and fads add new words to the language.

Political rhetoric also influences language. We hear sports metaphors (a success referred to as a homerun); war metaphors (victories or defeats); and business metaphors (ending up in the red or the black). Politicians like to "send a message" to enemies, political rivals, or the American people. Candidates like to be "the candidate of change" or "the education candidate."

Technology and science may have changed language more than any other factor in the past century. An estimated five hundred thousand technical and scientific terms have been added to English. Many of these words affect our daily lives. Fifty years ago, people didn't routinely use computers, cell phones, the Internet, or satellite dishes. They hadn't had an MRI or wondered if genetically modified organisms (GMOs) were safe to eat.

Text messaging, particularly among young people, has created a kind of shorthand variation of English: *CUL8R* means "see you later"; *BRB* means "be right back"; and *TTYL* means "talk to you later." ESL teachers might be surprised at how adroit their students are with technological language. Students who make English-speaking friends and want to adapt to U.S. culture will quickly learn this new language.

The merging of languages into English has contributed to the inconsistencies and exceptions to rules that make the language so difficult to learn. It has also increased the number of words one must learn to communicate in English. We can only be certain that English will continue to change and language will continue to be vital in new forms.

Work-related language (**jargon**) is often different from the language of the general public. To the professionals using it, jargon may be a kind of shorthand that makes long explanations unnecessary. Consider the multitude of terms used to refer to those learning English as an additional language (e.g., English as a Second Language students, English as a Foreign Language students, English Language Learners, and those with Limited English Proficiency) to name a few. Teachers may be referred to as TESOL, ESL, or EFL teachers, or simply bilingual teachers. The general public would be hard-pressed to understand the distinctions made by professionals using these terms.

Skill 3.4   **Identify factors that influence a speaker's or writer's choice of language variation for a given discourse (e.g., the context or setting of the discourse; the speaker's age, gender, culture, level of education, social class, vocation).**

Choice of language for a particular discourse refers to **register.** Register varies with many factors including context, age, gender, culture, level of education, social class, and vocation. British linguist Michael Halliday first defined the broadened term of **register** as three factors leading to variations in the formality between the participants:

- **field of discourse**: a reference to the subject matter being discussed

- **mode of discourse:** speaking or writing, and the choice of format
- **manner of discourse:** a reference to the social relations between the participants

Skill 3.5 **Apply strategies for identifying and addressing difficulties English Learners may encounter in comprehending regional dialects or other varieties of English.**

Learning to pronounce numbers provides an example of difficulties English Learners may encounter in different varieties of English. For instance, in American English, students are often directly taught that there are three auditory differences between *thirteen* and *thirty*:

- The *n* sound at the end of the *-teen* words is audible if you listen carefully
- The accent falls on the second syllable of the *-teen* words, and the first syllable of *thirty*, *forty*, etc.
- The *t* sound in the *-teen* words is a hard *t*, whereas the *t* sound in the tens is a soft *t*, pronounced like an English *d*

Direct instruction helps learners deal with everyday situations involving numbers, such as correctly offering money to a cashier.

Australian and British English, however, reverse the second and third points, pronouncing *thirty* with a hard *t* sound, and *thirteen* with an accented first syllable and a soft *t*. Such differences can cause confusion for a student with teachers from different areas or those listening to programs from different areas. Directly teaching these differences will help avoid confusion.

Other differences that can cause distress for students are those caused by changes in register and tone that are dependent upon audience and setting. **Register** is the term for speech that is appropriate in a particular social setting. For example, in talking to a preschool child, one might refer to a train as a "choo-choo" or a cat as a "kitty-cat." Such language would not normally be appropriate in an adult discussion. An example of regional differences in register is the way young students are expected to address teachers and other adults. In the southern states, a student may be expected to reply to an adult in conversation with, "Yes, ma'am," or "No, sir." In California, a teacher is more likely to say, "Oh, please call me Pam."

Students who watch American TV and movies for English comprehension often repeat words and phrases that are used disrespectfully or discourteously because they are unable to evaluate the appropriateness of the language in social settings. This situation may require the teacher to directly teach inappropriate language to protect students from using it.

Skill 3.6   Apply strategies for creating an instructional environment that respects English Learners' home language and variety of English.

It is counterproductive to punish the use of the home language in the school setting, even in a joking way. Students who have mastered a first language should have that accomplishment respected as they set about conquering their second language.

For students who are speaking "Spanglish," or another variety of mixed language, it is helpful to treat their variety of English as a separate language, which must occasionally be translated to be understood, and then to discuss when and where each variety is appropriate.

One method for doing this is to put phrases of similar meaning but different registers side by side and discuss when and where each would be appropriate. For example, would it be correct for a seventh grader to say to a peer, "Good morning, Arturo. Isn't this nice weather? Did you sleep well?" Probably not, and neither would it always be appropriate to say, "Yo, bro, que paso?" to an employer or the school principal. Different audiences and situations require appropriate changes in register and tone, and these must be taught to be understood.

One important strategy for showing respect for a student's first language is to learn how to pronounce his or her name correctly and teach the class to do the same. Changing Jose to Joe or pronouncing Xavier as X-ay-vier conveys the impression that the correct pronunciation is somehow no longer correct or not good enough.

Mispronouncing or changing names also contributes to an atmosphere in which children are led to disrespect their parents if the parents do not learn the second language, or do not speak it as well as their offspring. When asked by her teacher how her mother pronounced her name, Hermelinda replied, "She doesn't say the *H*, but she doesn't know anything." The school can go a long way in preventing such thinking by treating the home language with interest and respect.

Teaching the whole class a few words and phrases in the home language of a newcomer will help students appreciate the difficulty of learning a second language, and can create new respect for the student who has mastered it.

Skill 3.7   Demonstrate the ability to evaluate ELD programs for adequate attention to social and academic language functions.

Teachers should be able to evaluate ELD programs to ensure that the programs present activities that offer opportunities to increase understanding of social and academic language functions.

Basic Interpersonal Communication Skills (BICS), which learners must acquire to function in social situations, are generally less demanding than Cognitive Academic Language Proficiency (CALP), and are generally acquired earlier.

Language proficiency requires both BICS and CALP. While there are clear distinctions between them, there are underlying similarities that contribute to overall language learning. In addition, students should also recognize Common Underlying Proficiency (CUP). These are skills, ideas, and concepts that learners can transfer from their first language to their English learning. Both similarities and differences between languages can help learners understand and learn aspects of English.

COMPETENCY 4.1   DISCOURSE

Skill 4.1   Demonstrate understanding of the way sentences relate to one another to communicate meaning (e.g., conversations, texts).

Oral conversations are generally spontaneous, and the participants make up their speech as they interact with each other. They make corrections, revise their words, and try to clear up misunderstandings as they go. At times, oral conversations may seem to be disjointed as the interlocutors bring up new and old topics with their companions.

Written discourse, on the other hand, is more precise. It is produced over a longer time span and is subject to reflection, correction, and revision by its author. Once it is "published," however, it becomes very difficult to clear up misunderstandings or revise the text. The author of a text is held responsible for his or her words and cannot claim to have been speaking spontaneously.

Skill 4.2   Analyze oral and written discourse with respect to cohesion and coherence.

Oral discourse analysis is often referred to as conversational analysis. In oral discourse, the emphasis is on the behavior of the participants and social constraints such as politeness and face-saving phenomena. Oral discourse analysis is concerned with who initiates the conversation, turn-taking, how not to interrupt, and who speaks next.

Written discourse is generally analyzed for how the text hangs together. **Cohesion** is the "surface" characteristics of the semantic relationships between the elements of the text. **Coherence** is the deeper meaning of the logical elements of the text. Other elements of written discourse include theme, anaphora, topic progression, and grammatical choices at the clausal level.

Skill 4.3 **Identify similarities and differences between language structures used in spoken and in written English and apply strategies for teaching oral- and written-language structures to English Learners.**

Oral language structures are those used in greetings, the discourse itself, and endings. Certain types of oral language, such as that used in sermons, interviews, prayers, letters, advertisements, oaths, press releases, stories, and speeches, are formulaic. Speakers become disconcerted when the orator deviates from the rules or structure we expect to hear in these types of oral discourse.

Some of the first structures encountered by ELLs are referred to as **Basic Interpersonal Conversational Skills,** or **BICS**. These skills include the language needed to interact with peers, speak on the telephone, and arrive at meaning with adults. BICS can be modeled in the classroom. Many BICS are normal classroom language; for example, "Line up for lunch." "Where is the library?" "Raise your hand if you know the answer." "Can you tell me how to open this?" Other BICS include those used in the community: e.g., "May I have a hamburger, Coke, and fries?" "Next, please." "No thanks, I don't want any more," and "Yes, give me two fives and a ten."

Cognitive Academic Language Proficiency (CALP) refers to the formal language skills needed for successful academic learning—listening, speaking, reading, and writing. Cummins (1979) estimated that it takes five years or more to acquire CALP. More recent research suggests it may take even longer for those with no previous schooling and no primary language support (Peregoy and Boyle, 2008).

There are a myriad of **strategies** to develop oral language in ELLs. For very young children, games, mimicking, learning songs and rhymes, and simple poetry are all good strategies for developing oral language. While preschool and early elementary-age students are usually not self-conscious, it should never be assumed that learning a new language is easy for them. Many of the same techniques can be used with older students by simply adjusting the cognitive level of the activity. Total Physical Response, retelling stories, dictating stories, and disappearing dialogs are some of the strategies that can be used to develop oral language.

Skill 4.4 **Analyze text structures of different genres with respect to their language function (e.g., level of difficulty, featured language structures, writing style, complexity of syntax).**

The teacher will evaluate different genres with respect to the strategies required to understand them, and the responses students develop as they become aware of different genres. Level of difficulty involves more than vocabulary. The teacher must also consider the writer's style and complexity. Sentences such as this one, that are compound-complex, with numerous qualifiers and determiners, can be difficult to read, even if the words themselves are familiar.

According to Rabinowitz and Chi (1987), reading strategies must be consciously applied. Cognitive strategies are activities such as rehearsal, elaboration, and inference. Metacognitive strategies require monitoring one's own understanding, and social strategies include cooperation and clarification. Students transfer these strategies to the next reading task when they become aware of pattern similarities and recognize the genre (Anderson, 1983).

For example, instruction manuals or operating instructions require a different sort of reading than fiction. In reading instructions, such skills as skimming and scanning are necessary to find what is needed to complete the task or answer the question. The focus is on the information rather than on a personal response. Reading poetry, on the other hand, requires inference and a shift of focus to one's personal, introspective response to the words and phrases. Science fiction, fantasy, and magic realism require a willing suspension of disbelief by the reader. The reader's recognition of the structure of each genre helps with the process of strategy transfer.

The teacher must be able to evaluate such factors as schema: Do the students have background knowledge that can help scaffold the reading task? Does vocabulary need to be front-loaded to ensure comprehension?

There are many scales for measuring difficulty. Some, such as the Flesch-Kincaid and Flesch Reading Ease scores, provide a grade-level equivalent, which has the advantage of being easily understood. Others, such as the Lexile score, evaluate specific skills a student must have to understand a text and thus avoid the stigma of classifying a student as below grade level.

Skill 4.5 **Apply strategies for promoting English Learners' communicative competence by developing their discourse competence (i.e., ability to engage in oral and written discourse that is fluent, cohesive, and coherent and is responsive to the other participants in a communicative act), including utilizing the speaking and writing rubrics from the California English Language Development Test (CELDT) to identify areas for instructional practice.**

DISCUSSION ACTIVITIES

- **Describing pictures:** Each group is given a picture that all members of the group can see. The group's secretary makes a checkmark for each sentence the members of the group can come up with to describe the picture. (The secretary does not have to write out the sentence.) After two minutes, the checkmarks are added up, and the group tries to increase the number of checkmarks by describing a second picture.
- **Picture differences:** Students are grouped in pairs. Each pair is given a set of two pictures. Without showing their pictures to their partners, they must figure out what differences there are in the pictures.

- **Solving a problem:** Students are told that they will be on an educational advisory committee, which has to advise the principal on a problem involving students. They should discuss their recommendations and write them out as a letter to the principal. (The teacher needs to prepare the problem and copy it for each student or group.)

DRAMA ACTIVITIES

- **Creative drama:** This activity can be used in the language classroom to encourage dialog technique. Students either write their own play or learn one from English literature. The activity is time consuming but increases the confidence and morale of ELLs.

- **Role-plays and skits:** ELLs are each given a card describing a situation in addition to a task or problem. The participants can be given time to practice their role-play or they can be asked to improvise. This activity is usually done in pairs or small groups.

(Adapted from Ur, 1996)

Skill 4.6 **Demonstrate the ability to evaluate ELD programs for adequate attention to developing English Learners' discourse competence appropriate to their assessed English proficiency level.**

Teachers should be able to evaluate ELD programs to ensure that the programs present activities that offer opportunities to develop discourse competence appropriate to the English Learners' proficiency levels.

Discourse competence is defined as internalized functional knowledge of the elements and structure of a language. It is divided into:

- **textual competence**, which is the ability to create a monologue, such as a report or a speech, appropriate to one's proficiency level, and

- **interactional competence**, which includes the ability to understand and respond to communication from others. Discourse between speakers of English requires knowledge of certain protocols in addition to other aspects of language.

Speakers should have the necessary skills to maintain the momentum of a conversation as well as to correct misunderstandings. Typical spoken discourse follows predictable patterns. For example, one person might say, "I saw a good movie last night." The other person would ask, "What was it about?" The first person would then answer in a paragraph with a topic sentence: "It was about a bunch of guys who devised a plan to rob a casino," and then proceed to fill in the details.

ELLs might initially practice set conversations to learn the patterns of English discourse. Practicing in pairs using a question-and-answer format gives both participants an opportunity to learn the structure of discourse as well as information about the other person or the other person's culture. Such practice also gives students practice with other language skills and can increase vocabulary. The teacher may provide a set of questions, and learners can alternate asking and answering. Short skits that repeat a limited number of words also provide helpful practice. Allowing students time to converse informally, perhaps using suggested topics, continues to reinforce speech patterns.

COMPETENCY 5.0 PRAGMATICS

Skill 5.1 Recognize pragmatic features of oral and written language that influence or convey meaning (e.g., use of formal or informal registers, idiomatic expressions, gestures, eye contact, physical proximity).

Communication in a culture involves not only the language but also gestures, facial expressions, and body stance, among other elements. The teacher or students can model nonverbal elements. Then you can ask the ELLs how to communicate the same message in their culture. For example, the distance between different speakers and the way to indicate the height of a person may be different in different cultures.

In many cultures, children do not speak until called upon; in other cultures, children may shout out an answer as soon as a question is asked. Teaching turn-taking in speaking, the use of materials, and other classroom procedures may be a yearlong task.

Skill 5.2 Identify key pragmatic features of various discourse settings in English (e.g., the classroom, a social event, a store, different types of correspondence).

See Skill 5.5.

Skill 5.3 **Identify factors that affect a speaker's or writer's choice of pragmatic features (e.g., cultural and social norms, setting, goals, purpose, participants in a discourse, audience, subject matter).**

Comparing the **customs** of various cultures provides another opportunity for illustrating how context affects meaning, especially when students in a class represent a variety of cultures, For example, in other parts of the world, especially parts of Europe and the Middle East, people commonly greet each other by kissing on both cheeks, even if meeting for the first time. However, in many countries, including the United States, this greeting is not practiced and is culturally unacceptable in some contexts. For some people this practice would even be offensive or might be ridiculed. Describing and comparing cultural practices provides language practice and demonstrates meaning in context.

Explaining the nuances of English requires ongoing reinforcement. As examples surface, they should be explained and alternative ways to express the same message explored to clarify or expand on the meaning. Pragmatic features in communication can be indirect. For example, when parents ask their children, "Have you finished your homework?" they are implying a command that if homework has not been completed, the children should stop their current activities and finish their homework. The pragmatic features are found in what was actually said as well as what was not said. Students can generate their own questions that have farther-reaching implications.

Politics also affects the pragmatics of different situations. Many political leaders speak in the first-person plural form (*we*) when addressing a crowd to indicate that they are speaking from a position of power or for the greater good. This use of the "royal *we*" also absolves the politician from accepting individual responsibility.

Society imposes many rules that are unconsciously observed by its members. For example, English speakers normally read from left to right and therefore would alphabetize books from left to right on a shelf. Yet many languages are read from right to left. Teachers need to be aware of these differences and maintain a rich visual and textual environment in the classroom through pictures and texts. Visitors from different cultures (think of the numerous differences between American, Canadian, English, and Australian cultures) can help by discussing societal differences with the students.

Skill 5.4 **Identify strategies for promoting English Learners' communicative competence by developing their verbal and nonverbal sociolinguistic competence (e.g., making the pragmatic features of the school and other settings explicit for English Learners; promoting students' ability to engage in oral and written discourse that is appropriate for a given context, purpose, and audience).**

For students from other cultures, pragmatics involving nonverbal cues and body language can be confusing. It is the teacher's responsibility to be sensitive, to acknowledge these different behaviors when they become obvious in the classroom, and to guide students to behaviors appropriate to their audience, purpose, and setting.

Students may be unaware that others feel uncomfortable because they are standing too close or avoiding eye contact, yet these are common examples of cultural differences in nonverbal communication. In some cultures, it is considered impolite to look a teacher in the eye—exactly the opposite of behavior that North Americans expect! The problem could be addressed directly by discussing appropriate behaviors in different cultures, perhaps by focusing on behavior appropriate to the teacher as a model.

Other examples of nonverbal communication are gestures and using acceptable tone, volume, stress, and intonation in different social settings. Voice volume is a learned behavior. All students (not just ELLs) need to learn the appropriate volume for different settings such as the library, hall, gymnasium, supermarket, and movie theater. An appropriate correction for young children would be to ask everyone in the class to use their "inside" voices and not their "outside" (playground) voices when speaking in the classroom.

Skill 5.5 **Apply strategies for identifying and addressing difficulties English Learners have with respect to pragmatics.**

Pragmatics is the study of how context affects the interpretation of language. Situations dictate language choice, body language, the degree of intimacy, and how meaning is interpreted. For example, when customers drive through a fast-food restaurant, they expect a specific sequence of questions or statements: "Would you like a drink with that?" or "That'll be $3.80 at the second window." This sequence of events and cues is a typical pattern of interaction in a fast-food setting. Pragmatic knowledge sets customer expectations. Typically people expect to receive a certain level of service and to use a particular level of manners. These types of exchanges might be universal in a fast-food setting but would be completely inappropriate in a more formal setting, such as when dining at an elegant restaurant, where a server would not announce the cost of one's dinner.

Gestures, the appropriate distance between speakers, seating arrangements, nodding and shaking of the head, signs, and touch are all examples of nonverbal pragmatic conventions. These elements are different in different cultures and may be taught.

For students from other cultures, pragmatics involving nonverbal cues and body language can be confusing. It is the teacher's responsibility to be sensitive to and acknowledge these different behaviors when they become obvious in the classroom and guide students to behaviors appropriate to their audience, purpose, and setting. A teacher may not always be aware of the conventions being observed or violated. For instance, one Los Angeles teacher could have avoided an unpleasant confrontation in his classroom had he known that in Thailand, placing the sole of the foot toward another person is a serious insult.

Students may be unaware that others feel uncomfortable because they are standing too close or not making eye contact. These situations are common examples of cultural differences in nonverbal communication. In some cultures, it is considered impolite to look a teacher in the eye—exactly the opposite of behavior that is expected of North Americans! The problem could be addressed directly by discussing appropriate behaviors in different cultures, perhaps by focusing on behavior appropriate to the teacher as a model.

In the ESL classroom, pragmatics can be illustrated and practiced by repeating the same situation in different contexts. Students can write or act out how they would explain to three different people why they failed a test: their best friend, their teacher, and their parent. With a little imagination, different scenarios can be chosen that pique student interest and make learning fun: Explain an embarrassing event in different contexts, such as in front of a boy/girl you want to impress, a close friend, and an authority figure. For students with low language skills, pantomime can encourage participation, teach the concept, and set up an opportunity for using language to describe what has happened.

Skill 5.6   Demonstrate the ability to evaluate ELD programs for adequate attention to developing English Learners' sociolinguistic competence.

Teachers should be able to evaluate ELD programs to be certain the programs present activities that offer opportunities to increase sociolinguistic competence.

A good ELD program must address the fact that English Learners often demonstrate proficiency in a grammar classroom, but fail to apply their grammar lessons to the speaking and writing tasks they are assigned. In the same way, learners may feel competent in conversation with other students or with the teacher, but be unable to apply those sociolinguistic skills to situations outside of the classroom.

One thing to look for in an effective ELD program is whether activities provide opportunities for the students to interact with non-English Learners. Ordering in a restaurant, talking into a fast-food drive-through machine, or explaining a complaint to a nurse or doctor can present major challenges to language learners. A good program will provide opportunities to role-play these situations and prepare the student to face them in real life.

Authentic language experiences are even more valuable than scripted dialogs and role-plays. An effective program provides learners with opportunities to listen to native speakers and to try to make themselves understood by native speakers. Guest speakers such as store clerks or other service industry representatives can be invited into the classroom, and students can have such out-of-class assignments as asking a question of a stranger. Questions such as "Excuse me, do you have the time?" or "Do you know the way to the library?" can be practiced and then taken out into the larger community.

Speaking on the telephone is a particular challenge for English Learners, and listening to recorded messages to glean specific information, such as movie times or library or clinic hours, is a helpful exercise. The student can comfortably listen to the message as many times as necessary to learn the show times for *Avatar* without the nervousness that often results from a face-to-face encounter.

Sociolinguistic competence results when a learner not only knows the correct question or response, but is able to produce that question or response in the appropriate situations. Therefore, an effective program has to scaffold that process, providing opportunities for increased interaction with the larger world.

DOMAIN II   **FIRST- AND SECOND-LANGUAGE DEVELOPMENT AND THEIR RELATIONSHIP TO ACADEMIC ACHIEVEMENT**

COMPETENCY 6.0   **THEORIES, PROCESSES, AND STAGES OF LANGUAGE ACQUISITION**

Skill 6.1   **Analyze the significance for teaching and learning of contemporary theories of language acquisition.**

Contemporary theories of language acquisition have a solid basis in research on many different language learners in many different cultures. These theories have led to a solid basis upon which to base teaching practice and can guide teachers in their interactions with learners of all types.

Between two and three years of age, most children will be able to use language to influence the people closest to them. Research shows that, in general, boys acquire language more slowly than girls, which means we need to consider carefully how we involve boys in activities designed to promote early language and literacy.

Various theories have tried to explain the language acquisition process.

CHOMSKY: LANGUAGE ACQUISITION DEVICE

Chomsky's theory, described as nativism, asserts that humans are born with a special biological brain mechanism, called a Language Acquisition Device (LAD). His theory supposes that the ability to learn language is innate, that nature is more important than nurture, and that experience using language is only necessary in order to activate the LAD. Chomsky based his assumptions on work in linguistics. His work shows that children's language development is much more complex than what is proposed by behaviorist theory, which asserts that children learn language merely by being rewarded for imitating. However, Chomsky's theory underestimates the influence that thought (cognition) and language have on each other's development.

PIAGET: COGNITIVE CONSTRUCTIVISM

Piaget's central interest was children's cognitive development. He theorized that language is simply one way that children represent their familiar worlds, a reflection of thought, and that language does not contribute to the development of thinking. He believed that cognitive development precedes language development.

VYGOTSKY: SOCIAL CONSTRUCTIVISM AND LANGUAGE

Unlike Chomsky and Piaget, Vygotsky's central focus is the relationship between the development of thought and language. He was interested in the ways different languages affect a person's thinking. He suggests that what Piaget saw as the young child's egocentric speech was actually private speech, the child's way of using words to think about something, which progressed from social speech to thinking in words. Vygotsky views language first as social communication, which gradually promotes both language itself and cognition.

RECENT THEORIZING: INTENTIONALITY

Some contemporary researchers and theorists criticize earlier theories and suggest that children, their behaviors, and their attempts to understand and communicate are misunderstood when the causes of language development are thought to be "outside" the child or mechanistically "in the child's brain." They recognize that children are active learners who co-construct their worlds. Children's language development is part of their holistic development, emerging from cognitive, emotional, and social interactions. These theorists believe that language development depends on the child's social and cultural environment, the people in it, and their interactions. The way children represent these factors in their minds is fundamental to language development. They believe that a child's agenda and the interactions generated by the child promote language learning. The adult's role, actions, and speech are still considered important, but adults need to be able to "mind read" and adjust their side of the co-construction to relate to an individual child's understanding and interpretation.

Theories about language development help us see that enjoying "proto-conversations" with babies (treating them as people who understand, share, and have intentions in sensitive interchanges), and truly listening to young children are the best ways to promote their language development.

Brain research has shown that the single most important factor affecting language acquisition is the onset of puberty. Before puberty, a person uses one area of the brain for language learning; after puberty, a different area of the brain is used. A person who learns a second language before reaching puberty will always process language learning as if prepubescent. A person who begins to learn a second language after the onset of puberty will likely find language learning more difficult and depend more on repetition.

Other researchers have focused on analyzing aspects of the language to be acquired. Factors they consider include:

- **Error analysis:** recognizing patterns of errors
- **Interlanguage:** analyzing which aspects of the target language are universal
- **Developmental patterns:** the order in which features of a language are acquired and the sequence in which a specific feature is acquired

Skill 6.2   Demonstrate knowledge of cognitive processes involved in synthesizing and internalizing language rules (e.g.,, memorization, categorization, generalization and overgeneralization, metacognition).

COGNITIVE STRATEGIES

Cognitive strategies are vital to second-language acquisition; their most salient feature is the manipulation of the second language. The most basic strategies are: practicing, receiving and sending messages, analyzing and reasoning, and creating structure for input and output, which can be remembered by the acronym PRAC.

- **Practicing:** Practice constant repetition, make attempts to imitate a native speaker's accent, concentrate on sounds, and practice in a realistic setting to help promote the learner's grasp of the language.
- **Receiving and sending messages:** These strategies help the learner quickly locate salient points and then interpret the meaning: skim through information to determine "need to know" vs. "nice to know," use available resources (print and non-print) to interpret messages.
- **Analyzing and reasoning:** Use general rules to understand the meaning and then work into specifics, and break down unfamiliar expressions into parts.
- **Creating structure for input and output:** Choose a format for taking meaningful notes, practice summarizing long passages, use highlighters as a way to focus on main ideas or important specific details.

METACOGNITIVE STRATEGIES

The ESOL teacher is responsible for helping students become aware of their own individual learning strategies and constantly improve and add to those strategies. Each student should have his/her own toolbox of skills for planning, managing, and evaluating the language-learning process.

Some salient points for ELLs to keep in mind:

- **Center your learning:** Review a key concept or principle and link it to existing knowledge, make a firm decision to pay attention to the general concept, ignore input that is distracting, and learn skills in the proper order.
- **Arrange and plan your learning:** Take the time to understand how a language is learned; create optimal learning conditions, i.e., regulate noise, lighting, and temperature; obtain the appropriate books, etc.; and set reasonable long- and short-term goals.
- **Evaluate your learning:** Keep track of errors that prevent further progress and keep track of progress, e.g., reading faster now than the previous month.

SOCIOAFFECTIVE STRATEGIES

Socioaffective strategies are broken down into affective and social strategies. *Affective strategies* are those that help the learner control the emotions and attitudes that hinder progress in learning the second language and at the same time help him/her learn to interact in a social environment. There are three sets of affective strategies—lowering your anxiety, encouraging yourself, and taking your emotional temperature—which are easy to remember with the acronym LET.

- **Lowering your anxiety**: These strategies try to maintain emotional equilibrium with physical activities: Use meditation and/or deep breathing to relax, listen to calming music, and read a funny book or watch a comedy.
- **Encouraging yourself**: These strategies help support and motivate the learner. Stay positive through self-affirmations, take risks, and give yourself rewards.
- **Taking tour emotional temperature**: These strategies help learners control their emotions by understanding what they are feeling emotionally as well as why they are feeling that way. Listen to your body's signals; create a checklist to keep track of feelings and motivations during the second-language-acquisition process; keep a diary to record progress and feelings; and share feelings with a classmate or friend.

Social strategies affect how the learner interacts in a social setting. The following are three useful strategies for interacting socially: asking questions, cooperating with others, and empathizing with others, which can be remembered with the acronym ACE.

- **Asking questions**: Ask for clarification or help. Request that the speaker slow down, repeat, or paraphrase, and ask to be corrected when you are speaking.
- **Cooperating with others**: Interact with more than one person: Work cooperatively with a partner or small group and work with a native speaker of the language.
- **Empathizing with others**: Learn how to relate to others, remembering that people usually have more things in common than things that set them apart. Empathize with another student by learning about his/her culture and being aware and sensitive to his/her thoughts and feelings. Understanding and empathizing will help the other student but it will also help the empathizer.

Skill 6.3 **Demonstrate knowledge of similarities and differences between first- and second-language acquisition, including identifying the characteristic features of the stages of first-language acquisition and the proficiency levels of second-language acquisition as identified in the CELDT.**

Teaching students who are learning English as a second language poses some unique challenges, particularly in a standards-based environment. Teachers should teach with the students' developmental level in mind. Instruction should not be "dumbed-down" for ESOL students. Different approaches should be used to ensure that students get multiple opportunities to learn and practice English and still learn content.

L1 (acquired language) and L2 (learned language) learning follow many, if not all, of the same steps:

- **Silent period:** The stage when a learner knows perhaps five hundred receptive words but feels uncomfortable producing speech. The absence of speech does not indicate a lack of learning, and teachers should not try to force the learner to speak. Comprehension can be checked by having the learner point or mime in response to instructions. (Also known as the receptive or preproduction stage.)
- **Private speech:** When the learner knows about a thousand receptive words and speaks in one- or two-word phrases. The learner can use simple responses such as yes/no and either/or. (Also known as the early production stage.)
- **Lexical chunks:** The learner knows about three thousand receptive words and can communicate using short phrases and sentences. Long sentences typically have grammatical errors. (Also known as the speech emergence stage.)
- **Formulaic speech:** The learner knows about six thousand receptive words and begins to make complex statements, state opinions, ask for clarification, share thoughts, and speak at greater length. (Also known as the intermediate language proficiency stage.)
- **Experimental or simplified speech:** When the learner develops a level of fluency and can make semantic and grammar generalizations. (Also known as the advanced language proficiency stage.)

Researchers disagree on whether the development of formulaic speech and experimental or simplified speech is the same for L1 and L2 learners. Regardless, understanding that students must go through a predictable, sequential series of stages helps teachers recognize a student's progress and respond effectively. Providing comprehensible input will help students advance their language learning at any stage.

COMPETENCY 7.0   THEORIES, MODELS AND PROCESSES OF SECOND-LANGUAGE ACQUISITION

Skill 7.1   Demonstrate understanding of current research-based theories and models of second-language acquisition.

The major models of ESOL programs differ depending on the sources consulted. However, general consensus recognizes the following program models with different instructional methods used in different programs.

IMMERSION EDUCATION MODELS

In immersion programs, instruction is initiated in the student's nonnative language, using the second language as the medium of instruction for both academic content and the second language. Two of these models strive for full bilingualism: One is for language-majority students and the other for language-minorities.

- **English Language Development (ELD) or English as a Second Language (ESL) pull-out**: Pull-out programs include various approaches to teaching English to nonnative speakers. In 1997, TESOL standards defined these approaches as marked by an intent to teach the ELL to communicate in social settings, engage in academic tasks, and use English in socially and culturally appropriate ways. There are three well-known approaches to ELD or ESL:

  o **Grammar-based ESL:** This method teaches *about* the language, stressing its structure, functions, and vocabulary through rules, drills, and error correction.
  o **Communication-based ESL:** This approach emphasizes instruction in English that emphasizes *using* the language in meaningful contexts. There is little stress on correctness in the early stages and more emphasis on comprehensible input to foster communication and lower anxiety when students are taking risks.
  o **Content-based ESL:** Instruction in English that attempts to develop language skills and prepare ELLs to study grade-level content material in English. There is emphasis on language, but with graded introduction to content areas, vocabulary, and basic concepts.

- **Structured English immersion:** The goal is English proficiency. ELLs are pulled out for structured instruction in English so that subject matter is comprehensible. Used with sizable groups of ELLs who speak the same language and are in the same grade level or with diverse populations of language-minority students. There is little or no L1 language support. Teachers use sheltered instructional techniques and have strong receptive skills in the students' native or heritage language.

- **Submersion with primary language support:** The goal is English proficiency. Bilingual teachers or aides support the minority students in each grade level who are ELLs. In small groups, the ELLs are tutored by reviewing the content areas in their primary language. The teachers use the L1 to support English content classes; ELLs achieve limited literacy in L1.
- **Canadian French immersion (language-majority students):** The goal is bilingualism in French (L2) and English (L1). The targeted population is the language-majority. Students are immersed in the L2 for the first two years using sheltered language instruction, and then English L1 is introduced. The goal is for all students of the majority language (English) to become fluent in L2 (French).
- **Indigenous language immersion** (endangered languages, such as Navajo): The goal is bilingualism; the program is socially, linguistically, and cognitively attuned to the native culture and community context. This approach supports endangered minority languages and develops academic skills in minority language and culture as well as in the English language and predominant culture.

Skill 7.2   Demonstrate knowledge of cognitive and social strategies learners use in developing a second language (e.g., repetition, formulaic expressions, elaboration, self-monitoring, appeals for assistance, requests for clarification, role-play).

Language learners develop cognitive and social strategies to help them cope with the uncertainties of learning a second language. Among these are:

- **Repetition, elaboration, appeals for assistance, requests for clarification:** These are sometimes cries for reassurance that the ELL is on track or understands what he/she is being told or what he/she must do. Even when the ELL understands what is being required, assurance from an adult, peer, or teacher is an emotional need.
- **Formulaic expressions:** Some expressions are used in certain situations by all speakers of the language. For example, "May I help you?," "Good morning," "What can I do for you?" and "How's the weather today?" are all expressions used to establish social discourse but not necessarily used to request or give information.
- **Role-play:** Children, and even adults, engage in role-playing to internalize language and linguistic structures. By practicing the roles they see others acting out, children learn to act like the adults around them. Adults may engage in role-plays when they rehearse a speech to be given or act out their part in requesting a raise from their boss.

Skill 7.3   Demonstrate understanding that language is acquired in a natural process wherein productive and expressive skills (speaking and writing) are facilitated by the development of receptive skills (listening and reading).

Language is not learned in a vacuum. The four language skills are interactive, with each one supporting and improving the other skills. Improving the receptive skills of listening and reading improves the productive and expressive skills of speaking and writing. For this reason, ESOL teachers should provide ample opportunities for their students to hear English, their target language. Listening to oral language helps the ELLs to:

- Develop language models of vocabulary, language patterns, and structures
- Develop background knowledge and activate prior knowledge, ideas, and past experiences
- Transfer listening strategies to reading and develop active construction of meaning

Young children should be taught in print-rich environments with ample opportunities to hear spoken English while having stories read to them. Current thinking emphasizes that the oral language being heard should come from speakers of a variety of backgrounds in order to accustom the ear to the many varieties of English being spoken in the world today. As ELLs improve their receptive vocabularies and their knowledge of language structures, they feel more confident in expressing themselves orally and in writing. For many learners, there is a "silent period" in which the learner absorbs the sounds of the language before feeling confident enough to express him- or herself, though young children may engage in "private speech," when they try out the new language.

COMPETENCY 8.0 **COGNITIVE, LINGUISTIC, AND PHYSICAL FACTORS AFFECTING LANGUAGE DEVELOPMENT**

Skill 8.1 **Demonstrate knowledge of research-based cognitive, linguistic, and physical factors affecting second-language development (e.g., prior knowledge, cognitive/learning styles, positive and negative language transfer, age, disabilities, lack of formal school experience).**

PRIOR KNOWLEDGE

Schemata, or the prior knowledge students have when beginning a new foreign language, is a valuable asset to be exploited in their language learning. The schema theory (Carrell and Eisterhold, 1983) explains how the brain processes knowledge and how this facilitates comprehension and learning. A schema is the framework around information that is stored in the brain. As new information is received, schemata are activated to store the new information. By connecting what is known with what is being learned, understanding is achieved and learning can take place. If students lack sufficient prior knowledge, they cannot be expected to understand a new lesson.

Children may or may not have prior educational experiences upon which to build their new language skills. However, even children who have little or no formal education may have been taught the alphabet or simple mathematics by their parents. Children from oral cultures may have quite sophisticated language structures already in place upon which to base new language learning.

COGNITIVE/LEARNING STYLES

A student's learning style includes cognitive, affective, and psychological behaviors that indicate his/her characteristic and consistent way of perceiving, interacting with, and responding to the learning environment (Willing, 1988).

Willing identified four main learning styles used by ESL learners in Australia:

- **Concrete learning style:** people-oriented, emotional, and spontaneous
- **Analytic learning style:** object-oriented, with the capacity for making connections and inferences
- **Communicative learning style:** autonomous, prefers social learning, likes making decisions
- **Authority-oriented learning style:** defers to the teacher, does not enjoy learning by discovery, intolerant of facts that do not fit (ambiguity)

Reid (1987) identified four perceptual learning tendencies:

- **Visual learning:** learning mainly from seeing words in books, on the board, etc.
- **Auditory learning:** learning by hearing words spoken and from oral explanations, from listening to tapes or lectures
- **Kinesthetic learning:** learning by experience, by being involved physically in classroom experiences
- **Tactile learning:** hands-on learning, learning by doing, working on models, lab experiments, etc.

POSITIVE AND NEGATIVE LANGUAGE TRANSFER

L1 transfer refers to the effect the native tongue has on the language being acquired. It can be positive or negative. **Negative transfer** is illustrated in many of the errors ELLs make when using the new language. An example would be Chinese learners who overuse expressions of regret when apologizing because in their native language it is customary to do so.

Positive transfer occurs when similar structures in the L1 facilitate the learning of the new language. An example of this would be when cognates are able to transfer to the target language.

AGE

According to Ellis (1985), age does not affect the "route" (order) of second-language acquisition (SLA). Thus, children and adults acquire language in the same order, that is, they go through the same stages. With respect to rate of acquisition, teens appear to surpass both children and adults, especially in learning the grammatical system (Snow and Hoefnagel-Hohle, 1978). Older learners seem to be more efficient learners. The achievement of a foreign language is strongly related to the amount of time spent on the language, and the earlier a second language is started, the better the pronunciation (Burstall et al., 1974). Krashen (1982) disagrees, believing instead that SLA is related to the amount of comprehensible input (i.e., the younger child will receive more comprehensible input) and that younger learners are more open emotionally to SLA.

Other theorists have formulated different hypotheses about age in SLA related to affective factors. In the critical period hypothesis, Penfield and Roberts (1959) state that the first ten years are the best age for SLA as the brain retains its plasticity. After puberty, this plasticity disappears and the flexibility required for SLA is lost. Guiora et al. (1972) believe that around the age of puberty, the ability to acquire native-like pronunciation of the foreign language is no longer present.

Cognitive explanations are also used to explain the effects of age on SLA. These theories assert that children are more prone to use their Language Acquisition Device (LAD), while adults are better able to use their inductive reasoning because of more fully developed cognitive faculties. Rosansky (1975) explains SLA in terms of Piaget's "period of concrete operations." Rosansky believes the child is more open and flexible to new language than an adult who identifies more closely with the differences in the native language and the language to be acquired. Krashen (1982) believes that adolescents and adults probably have greater access to comprehensible input than children and that this is the real causative variable, rather than age itself.

DISABILITIES

Students with disabilities are guaranteed an education under Public Law 94-142 of 1975. A key feature of the law is the requirement of an individualized education program (IEP) for any student receiving special funds for special education. However, the classification of many ELLs or the "dumping" of ELLs in special education classes has been of concern to many educators. Those testing ELLs for placement in different classes must be certain that the tests used are both reliable and valid. Reliability can be established using multiple assessment measures, objective tests, multiple raters, and clearly specified scoring criteria (Valdez-Pierce, 2003). For a test to be valid, it must first be reliable (Goh, 2004).

Learning disabilities refer to physical, emotional, cognitive, or social components, which severely limit what is considered to be "normal" functioning behavior. Children who fall into this category can be one or more of the following: emotionally challenged, hearing-, vision-, or speech-impaired or learning disabled.

EDUCATIONAL EXPERIENCE

ELLs come to the United States for many different reasons: in search of a better life, fleeing war zones and oppressive governments, or to escape economic difficulties. In many cases, ELLs have entered the school system in their native land and done very well. In other cases, they have had little or no educational experience. In either case, it is imperative that, previous to or upon enrollment, assessment of the student take place—if possible, in their L1. By building on their previous knowledge with regard to literacy, language, and experience, L2 instruction will be more successful (Au, 1993, 2002; Ovando et al., 2006).

Shumm (2006) emphasizes that not only are reading-level characteristics important, but also the differences between L1 and L2, as these may influence the assumed level of the student. Some of the questions she proposes for eliciting these similarities and differences are useful for further evaluation of reading-level characteristics:

- Is the L1 writing system logographic, as is Arabic; syllabic, as is Cherokee; or alphabetic, as are English and Greek?
- How does the L1 syntax compare with L2 syntax?

- Are the spelling patterns phonetic with consistent grapheme-phoneme relationships (e.g., Spanish or French), or are there multiple vowel sounds (e.g., English)?
- Do students read from left to right and top to bottom in their L1?
- Are there true cognates (Spanish: *instrucción*, and English: *instruction*) and false cognates (Spanish: *librería* [bookstore], and English: *library*) that will help or confuse the ELL?
- Are the discourse patterns and writing styles of L1 and L2 similar or different?
- Are questions with known answers asked (teacher questions) or are rhetorical questions (found among many working-class families) asked?
- Is L1 writing style circular, with long sentences and many details (e.g., Spanish), or linear, with the minimum number of facts or supporting details needed to support the main idea (e.g., English)?

Skill 8.2	**Analyze the pedagogical implications of cognitive, linguistic, and physical factors for the instruction of English Learners (e.g., with respect to assessing a student's language proficiency level, accessing prior knowledge, scaffolding language tasks, providing opportunities for comprehensible input and output, promoting communicative classroom interactions, monitoring students' progress, providing constructive feedback, building on students' prior knowledge of their primary language to promote English language development).**

- **Assessing a student's language proficiency level and prior knowledge** is of critical importance when placing students in ESOL programs. **Diagnostic tests** are used to determine an ELL's areas of strength and weakness so that appropriate types and levels of teaching and learning tasks are given. While standardized language proficiency tests are fairly accurate, they do have certain limitations. A student's performance can be affected by nonlinguistic variables such as anxiety, fatigue, disinterest, or even lack of familiarity with the testing procedure. Thus, students are sometimes placed in the wrong classroom. As the teacher, it is your responsibility to speak to the principal concerning procedures for retesting. A teacher's judgment is likely to be more accurate than a student's test scores.
- **Scaffolding language tasks,** or supporting children of all ages, consists of demonstrating, guiding, and teaching in a step-by-step process so that ELLs are able to communicate effectively and develop their language skills (Cazden. 1983; Ninio and Bruner, 1976). The amount of scaffolding depends on the support needed and the individual child. Scaffolding allows the ELL to assume more and more responsibility as he or she is able. Once ELLs feel secure in their abilities, they are ready to move on to the next stage.

Educational scaffolding consists of several linked strategies, including modeling academic language and contextualizing academic language using visuals, gestures, and demonstrations to help students while they are involved in hands-on learning. Some efficient scaffolding techniques include: providing direction, clarifying purpose, keeping the student on task with proposed rubrics that clarify expectations, offering suggestions for resources, and supplying lessons or activities without problems.

Tompkins (2006) identified five levels of scaffolding for learning and problem solving to show how ELLs moved from needing considerable support to the independent level, when they are ready to solve problems on their own.

- **Modeling**: The instructor models orally or through written supports (a paragraph, a paper, or an example) the work expected of the ELL. Projects from previous years can provide examples of the type of work expected.
- **Shared:** ELLs use their pooled knowledge of the project (and that of their teacher) to complete the assignment.
- **Interactive:** The teacher allows ELLs to question him/her on points that need clarification or that are not understood, i.e., everyone is a learner. It is especially satisfying for the student when the teacher admits that he/she does not know the answer and helps the students locate it.
- **Guided:** Well-posed questions, clues, reminders, and examples are all ways of guiding the ELL toward the goal.
- **Independent levels:** The learner achieves independence and no longer needs educational scaffolding.

PROVIDING OPPORTUNITIES FOR COMPREHENSIBLE INPUT AND OUTPUT

In language learning, input is defined as the language information to which the learner has access. Learners receive input from their parents, their community, TV, the teacher, the textbook, readers, audio- and videotapes, other students in the classroom, etc. It is generally accepted that comprehensible input is key to second-language learning. Even so, input alone may not lead to second-language acquisition. The kind of input received must also be taken into consideration.

Krashen (1981, 1982, 1985) believes that humans acquire language in only one way: by understanding messages, that is, receiving comprehensible input. Krashen defines comprehensible input as $i + 1$, or input that is just beyond the learner's present ability. In this way, the learner can move from what he/she knows to the next level in the natural order of acquisition.

Other theorists report that the frequency in which certain items occur in the target language appears to contribute to output (Dulay and Burt, 1974; Schmidt and Frota, 1986). Collier's (1995) research suggests that classes in schools that are highly interactive, emphasizing student problem solving and discovery through thematic experiences across the curriculum are likely to provide the kind of social setting for natural language acquisition to take place simultaneously with academic and cognitive development. She states, "Collaborative interaction in which meaning is negotiated with peers is central to the language acquisition process, for both oral and written language development."

- **Monitoring students' progress** is an ongoing, continuous process in which the student's language and content area learning is evaluated. Without proper monitoring, students are at risk of long-term failure of instruction. With proper assessment, they may be earlier candidates for reassignment to higher ESL levels or leaving the ESL program.

- **Providing constructive feedback** is a key element in the success of all students. Feedback should:

  o Illustrate what the results of the student's actions were, e.g., "Your transitions helped me understand the paper."
  o Contain information that shows the student what he/she is doing right or wrong in the specific task, e.g., "You used the word 'got' three times. 'Got' is a very general verb. Try to use verbs that are more specific."
  o Be immediate
  o Be specific to student utterances
  o Be focused, not excessive in the amount of information provided or the number of things to think about
  o Be separate from evaluation

- ELLs must have **prior background knowledge** before they are able to develop enough language to succeed in content classrooms. Frequently, they are unable to relate to the present experience because they are unfamiliar with the topic at hand, but if appropriate experiences are presented, ELLs are better able to deal with the situation. Carrell and Eisterhold (1983) stress the importance of teachers activating prior knowledge in order for ELLs to succeed in content classrooms. One way to activate background knowledge is through eliciting shared information from students before introducing new topics.

COMPETENCY 9.0   AFFECTIVE FACTORS AFFECTING LANGUAGE
DEVELOPMENT

Skill 9.1   Demonstrate knowledge of affective factors affecting second-
language development (e.g., motivation, inhibition, attitudes, levels
of anxiety and self-esteem, teacher expectations, classroom
environment).

The term **affective domain** refers to the range of feelings and emotions in human
behavior that affects how a second language is acquired. Self-esteem, motivation,
anxiety, and attitude all contribute to the second-language acquisition process. Internal
and external factors influence the affective domain. ESOL teachers must be aware of
each student's personality and stay attuned to affective factors in their students' lives.

MOTIVATION

Researchers Gardner and Lambert (1972) have identified two types of motivation in
relation to learning a second language:

- **Instrumental Motivation:** acquiring a second language for a specific reason,
such as a job
- **Integrative Motivation:**   acquiring a second language to fulfill a wish to
communicate within a different culture

Neither type stands completely alone. Instructors recognize that motivation can be
viewed as either a "trait" or a "state." As a trait, motivation is more permanent and
culturally acquired. As a state, motivation is considered temporary because it fluctuates,
depending on rewards and penalties.

INHIBITION

ELLs may be inhibited about trying to say things in their target language—English. They
worry about what others will think of their speech. They are afraid of making mistakes
or losing face. They may be shy about speaking in front of others.

ATTITUDES

Attitudes typically evolve from internalized feelings about oneself and one's ability to
learn a language. On the other hand, one's attitude about a language and the speakers
of that language is largely external and influenced by the surrounding environment of
classmates and family.

If nonnative speakers of English experience discrimination because of their accents or cultural status, their attitude toward the value of second-language learning may diminish. Schools can significantly improve attitudes toward second-language learners by encouraging activities between native speakers and ELLs. This can be particularly beneficial to both groups if students learning the ELL's first language work on projects together with ELLs. When native speakers get a chance to appreciate the ELL's language skill in their first language, attitudes change and ELLs have an opportunity to shine.

ANXIETY

Anxiety is inherent in second-language learning. Students are required to take risks, such as speaking in front of their peers. Without a native's grasp of the language, second-language learners are unable to express their individuality, which is even more threatening and uncomfortable. However, not all anxiety is debilitative. Bailey's (1983) research suggests that "facilitative anxiety" (anxiety that compels an individual to stay on task) is a positive factor for some learners, closely related to competitiveness.

SELF-ESTEEM

Learning a second language puts learners in a vulnerable frame of mind. While some learners are less inhibited than others about taking risks, all learners can experience stress if forced to go beyond their comfort level. Using teaching techniques that decrease stress and emphasize group participation rather than focusing on individuals getting the right answer reduce anxiety and encourage learners to attempt to use the new language.

TEACHERS' EXPECTATIONS

Teachers' expectations regarding learning objectives and goals should be high for all students including ELLs. Teachers' expectations in terms of behavior should be clearly stated and posted in the classroom.

CLASSROOM CULTURE

The teacher is responsible for establishing an effective classroom community where all students feel safe, are responsible and respectful, and work cooperatively with their classmates. Students will engage in activities that are meaningful and functional. Teachers should provide demonstrations and scaffolding as needed, yet students should be encouraged to make guesses and take risks in their learning activities. The teacher should allow students to have choices about the activities they will be involved in, e.g., which book they will read.

Skill 9.2   Analyze the pedagogical implications of affective factors for the instruction of English Learners (e.g., with respect to lowering students' affective filters, providing supportive and constructive feedback, creating an inclusive classroom environment, valuing and validating students' home cultures and languages).

LOWERING AFFECTIVE FILTERS

Krashen identified three areas in which affective filters may inhibit language learning: **anxiety, motivation,** and **self-confidence.** Teachers can lower the affective filter by establishing a classroom environment where all children feel safe and appreciated, where different cultures interact in a harmonious way, and where all students are encouraged to reach their maximum potential.

PROVIDING CONSTRUCTIVE FEEDBACK

Ur (1996) defines **feedback** as "information given to the learner about his or her performance of a learning task, usually with the objective of improving this performance." This can be as simple as a thumbs up, a grade of 75% on a quiz or test, a raised eyebrow when the student makes a mistake, or comments in the margin of an essay.

Feedback has two main aspects: assessment and correction. Typically, a grade assigned on a written paper, saying "No" to an oral response, simply calling on another student, or a comment such as "Fair" at the end of a written paragraph are used in the language classroom as ways of assessing performance. In correction, comments on a specific aspect of the ELL's performance are given: better or additional alternatives may be suggested, an explanation of why the ELL's answer is incorrect or partially correct may be given, or the teacher may elicit a better oral response from the student.

Research suggests that not all errors need correcting. Different theories look at mistakes in different ways:

- **Audio-lingualism:** Learners should make few mistakes because they learn in small, controlled steps, so corrections are meaningless.
- **Interlanguage:** Mistakes are an important factor in language learning; by correcting them the learner's interlanguage approaches the target language (Selinker, 1972, 1992).
- **Communicative approach:** Not all mistakes need to be corrected. only those mistakes that interfere with meaning should be corrected.
- **Monitor theory:** Correction does not lead to language acquisition. Learners need comprehensible input so they can acquire the target language (Krashen, 1982).

INCLUSIVE CLASSROOM ENVIRONMENT

One important element of the effective classroom is an inclusive classroom environment. This type of environment assures the teacher and the students that they are respected and connected to the other members of the classroom.

VALUING AND VALIDATING STUDENTS' HOME CULTURES AND LANGUAGES

Culture encompasses the sum of human activity and symbolic structures that have significance and importance for a particular group of people. Culture is manifested in language, customs, history, arts, beliefs, institutions, and other representative characteristics of the group, and is a means of understanding the lives and actions of people.

Culture constitutes a rich component of language learning. It offers a means of drawing learners into the learning process and greatly expands their understanding of a new culture, as well as a deeper understanding of their own.

Second-language acquisition, according to the findings of Saville-Troike (1986) places the learner in the position of having to learn a second culture. The outcome of learning a second culture can have negative or positive results, depending not only on how teaching is approached, but also on outside factors. The way people in the new culture respond to ELLs makes them feel either welcome or rejected. The attitudes and behavior of the learner's family are particularly important. If the family is supportive and embraces the second culture, the effect is typically positive. However, if the family is perceived to reject the primary culture, then the child risks feeling alienated from both cultures. In some cultures, children who learn a second language at the expense of their primary language might be viewed as "turncoats" by family and friends. This can cause negative feelings about school in general and can adversely affect second-language acquisition.

Teachers need to be aware of the importance of culture in order to establish an inclusive classroom environment and effective classroom culture. By learning about their students' cultures, teachers can provide better instruction based on relevant topics and issues.

COMPETENCY 10.0   SOCIOCULTURAL AND POLITICAL FACTORS AFFECTING LANGUAGE DEVELOPMENT

Skill 10.1   Demonstrate knowledge of sociocultural and political factors affecting second-language development (e.g., family expectations, acculturation patterns, value systems, prior educational experiences, school culture and organization, differential status of the primary language or dialect and the target language, language planning and policies, community influences).

Family expectations for many children are high. Many parents have a positive effect on their children's academics. They frequently express the desire that their children have more education and more opportunities than they did.

Acculturation patterns: Acculturation is the process of becoming accustomed to the customs, language, practices, and environment of a new culture. Factors that influence this process include the learner's desire and ability to become a part of the dominant culture.

Acculturation occurs when two distinct cultures come in contact, altering the original cultural patterns of either or both groups. The cultural groups remain distinct. Definitions acculturation describe this as a two-way process, but research and theory continue to explore the adjustments and changes that the aboriginal peoples, immigrants, and other minorities experience when in contact with the dominant culture. Thus, acculturation is now believed to be the process by which cultural learning is imposed upon the weaker cultures simply because they are weaker. Acculturation then becomes a process of learning a second culture, and the minority culture becomes displaced. **Transculturation** is acculturation by an individual, while acculturation is the same process for a large group.

Accommodation theory emerged in the 1970s as an explanation of the motivations underlying, and the consequences of, adapting our language and communication patterns to others. Since its emergence, it has been applied in a wide variety of disciplines and expanded many times. It can be used to facilitate or impede second-language learning as well as to refer to immigrants' acceptance into host communities. Teachers can facilitate language learning by accommodating their language—vocabulary, structure, and pronunciation—to make it more understandable for those who are striving for proficiency. Immigrant groups or ethnic groups accommodate their cultural heritage to the host or dominant culture in an effort to show their flexibility and willingness to assimilate.

Biculturalism often exists in countries with a history of national or ethnic conflict when neither side has obtained a complete victory. The conflict may be between colonizers and indigenous people(s) or between rival groups of colonizers. The term was first used in Canada to describe the coexistence of the English-speaking and French-speaking cultures. Examples in the United States are the bicultural distinctions that exist between its Caucasian and Mexican citizens or between its Caucasian and African American citizens.

Value systems: Different cultures have different value systems. American values include: personal control over the environment, the importance of time, individualism, and self-help. Other cultures may value tradition, group orientation, past orientation, formality, indirectness, and face-saving. Often people are unaware of their values until challenged about them. Students need to compare and contrast values to heighten their awareness of possible differences.

Prior educational experiences: In schools in the United States, students are expected to sit quietly at their desks, line up to go to the cafeteria or library, be on time, and raise their hands to answer the teacher's questions. Schools in other countries may have expectations and traditions that are completely different. Students may mill around the classroom, walk as a group to other parts of the school, find time unimportant, and shout out answers as soon as they know them. Children must be taught what is expected in their new classroom. This process may take gentle reminders for long periods of time.

School culture and organization: U.S. schools are organized around middle-class European-American experiences. These traditions may be different from those of other cultures. Teachers need to be aware of this. They can then ensure classroom participation of all students in different modalities. It is helpful to use journals and individual conferencing so that students have a chance to express their private concerns to the teacher without peer scrutiny.

Differential status of the primary language or dialect and the target language: Bilingualism is the use of two languages by an individual. Diglossia refers to two languages in the community. Usually when two languages appear in a community, there is a high-language variety and a low-language variety. The high variety tends to be used in interactions outside the home and the low variety is more common with family and inside the home. The high variety is the language of official communication and almost always has the higher status.

Language planning and policies: Tollefsen (1991) claims that language policies are ideological, with the purpose of sustaining existing power relationships. He states, "Language education has become increasingly ideological with the spread of English for specific purposes, curricula and methods that view English as a practical skill, a 'tool' for education and employment."

See Skill 9.2 for community influences.

Skill 10.2 **Analyze the pedagogical implications of sociocultural and political factors for the instruction of English Learners and for program organization (e.g., with respect to creating a culturally and linguistically inclusive classroom and school environment, providing culturally and linguistically inclusive instruction, respecting linguistic and cultural differences, promoting family and community involvement, evaluating program organization).**

Creating a culturally and linguistically inclusive classroom and school environment: Teachers play a pivotal role in creating a classroom environment that is culturally and linguistically inclusive. Demonstrating a positive attitude toward "foreign" clothing, speech, music, food, and other elements of different cultures is the responsibility of the teacher. This positive attitude will help the other students in the class respond affirmatively toward different cultures.

Providing culturally and linguistically inclusive instruction: Teachers can highlight the music, food, and art of different cultures in the classroom. However, it is more important to make the students aware of the feelings, values, and belief systems of other cultures.

Respecting linguistic and cultural differences: Social rules for communication are different among the various cultures of society. In some cultures, children are not allowed to speak until spoken to—the very opposite of what teachers expect when they ask questions of the class. A teacher unaware of cultural differences may not understand that a child is respecting the adult authority figure and waiting to be invited to speak. Another cultural difference may be caused by students' reluctance to call attention to themselves by "'showing off." These students may feel that by "showing off" they make their friends look ignorant if they don't know the answer.

Another method of demonstrating sensitivity is to use appropriate "teacher talk" in the classroom. The wait time for student responses differs in different cultures. Students who are struggling to formulate their answers may need more time than the teacher normally gives for responding. Also, if the questions are rhetorical, students may be reluctant to answer them, as they see no point to such questions.

Promoting family and community involvement: Often in schools, parents, grandparents, and other people involved in children's lives want to take an active role in the educational process. They may all seem to have an opinion on the appropriate method for teaching students how to read or learn English. Sometimes this can lead to controversy and misunderstandings.

By providing opportunities for the public to come into the school and participate in activities, teachers have the opportunity to share information about the methodologies and strategies being implemented. In this way, the public can begin to understand the differences between ESOL instruction today and what it may have been in their native cultures when they attended school. This comparison addresses what is often the biggest concern expressed by adults regarding current educational trends.

Taking the time to educate parents and other family members not only helps to enhance understanding and open communication, it can also provide more support for students than the school alone would ever be able to provide.

Some strategies for educating parents and family members about ESOL methodology include:

- Bingo games in which the correct answer on the Bingo board is a fact about English-language instruction
- small parent workshops offered on various topics
- newsletter pieces or paragraphs
- individual parent meetings
- inviting parents to observe lessons
- small pieces of information shared during other social occasions when parents are invited into the school

Communicating general information about English and appropriate English-language instruction is a good idea. It is just as important to share specific information about students with parents, other school personnel, and the community. Once the teacher has gathered sufficient information about the students, he/she must find appropriate methods to share it with those who need it. Again, depending on the audience, the amount and type of information shared may vary. Some ways to share information with parents/guardians include:

- individual parent meetings
- small group meetings
- regular parent updates through phone calls
- charts and graphs of progress sent home
- notes sent home

Evaluating program organization: Collier and Thomas (1999-2000) state that there are five organizing principles that encourage high academic standards for ELLs:

- Facilitate learning through joint, productive activities among teachers and students
- Develop students' competence in the language and literacy of instruction throughout all instructional activities
- Contextualize teaching and curriculum in the experiences and life skills of home and community
- Challenge students toward cognitive complexity
- Engage students through dialog, especially in instructional conversation

SUBAREA II   ASSESSMENT AND INSTRUCTION

DOMAIN III   ASSESSMENT OF ENGLISH LEARNERS

COMPETENCY 11.0   PRINCIPLES OF STANDARDS-BASED ASSESSMENT AND INSTRUCTION

Skill 11.1   Demonstrate understanding of how the California English Language Development (ELD) standards support the English Language Arts (ELA) standards (e.g., as described in the section entitled "Universal Access to the Language Arts Curriculum" in the Reading/Language Arts Framework for California Public Schools, Kindergarten Through Grade Twelve).

ELD standards support the ELA standards through learning experiences that are understandable and meaningful from the beginning of an ELL's schooling in California. ELLs are engaged in language study through activities such as singing, drama, and reading aloud. Teachers model and teach language patterns and vocabulary students need to continue their study of language arts and other content areas. Activities are designed for further study of English language arts and content standards.

Instructional opportunities are planned by the teacher and supported by the appropriate materials. Teachers create an environment that is conducive to ELD and provide the ELL constructive feedback about the accuracy of oral and written work. The goal is to bring students up to grade level in academic language as soon as possible through high-quality materials and well-qualified teachers.

(Adapted from Reading/Language Arts Framework for California Public Schools, 1999)

Skill 11.2   Apply strategies for ensuring that differentiated, standards-based assessment and instruction address the needs of English Learners (e.g., taking into account the range of English proficiency levels represented in the classroom; providing multiple opportunities to develop English Learners' knowledge, skills, and abilities as outlined in the ELD and content standards; matching the purpose and level of an assessment to an appropriate assessment task; creating an appropriate testing environment; using multiple measures for assessing English Learners' performance with respect to a given standard).

Differentiated instruction is instruction geared to the different English and knowledge levels of students in the classroom. Since all teachers are required to teach the curriculum grade-level standards, it is challenging to provide appropriate instruction to students whose English level may be low.

Teachers need to create lesson plans that reflect the ELD standards for each proficiency level of ELL students. Various methods of assessment can be planned to demonstrate the English level of each student and at the same time contribute to content advancement. For example:

- Students can collaboratively prepare a report/fact sheet based on the topic in the content area
- Each student can presents the facts on the topic of their research orally
- Each student can write a paragraph to display on a poster

An appropriate testing environment is achieved by using both collaborative group work with individual responsibilities. Students should not feel threatened by ongoing evaluation during the presentation of a group project. The teacher can create a relaxed environment by guiding the students through the research process and evaluating for understanding in an informal manner.

Skill 11.3 **Demonstrate understanding of how to use formative and summative assessment to design and implement differentiated, standards-based instruction (e.g., Wiggins and McTighe's "backwards" lesson planning, curriculum calibration, curriculum mapping).**

Formative and summative assessments are essential to teaching. **Formative assessment** occurs during the learning process while both the teacher and the student have the opportunity to modify outcomes. **Summative assessment** usually takes place at the end of a specific task or at the end of the course. It may be represented by a single grade.

To implement **"backwards" lesson planning** (Wiggins and McTighe, 1998), teachers should:

- Identify the expected outcomes
- Determine what is an acceptable competency in the outcome and results
- Plan instructional strategies and learning experiences to achieve the competencies

Backwards lesson planning differs from traditional lesson planning in that outcomes are used to plan the curriculum/lesson rather than the traditional approach which defines topics to be covered.

Curriculum calibration involves an examination of content standards across grade levels. Once the content standards have been agreed upon, practical strategies are designed to align teachers and publishers' textbooks with the grade-level standards previously established. The goal is to raise expectations and increase achievement for all students.

Curriculum mapping is an outline of the unit or course in a schematic form that helps teachers plan their instructional goals. The map can be used to coordinate interdisciplinary studies and assist in scheduling testing or field trips without interfering with teaching and learning. A key component is taking advantage of technology (e.g., PCs and Internet/Intranet capabilities) so that teachers and administrators become familiar with the work that is going on throughout the school/district in real time instead of having to wait for outside committees to determine actions. Teachers are able to revise their work based upon what they discover others are doing.

Skill 11.4 Demonstrate an ability to use ELD and content standards to design and provide differentiated instruction and assessment based on students' assessed English proficiency level.

Teachers are expected to teach content standards to all students. Yet, the ELD standards vary according to each student's ability level. In grouping students for project work, it may be possible to pair nonnative speakers (who have content knowledge but lack the English language skills to express themselves) with native speakers (who don't have content knowledge but can read and write in English). In this way, the teacher draws upon the prior knowledge of each student and the language they use for differentiated instruction goals.

Assessment is based on how well the students understand the vocabulary and various concepts taught in the unit. ELD is assessed based on the demonstrated ability of the student to read and write in English. Assessment for all students can be achieved in distinctive ways, including orally, as ELLs' oral abilities often exceed their ability to read and write.

COMPETENCY 12.0 ROLES, PURPOSES, AND TYPES OF ASSESSMENT

Skill 12.1 Demonstrate knowledge of State-mandated standardized assessments, including the role and use of data from the California English Language Development Test (CELDT) in designing, monitoring, and refining instruction and in identification, placement, and redesignation/reclassification.

The California English Language Development Test (CELDT) results for newly enrolled students are used to identify the English level of students as English learners or as Initial Fluent English Proficient (IFEP). Annual assessments of English learners are used to evaluate their progress in learning English and for reclassification. The CELDT results must be used as one of four criteria when considering reclassification of English learners. Other factors to be considered are a student's performance in basic skills, the teacher's evaluation, and a parent or guardian's opinion and consultation. All English learners are required to take the CELDT annually until they are reclassified.

Skill 12.2   Demonstrate understanding of the role and purposes of assessment in programs for English Learners (e.g., identification, placement, progress, redesignation/reclassification, diagnosis, instructional planning, program evaluation).

There are a multitude of tests for evaluating, assessing, and placing ELLs in appropriate programs. Each test can evaluate a narrow range of language skills (such as discrete tests designed to measure subsets of grammar skills or vocabulary).

Language tests should be chosen on the basis of the information they give, the appropriateness of each instrument for the purpose, and the soundness of the test content. Language has more than two hundred dimensions which can be evaluated, and yet most tests assess less than twelve of them. Therefore, all language testing should be done cautiously, backed up by teacher observations, oral interviews, family-life variables, and school records.

LANGUAGE PLACEMENT AND PROFICIENCY TESTS

A language placement test is designed to place a student within a specific program. The school district may design its own instrument or use a standardized test.

Language proficiency tests measure how well students have met certain standards in a particular language. The standards have been predetermined and are unrelated to any course of study, curriculum, or program. These tests are frequently used when students enter or exit a particular program.

Examples of language proficiency tests include:

- ACT Oral Proficiency Interview (OPI)
- Test of Spoken English (TSE)
- Test of English as a Foreign Language (TOEFL)
- Foreign Service Officer Test (FSOT), Oral Assessment (OA)
- IDEA Proficiency Test (IPT)
- Language Assessment Scales (LAS)

LANGUAGE ACHIEVEMENT TESTS

Language achievement tests are related directly to a specific curriculum or course of study. These tests include subsets of language skills, reading comprehension, parts of speech, and other mechanical parts of the language such as spelling, punctuation, and paragraphing.

Examples of language achievement tests include unit exams and final exams.

DIAGNOSTIC LANGUAGE TESTS

Diagnostic language tests are designed to identify individual students' strengths and weaknesses in languages. They are generally administered by speech therapists or psychologists in clinical settings when specific language learning problems are present.

Skill 12.3   Demonstrate knowledge of assessment issues related to reliability, validity, and test bias and their significance for English Learners.

Certain factors may affect the assessment of ELLs who are not familiar with assessment in the U.S. or California classroom. Among these is lack of familiarity with standard testing techniques. Students may be disconcerted when they are not allowed to ask questions of the teacher, when time constraints are imposed, or when they are only permitted to work on certain sections of a test at a time.

Students may also be uncomfortable when ELLs are allowed specific accommodation during a test session. Accommodations allowed by the test publisher or those prescribed by the state of California need to be introduced in the regular classroom so that ELLs and other students are familiar with them before the testing session begins.

The constructs of reliability and validity are crucial in assessing ELLs because of the high stakes involved in testing in today's schools. Decisions about schools, teachers, and students are based on these tests. A reliable assessment for ELLs will have the following three attributes: validity, reliability, and practicality.

VALIDITY

An assessment can only be considered "valid" if it measures what it claims to measure. If an ELL test claims to measure oral proficiency, then the test should include a section in which instructors ask the ELL to pronounce certain words, listen to the instructor's pronunciation and determine if it is correct, and/or respond directly to the instructor's questions.

According to Diaz-Rico and Weed (1995), *"...empirical validity is a measure of how effectively a test relates to some other known measure."* There are different types of validity: predictive and concurrent (Diaz-Rico and Weed, 1995). "Predictive" empirical validity is concerned with the possible outcomes of test performance, while "concurrent" empirical validity is connected with another variable for measurement. For example, if a learner shows a high level of English speech proficiency in class, then the instructor would expect the learner to perform well during an oral proficiency exam.

Test Bias

Avalos (in Schumm: *Reading Assessment and Instruction for All Learners*, 2006.) states that there are four types of bias that can affect validity:

- **Cultural bias:** Concerns acquired knowledge from participating in and sharing certain cultural values and experiences. Asking questions about birthday or holiday celebrations presumes a middle-class family experience. Immigrants may not celebrate birthdays because they live in poverty or may celebrate a birthday differently (e.g.,, with an extended family and piñatas).
- **Attitudinal bias:** This refers to the negative attitude of the examiner toward a certain language, dialect, or culture. Just as low expectations from instructors can produce poor results (the Pygmalion effect), the same thing happens during testing when a negative attitude conveyed by the assessor, teacher, or school culture can produce negative test results.
- **Test bias or norming bias:** This type of bias refers to excluding ELLs or different populations from the school's population used to obtain the norm results.
- **Translation bias:** Occurs when the test is literally translated from L2 to L1 by interpreters or other means. The "essence" of the test may be lost in such translation because it is difficult to translate cultural concepts.

RELIABILITY

A test can only be considered "reliable" if similar scores result when the test is taken a second time. Factors such as anxiety, hunger, tiredness, and uncomfortable environmental conditions should not cause a major fluctuation in the learner's score. Typically, if a learner earns a score of 90% on a test that was created by the instructor, then averages predict that the learner probably scored 45% on one half of the test and 45% on the other half, regardless of the structure of the test items.

PRACTICALITY

A test that proves to be both valid and reliable may unfortunately prove to be cost- or time-prohibitive. The ideal test would be one that is easy to administer and easy to grade, as well as one that includes test items similar to what the learners have experienced in class. However, when writing journals are used for assessment, practicality becomes an issue. Journals are an excellent method for learners to explore their critical literacy skills and track language achievement progress, but they can be difficult to grade due to the subjective nature of the content, and they may not be a fair representation of what learners have encountered in class.

Skill 12.4 **Demonstrate applied knowledge of how to identify and address cultural and linguistic bias in student assessment (e.g., in relation to test administration, established norms, test content) and understand the process by which test developers work to eliminate bias.**

Teachers must be able to recognize tests that have cultural and/or linguistic bias. This prevents injustices from being done when students are classified and assessed.

- **Teacher bias** may occur when teachers are not fully trained in the application of tests; fully training test administrators is one way to eliminate this problem.
- **Cultural bias** occurs when test questions have contexts that are unfamiliar to the students. This frequently occurs when tests items are written using white middle-class contexts that are often unfamiliar to minorities. Using tests written by a multicultural team will reduce cultural bias. Also, doing trial runs of tests helps pinpoint areas of difficulty.
- **Linguistic bias** occurs if English is the only option offered to Limited-English-Proficient (LEP) students. Whenever possible, students should be tested in both their native language and English until such time as they are Fluent-English-Proficient (FEP).

Skill 12.5 **Demonstrate understanding of various types of classroom assessments for English Learners and their purposes, features, and limitations (e.g., textbook assessments, performance-based assessments, curriculum-based assessments, authentic assessments, teacher-made tests).**

Hughes (1989) makes a number of distinctions between test types:

Proficiency tests: These tests are designed to measure students' proficiency in the target language irrespective of any prior training in that language. Their criteria are based on what candidates have to be able to do in the language in order to be considered proficient for a particular purpose (e.g.,, for college/university or to be a UN translator).

Achievement tests: Unlike proficiency tests, achievement tests are directly related to language courses and establish how successful the students or the course itself is in achieving the objectives.

Diagnostic tests: These tests are used to identify students' strengths and weaknesses. The aim is to determine what still needs to be taught to the students and who can benefit from individual instruction.

Placement tests: Placement tests are typically used to determine the class level in which the student should be placed according to his/her abilities.

Direct versus indirect testing: These are two approaches to test construction. Direct testing requires the candidate to perform precisely the skill to be measured. For example, if we want to know how well candidates can write compositions, the test would ask them to write a composition. Indirect testing tries to determine the abilities that underlie the skills that are important for the testing purpose. An example would be a paper-and-pencil test for testing pronunciation ability in which the candidates have to identify pairs of words that rhyme with each other.

Discrete-point versus integrative testing: Discrete-point testing refers to the testing of one element at a time, item by item. This type of test might contain a number of items, with each one testing a particular grammatical structure. Integrative testing makes use of a combination of language elements for a candidate to complete a task. This could range from taking notes while listening to a lecture to writing a composition.

Norm-referenced versus criterion-referenced testing: A norm-referenced test relates one candidate's performance to that of other candidates. It does not show directly what the student is capable of doing in the language. For example, the test score would place the student in the top ten percent of candidates who have taken the test or indicate that a candidate did better than sixty percent of those who took it. A criterion-referenced test classifies people according to whether or not they are able to perform a task or set of tasks successfully. The candidates who perform the tasks successfully pass irrespective of how the rest of the candidates did on the test.

Objective testing versus subjective testing: The difference in these two types of tests is in the method of scoring. If no judgment is required by the scorer during the scoring process, then the test is objective (e.g., a multiple-choice test). However, if judgment of the scorer is required, then the test is subjective (e.g., a written paper).

Communicative language testing: A lot of discussions have emphasized the importance of measuring students' ability to take part in acts of communication (including reading and listening) and the best way to do this. A number of informal testing methods can be used. For example, teachers can observe students working on a task in groups or students' or they could structure an assessment so that comprehension of a reading passage enabled students to successfully complete a task.

See Skill 12.3

Skill 12.6 **Demonstrate understanding of the importance of selecting and using appropriate classroom assessments (e.g., district benchmarks, textbook assessments, differentiated levels of discussion questions for checking understanding) that enable English Learners to demonstrate their knowledge and skills according to their English proficiency level.**

District benchmarks: The student's performance can be compared to others in the school and district through district benchmarks. This gives the teacher invaluable information about the relationship of the student to the grade-level standards.

Textbook assessments: Textbook content should reflect the district/state's standards for each grade level. By using textbook assessments, the teacher can monitor progress and students' mastery of the content.

Differentiated levels of discussion questions to check for understanding: As each ELL's performance is different, the teacher uses differentiated levels of discussion questions to evaluate the comprehension and mastery of content. These questions should be evaluated using the guidelines established for ELD proficiency.

COMPETENCY 13.0   LANGUAGE AND CONTENT-AREA ASSESSMENT

Skill 13.1   Demonstrate knowledge of the characteristics, advantages, and limitations of various informal and formal ELD assessments (i.e., oral-language, reading, and writing assessments) and content area assessments for English Learners.

The following are examples of **alternative assessments** that offer options for an instructor:

- **Portfolios:** Portfolios are a collection of a student's work over a period of time (report cards, creative writing, drawing, and so on) that also function as an assessment, because they indicate a range of competencies and skills and are representative of instructional goals and academic growth.
- **Conferencing:** This assessment tool allows the instructor to evaluate a student's progress or decline. Students also learn techniques for self-evaluation.
- **Oral interviews:** Teachers can use oral interviews to evaluate the language the students are using or their ability to respond when asked questions—both of which have implications for further instructional planning.
- **Teacher observation:** During this type of assessment, the instructor observes student behavior during an activity when the student is alone or in a group. Before the observation occurs, the instructor may want to create a numerical scale to rate desired outcomes.
- **Documentation:** Documentation is similar to teacher observation. However, documentation tends to transpire over a period of time, rather than in isolated observations.
- **Interviews:** This type of assessment allows instructors to evaluate the student's level of English proficiency as well as identify potential problem areas that may require correctional strategies.
- **Self-assessment:** Students benefit tremendously from self-assessment because through the process of self-analysis they begin to "think" for themselves. Instructors need to provide guidance as well as the criteria related to success.

- **Student journals:** Students benefit from journals because they are useful for keeping records as well as promoting an inner dialog.
- **Story or text retelling:** Students respond orally and can be assessed on how well they describe events in the story or text as well as their response to the story and/or to their language proficiency.
- **Experiments and/or demonstrations:** Students complete an experiment or demonstration and present it through an oral or written report. Students can be evaluated on their understanding of the concept, explanation of the scientific method, and/or their language proficiency.

See Skill 12.2

Skill 13.2   Demonstrate conceptual understanding and applied knowledge of how to interpret and use assessment results in the areas of oral language, reading and writing, and the content areas, including being able to identify student variations in performance that are not related to language acquisition and that may require special attention or referral (e.g., Gifted and Talented Education [GATE], Student Success Team [SST], Special Education, intervention programs).

Potentially **gifted students** are identified as gifted in three different ways:

- **Demonstrated high ability**: The students may then be referred by parents or teachers to a screening committee for further consideration.
- **High achievement:** Based on high achievement on standardized tests, students may be recommended for further screening.
- **High IQ score:** Students with a full-scale IQ score of 132 or above on a privately administered intelligence test will be screened for possible GATE placement.

STUDENT SUCCESS TEAMS (FORMERLY STUDENT STUDY TEAMS)—SST

If a student is determined to be at risk of retention, after consulting with parents or guardians, the regular classroom teacher, or multiple teachers, it may be decided that retention is not in the best interest of the student. In this case, an early school-wide identification and intervention process designed to prevent school dropouts may be initiated. The student and parents form part of the discussion process. A student's strengths are identified so that an improvement plan can be designed by teachers and school administrators. Follow-up meetings are programmed to provide continuous monitoring so that maximum achievement is realized. (Adapted from California Department of Education, http://www.cde.ca.gov/ls/ai/dp/sb65sst.asp)

SPECIAL EDUCATION

Teachers are often the first to recognize that children are struggling with classwork and have limitations that are not related to ELD. Proper assessment helps teacher(s) and administrators determine if the child's abilities are being challenged. Should this be the case, further testing can be recommended. Teachers can initiate the process for more thorough evaluation of the individual's abilities, strengths, and weaknesses.

To be eligible for special education, a student must have one of thirteen recognized disabilities:

- Specific learning disability
- Speech and language disability
- Other health impairment
- Severe emotional disturbance
- Autism spectrum/pervasive developmental disorder
- Mental retardation (limited cognitive ability)
- Hearing impairment
- Deafness
- Deaf-blindness
- Multiple disabilities
- Orthopedic impairment
- Traumatic brain injury
- Visual impairment

If the student already has an Individual Education Plan (IEP), assessments are used to revise the IEP and establish appropriate services. Eligibility for special education services as well as accommodations provided under the 504 plan must be determined through assessments.

INTERVENTION PROGRAMS

Programs are established to intervene if students show cognitive difficulties (typically in mathematics and English language arts) or noncognitive difficulties (attendance problems or behavior problems). Depending on the type of problem exhibited by the student, appropriate interventions can be initiated using the resources of the school and district. For cognitive problems, students can be referred to SST programs. For noncognitive problems, additional information can be found in the following documents:

- *School Attendance Improvement Handbook* (PDF; 1.51 MB; 92pp.)
  http://www.cde.ca.gov/ls/ai/cw/documents/schoolattendance.pdf
  This handbook provides strategies to improve school attendance.

- *Resilience and Youth Development Module* (PDF; outside source).
  http://chks.wested.org/using_results/resilience
  Prepared by WestEd and the Safe and Healthy Kids Program Office, California Department of Education, 2002.

Skill 13.3   Demonstrate an ability to analyze student assessments and assessment results in order to modify and differentiate instruction, to plan strategies for reteaching specific content and/or skills as necessary, and to select or design classroom modifications/interventions to address individual English Learners' needs.

Teachers can use the results of student assessment to modify and differentiate instruction with all students. When students do not reach the standards, teachers need to look carefully at students' work and decide exactly what needs to be re-taught, if necessary, and how.

Re-teaching a skill can often be achieved by incorporating it into the next task being taught without any undue emphasis. It is also possible that the standard was not reached because the material was too complex for the students and needs to be simplified. It may be that the students did not have sufficient background on the topic.

In some cases, failure to reach a standard may be one of a series of standards a student has failed to meet and consideration should be given to initiating the process of intervention on behalf of the student. Only the teacher can analyze the assessment and set new goals for future success.

Skill 13.4   Apply strategies for differentiating and scaffolding ELD and content-area assessment tasks for English Learners.

Differentiated instruction helps teachers cope with diverse learning and learners in the classroom. Differentiated instruction implies that teachers will decide what all students will learn about a topic, what some will learn and what a few will learn. Students are not placed in learning levels, but instead the instruction is organized so that all students have the opportunity to explore the topic. Upper levels of mastery are more complex and may be achieved by those who are eager to gain a deeper understanding of the task and material. However, since all materials are available to all students, the student is in charge of the learning and the teacher becomes a facilitator or coach.

Teachers can use **scaffolding techniques** with ELLs by helping the learner focus on the key parts of an assignment. Through questioning, teachers provide opportunities for students to verbalize what they know (or demonstrate what they do not know) about the task. Tasks can also be broken down into smaller segments, which allows students to think and talk about the task more successfully.

DOMAIN IV   FOUNDATIONS OF ENGLISH LANGUAGE/LITERACY
                 DEVELOPMENT AND CONTENT INSTRUCTION

COMPETENCY 14.0   FOUNDATIONS OF PROGRAMS FOR ENGLISH
                       LEARNERS

Skill 14.1   Demonstrate understanding of the historical, legal, and legislative
              foundations of educational programs for English Learners, including
              federal laws, state laws and policies, judicial decisions, and
              demographic changes and their effects on educational programs for
              English Learners (e.g., No Child Left Behind Act of 2001 [NCLB], Title
              III; Individuals with Disabilities Education Improvement Act of 2004
              [IDEA]; Proposition 227; Williams v. State of California ; Lau v.
              Nichols).

Several legal precedents have established that schools must provide equal educational
opportunities for ELLs. This has led directly to improved language instruction and
accommodations for language deficiencies. The Civil Rights Act of 1964 established
that schools, as recipients of federal funds, cannot discriminate against ELLs: "No
person in the United States shall, on the grounds of race, color, or national origin, be
excluded from participation in, be denied the benefits of, or be subjected to
discrimination under any program or activity receiving federal financial assistance."

In 1970, this mandate was detailed more specifically for ELLs in the **May 25
Memorandum**: "Where inability to speak and understand the English language
excludes national origin-minority group children from effective participation in the
educational program offered by a school district, the district must take affirmative steps
to rectify the language deficiency in order to open its instructional program to these
students." The memorandum specifically addressed the practice of placing ELLs, based
on their English-language skills, in classes with mentally retarded students, excluding
them from college preparatory classes, and failing to notify parents of ELLs of school
activities, even if translation is required.

LAU V. NICHOLS

Lau v. Nichols (1974): A 1969 class action suit filed on behalf of the Chinese community
in San Francisco alleged that the school district denied "equal educational opportunity"
to their children because the classes the children were required to attend were not
taught in the Chinese native language. The Supreme Court ruled in favor of the
plaintiffs, and determined a set of requirements that academic programs must provide.

Related to Lau v. Nichols, the Office of the Department of Health, Education and
Welfare created a committee of experts, who established guidelines and procedures for
local educational groups serving the LEP population. The "Lau Remedies" became
guidelines for all states to assist in the academic needs of LEP students; the "Lau
Remedies" also provided guidelines for "exiting" LEP programs.

Per Lau v. Nichols, the Supreme Court ruled that no student shall be denied "equal access" to any academic program, due to "limited English proficiency."

CASTANEDA V. PICKARD

In Castaneda v. Pickard, which was filed against the Raymondville, Texas Independent School District (RISD), Mexican-American children and their parents claimed that the district was discriminating against them, because of their ethnicity. They argued that classrooms were segregated using a grouping system based on racially and ethnically discriminatory criteria. School districts were required to establish bilingual education according to the Lau vs. Nichols ruling, yet, there was no way to evaluate the adequacy of the school's approach. Consequently, sometimes it could result in inadequate separation.

The case was tried and on August 17, 1978 the judge ruled in favor of the defendant, stating that the district had not violated any of the plaintiff's constitutional or statutory rights. The ruling was appealed and in 1981, the Fifth Circuit Court of Appeals ruled in favor of the plaintiffs. In addition, the Castañeda vs. Pickard case established three criteria for a program that serves LEP students. These measures determine whether a school district is serving the LEP students and if the program addresses the needs of these students. The principles are as follows:

- It must be based on "a sound educational theory."
- It must be "implemented effectively," with adequate resources and personnel.
- After a trial period, it must be evaluated as effective in overcoming language handicaps.

A NATION AT RISK REPORT

The 1983 **A Nation at Risk** report, produced by the National Commission on Excellence in Education, concluded that the U. S. educational system was failing to meet the national need for a competitive workforce. This prompted a flurry of education reforms and initiated the National Assessment of Educational Progress (NAEP), which keeps an ongoing record of school performance. While general participation is voluntary, all schools that receive Title I money must participate. This funding is set aside for low socioeconomic and minority students, which includes a large percentage of ELLs.

PROPOSITION 227

In 1998, California passed **Proposition 227,** mandating sheltered English immersion for a temporary transitional period not to normally exceed one year. The statute permits parents to request a waiver and receive bilingual education (or enroll in an alternative program). According to Unrau (2008), the California Department of Education states that a structured immersion program must contain the following elements:

- a curriculum designed specifically for ELLs
- teachers who are trained in second-language acquisition methods
- instructional strategies designed for language learning

WILLIAMS V. STATE OF CALIFORNIA

Williams v. State of California was filed as a class action suit in 2000 and settled in 2004. Williams claimed that state education agencies, including the California Department of Education (CDE), failed to provide public school students with equal access to instructional materials, safe and decent school facilities, and qualified teachers.

As a result of the Williams case, the CDE has proposed changes to the School Accountability Report Card (SARC) template that all schools must update and publish annually. The proposed changes will help all schools report the overall condition of their facilities, the number of teacher misassignments and vacant teacher positions, and the availability of textbooks or instructional materials. The proposed changes were submitted to the State Board of Education and approved at its meeting on November 9, 2004.

NO CHILD LEFT BEHIND ACT (NCLB)

Most recently, the **No Child Left Behind Act (NCLB)** (2001) established requirements that school districts must meet to continue to receive federal funds. The law has a number of requirements, but the one that has affected ELLs most is the system of evaluating school performance based on disaggregated data. Schools can no longer rely on high-performing students to average out the low performance of language-challenged students. While the law is far from perfect, it prohibits schools from burying the low performance of any subpopulation in a school-wide average.

Despite its many positive results, since its inception the NCLB has been frequently criticized. Some of the criticisms and arguments against the NCLB are:

Some of the Criticisms of NCLB

- Schools, districts, and states manipulate the test results. (NEA: 2008-2009 Adequate Yearly Progress (AYP) Results.)

- Standardized tests are problematic and encourage teachers to teach to the test. (Menken, 2006),
- There are incentives against low-performing students. The law imposes punitive measures on schools, encouraging some schools to lower standards rather than raising them. (NEA: 2008-2009 Adequate Yearly Progress (AYP) Results.)
- Since NCLB is egalitarian, no provisions are made for gifted, talented, and high-performing students. (Cloud, 2007)
- Some states refuse to produce non-English assessments and in others the emphasis is on monolingual instruction. (Menken, 2006)
- High schools are essentially ignored by the NCLB in areas of funding, measurements, and improvement strategies. (Alliance for Excellent Education, 2007)
- The law increases segregation in public schools.
    - African Americans score considerably lower on almost every indicator of academic skills than whites do. High-minority and high-poverty schools score lower on standardized tests than low-minority and low-poverty schools. (Children's Defense Fund. 2005).
    - Statistics show that 71 percent of African Americans attend high-minority schools and 72 percent of African Americans attend high-poverty schools.
    - African-Americans are four times as likely to not meet proficiency scores as their white counterparts. (Knaus, 2007).
    - Low-performing schools must offer parents the opportunity to transfer their child to a non-failing school within the district after failing to make adequate yearly progress (AYP) for two years. Normally, parents with more education and resources are the most likely to take advantage of this provision. By making informed choices about where to transfer their child, de facto segregation by both race and class occurs. (Orfield, Eaton, and The Harvard Project on School Desegregation, 1996).
- There is inadequate funding.
    - Despite federal mandates, funding has been inadequate to meet the criteria established in the Act, leading some to remind the states that education is a state responsibility. (Merrow, 2001).
    - Nevertheless, the punitive nature of the law requires states to improve their AYP but does not grant the funding necessary for them to do so. The NEA in conjunction with school districts in Michigan, Texas, and Vermont has sued the NCLB Act claiming funding issues were unclear. (Education Matters, 2008)

Skill 14.2 Demonstrate knowledge of federal and state requirements for program implementation (e.g., NCLB, Title III; IDEA; Proposition 227; Williams v. State of California; Lau v. Nichols).

Title VII defines an LEP as one who:
(A)

- was not born in the U.S. or whose native language is a language other than English and comes from an environment where a language other than English is dominant, or a Native American or Alaska Native or who is a resident of the outlying areas and comes from an environment where a language other than English has had a significant impact on the individual's development of English;
- is migratory and whose native language is other than English and comes from an environment where a language other than English is dominant; and

(B) has sufficient difficulty speaking, reading, writing, or understanding the English language that those difficulties may deny such individual the opportunity to learn successfully in classrooms where the language of instruction is English or to participate fully in our society.

Several legal precedents have established that schools must provide equal educational opportunities for ELLs. This legal support has led directly to improved language instruction and accommodations for language deficiencies.

See Skill 14.1 for background information on Lau v. Nichols, Castaneda v. Pickard, and A Nation at Risk

The No Child Left Behind Act (2000) has several core provisions including:

- All students must be proficient in reading and math by 2014, as defined and mandated by state standards
- States must assess students in math and reading once a year in grades 3-8 and at least once during high school.
- Every public school must be evaluated to see if it has made Adequate Yearly Progress (AYP). This is based primarily on the percentage of students scoring 'proficient' or above on state assessments, overall and for each of the following categories of students: economically disadvantaged students, students from major racial and ethnic groups, students with disabilities, and students with limited English proficiency (LEP).
- Schools that receive Title I funding and are identified as "needing improvement" must develop a school improvement plan. For each year that the school does not make AYP, the school must undertake specific actions to overcome its deficiencies. These schools are required to spend federal funds to implement federally mandated strategies—public school choice, supplemental education services (SES), corrective action, and restructuring.

(Adapted from Alliance for Excellent Education, 2007).

In 2000, Eiezer Williams filed a class action suit, **Williams v. State of California**, on behalf of millions of California students. In 2004, the case was settled, and two fundamental precedents established:

1. The state is required to provide trained teachers, adequate materials, and safe facilities for all students.
2. All students have the right to an equal education.

The impact for English Learners is noteworthy because the case established the right of English Learners, like all other students:

1. to have adequate texts and materials for the classroom and to take home
2. to have teachers who are trained to teach them
3. to have the standards they are required to meet clearly posted
4. to have their parents file complaints if the requirements are not met within their school

The reauthorized **Individuals with Disabilities Education Act (IDEA)** was signed into law on Dec. 3, 2004, by President George W. Bush. The provisions of the act became effective on July 1, 2005, with the exception of some of the elements pertaining to the definition of a "highly qualified teacher" that took effect upon the signing of the act. The final regulations were published on Aug. 14, 2006.

Each state that receives assistance under Part B of the Act, and the Secretary of the Interior, must provide for the collection and examination of data to determine if significant disproportionality based on race and ethnicity is occurring in the state and the local educational agencies (LEAs) of the state with respect to:

- The identification of children as children with disabilities, including the identification of children as children with disabilities in accordance with a particular impairment described in section 602(3) of the Act
- The placement in particular educational settings of these children
- The incidence, duration, and type of disciplinary actions, including suspensions and expulsions

The identification of English Learners who actually are learning disabled is compounded by the lack of first-language testing materials that would identify learning problems, and by teachers who have not been trained in the language-acquisition process, in particular, the "silent period," during which time a new learner may appear unresponsive, uncooperative, or generally "lost." IDEA is designed to examine and reduce the number of students who are inappropriately classified as learning disabled.

In 1998, **Proposition 227** was passed in California, mandating that English learners be taught following a specific pattern. Instruction was to be "overwhelmingly in English," and students were to have immersion classes with sheltered, or structured, English instruction for a maximum of one year. Parents were given the alternative of signing a waiver if they wished their student to receive bilingual education.

Since California currently has more than 1/3 of the five million English learners in the United States, the proposition had great impact. After five years, the California Department of Education commissioned the American Institute for Research to conduct a study of the results of Proposition 227. The following are findings of that study:

- The performance gap between English Learners and other students remained constant over the five years of the study. This finding is significant because during the period in question there was a substantial increase in the number of ELLs participating in statewide testing.
- The likelihood of an ELL student reclassifying to English-proficient status after ten years in California schools is less than 40 percent.
- The methods recommended by Proposition 227 have been shown to have no significant impact on the success of English Learners.

The recommendation of the study was that schools put less emphasis on specific methods and focus more on rewarding academic success and implementing appropriate interventions when failure occurs. (Parrish, 2006)

Section (9) of **Title III, the renewed No Child Left Behind Act**, would seem to set itself in direction opposition to Proposition 227:

(Section 3102. Purposes)
The purposes of this part are:

(8) to hold State educational agencies, local educational agencies, and schools accountable for increases in English proficiency and core academic content knowledge of limited English proficient children by requiring:

(A) demonstrated improvements in the English proficiency of limited English proficient children each fiscal year; and

(B) adequate yearly progress for limited English proficient children, including immigrant children and youth, as described in section 1111(b)(2)(B); and

(9) to provide State educational agencies and local educational agencies with the flexibility to implement language instruction educational programs, based on scientifically based research on teaching limited English proficient children, that *the agencies believe to be the most effective for teaching English* (emphasis added).

It can be seen that the best policies and methods for teaching English Learners remain very much open to debate, even at the highest levels of policy making.

Skill 14.3   Demonstrate understanding of the political foundations of educational programs for English Learners (e.g., views and attitudes about bilingualism, heritage-language movement, English-only movement).

Views on how to deal with the multitude of languages spoken in the United States have varied widely over the years, and had considerable impact on the educational system.

ENGLISH-ONLY PROGRAMS

While the federal government has never imposed legislation mandating an official language, many states have adopted forms of **Official English** legislation. In his book *Language Loyalties* (1992, pp. 2-3), James Crawford summarizes the opposing views of those who advocate English only:

- **For supporters,** reaffirming the preeminence of English means reaffirming a unifying force in American life. English is an essential tool of social mobility and economic advancement. The English Language amendment would send a message to immigrants encouraging them to join in rather than remain apart.
- **For opponents,** Official English or English Only are attempts to coerce conformity by terminating services in other languages. The amendment poses a threat to civil rights, educational opportunities, and free speech. It insults groups whose roots in this country go deeper than those of English speakers: Mexican Americans, Puerto Ricans, and Native Americans.

As summarized in the ERIC Digests, (www.ericdigests.org/1999-4/english.htm), language-minority children are positively affected by the opportunity to use their mother tongue in school. These children can use their background knowledge in the first language to make sense of the unfamiliar one. Even when the written form of the first language and English are distinctly different—as are Chinese characters and the English alphabet, for example—the children are able to apply the visual, linguistic, and cognitive strategies used in their first language to reading and writing in English (Freeman and Freeman, 1992). These essential resources are unavailable when children are thrown into an English-only situation in which they are expected to learn unfamiliar content in an unfamiliar language. Without the bridge provided by their first language, their chances of academic success are severely reduced.

Moreover, researchers (Wong-Fillmore, 1992; Gibson, 1998) have maintained that the consequences of losing a mother tongue for language-minority children are often extensive and severe. Family communication may deteriorate.

As education in the United States becomes increasingly verbocentric (Leland and Harste, 1994), with language the dominant means of teaching and learning, the limited language skills possessed by children who have lost their mother tongue without complete mastery of their second language are inadequate to support their learning.

TWO-WAY IMMERSION PROGRAMS

Two-way immersion programs serve both an English-only population and a population of students who speak a partner language in their families and communities. (Howard and Sugarman, 2007). These programs focus on developing proficiency in two languages while also developing the academic skills of all the students in the program. While there are many positive benefits, such K-12 schools face definite challenges. For instance, the English-speaking population tends to be middle class, while the heritage-language population is working class (Christian, 2007). This cultural and socioeconomic difference in population can contribute to making social interaction problematic. In one two-way immersion school the majority of the English-speaking students had computers available at home, while the majority of the partner-language students did not. When the fifth graders study California missions, the English-speaking parents often take their students to visit those missions, while the partner-language students have no such advantage.

Two-way immersion programs are largely elementary-level public schools, charter schools, magnet schools, or private schools. A coalition of parents can request a two-way immersion program from their school district. (Cloud, Genesee, and Hamayan, 2000).

HERITAGE LANGUAGE MOVEMENT

The **heritage language movement** is often based in ethnic communities and has the purpose of teaching academic language and history in the heritage language in order to maintain connections within families and communities.

Historically, in the United States the strongest efforts in this movement have occurred outside mainstream schooling where education in languages other than English was characterized almost exclusively as foreign language teaching (Valdes, 2001). Because these schools have been organized privately, no centralized government records have been maintained.

Linguist Joshua Fishman undertook studies in 1960 and again in 1980 to identify and document such schools. The more recent study identified more than six thousand heritage language schools, teaching 145 different languages, 91 of which were indigenous American languages. The most common languages taught in heritage language schools were Chinese, French, Hebrew, Italian, Japanese, Korean, Polish, Portuguese, Spanish, Ukrainian, and Yiddish (Fishman, 2001). Some, such as the German Language School Conference and the Chinese School Association, are organized into regional or national networks.

Skill 14.4   **Demonstrate understanding of basic empowerment issues related to the education of English Learners (e.g., creating a positive affective environment for all students, including English Learners, in the classroom and the school; promoting inclusive parent and community involvement; valuing cultural and linguistic diversity; respecting parent program choices).**

Students who enter the classroom without a full command of the language of instruction are at an affective disadvantage. They may suffer from various forms of cultural or linguistic shock which has an impact on their ability to process new vocabulary. They may shut down for a period of time. They normally undergo what Krashen has named the "silent period," when they begin to try to make sense of the new words and structures but do not speak or participate in language activities.

Teachers can help to create a positive emotional environment for English Learners by recognizing and acknowledging what the student already knows. This can be done by learning the correct way to pronounce the new student's name, by finding a buddy who speaks the ELL's primary language, by pointing out on the map where the ELL has come from, by helping other class members learn some words in the ELL's primary language, or utilizing other techniques of inclusion.

Honoring parents who do not speak English can help significantly to reduce the disjunction between ELLs and their non-English-speaking parents. Parents can be invited to cook, play music, or simply visit the classroom.

State law mandates that parents be notified in their primary language of their right to place their child in bilingual or other alternative programs. It is the teacher's responsibility to ensure that this information is actually delivered in a comprehensible fashion, and that the parents' choices are honored.

Skill 14.5   **Demonstrate understanding of equity issues related to the education of English Learners (e.g., achievement gap, dropout rates, expulsion and detention rates, retention/promotion, tracking, access to AP classes, segregation, length of program, special education placement, gifted education placement, teacher qualifications, teacher retention, funding and resources).**

Remarkably, the achievement gap between English Learners and the mainstream community has remained constant through the five years of the California Department of Education's study of California schools (2002-2006), in spite of a large increase in the number of English Learners during the same period.

According to the Department of Education figures, in 2007-2008, California dropouts were made up of 12 percent white students, 8 percent Asian students, and 25 percent Latino students. Since bilingual aides, teachers, and instructional materials are much more readily available for Spanish-speaking students than for the Asian population, these figures would argue that something other than "appropriate additional support" is at play.

Tracking is another area that will require more concentrated effort. While a significant number of seventh and eighth graders drop out of school, for instance, California did not keep records on these numbers until 2010, according to State Superintendent Jack O'Connell. According to the April 20, 2010, report of the California legislative analyst, successful application for the state fiscal stabilization funding (SFSF) will require a complete preschool through college data-collection system to address this need.

Identification of English Learners with special needs is problematic because of the lack of testing materials in students' heritage languages. When materials are available, it may be the case that students do not read or write in their primary language. The same problem also complicates students' placement in Advanced Placement (AP) or Gifted and Talented Education (GATE) classes.

Teachers are required under the 2001 No Child Left Behind Act, to be "highly qualified," which means they must have:

1. at least a B.A. degree
2. a state license or credential
3. demonstrated subject matter competency

If students are taught for more than four consecutive weeks by a non-highly qualified teacher, the school is obliged to send parental notification.

Schools that fail to meet state standards for providing "highly qualified" teachers will face state interventions. After one year of noncompliance, the school must provide an action plan for bringing the school into compliance.

Because experienced teachers are more frequently employed at high-performing schools and new teachers are more frequently placed in low-performing schools, and because the highest concentration of English Learners is in low-performing schools, it is perhaps inevitable that English Learners are less likely than others to have highly qualified teachers. Some teachers and school reform advocates are calling for a more equitable distribution of the highly qualified teachers now in classrooms. Court cases are currently challenging the right of districts to call teaching interns "highly qualified."

Federal funding, such as Local Agency Program (LAP) funding, attempts to address the inequity by providing funds only to schools that demonstrate improvement.

Skill 14.6 **Demonstrate understanding of the impact of district and school philosophies on educational policies and practices for English Learners.**

Teachers recognize that there have been many changes since the days when students were punished for speaking their heritage language on school grounds, and a new student's name was routinely translated to an English version. However, the legislation governing instruction of English Learners allows wide latitude for interpretation within districts and schools.

How much of the instructional day, for instance, is required to be conducted "overwhelmingly" in English? What constitutes "appropriate additional support?" How is a school to provide accurate placement for students without first-language assessment materials to determine special needs? How is the school to recognize and record progress in English literacy that remains well below state grade-level standards? Many of these questions are decided at the district level, making best practices difficult to identify and disseminate, and allowing for a wide variance in the quality of services offered.

Skill 14.7 **Demonstrate knowledge of the philosophy/assumptions, characteristics (e.g., placement and exit criteria, program length, class composition, language components), and research on the effectiveness of various types and models of programs for English Learners in California. For example:**

a. Alternative course of study (e.g.,, transitional/developmental bilingual educational programs, dual-language programs, heritage-language programs)

Alternative programs such as **dual language** and **heritage language** programs are based on research indicating that students learn more efficiently when literacy skills and content are taught in the language with which they are most familiar. Learning to read in a phonetic language such as Spanish, in which each letter represents only one sound, is faster and easier than learning to read in English, so learners are able to develop basic skills more readily. The skills acquired in developing first-language literacy readily transfer to literacy in the second language. As spoken-language vocabulary increases with exposure, second-language literacy is more effectively taught, so a delay in teaching second-language literacy actually saves time.

Newcomer centers are transitional programs that provide middle-grade elementary students with the opportunity to have core subjects—math, science, and social studies—taught in the primary language for a maximum of one year, with an ESL class as part of the instructional day.

Such programs also subscribe to the philosophy that bilingualism is an important asset that is best developed early.

b. Structured English Immersion (SEI)

Structured English Immersion (SEI) classes endeavor to teach content in a way that carefully builds vocabulary and sentence structures to facilitate understanding. California law mandates at least a full hour of English instruction in such classes, with the class made up of students who are no farther apart than one CELDT level. Content throughout the day is delivered in "sheltered" or "structured" English—a method that reduces unnecessary language and tries to make English content comprehensible. The word *sheltered* implies some sort of disability on the part of second-language learners and is therefore avoided in California, though it is in wide use in other states.

c. English-language mainstream programs with additional and appropriate support

Putting English Learners into mainstream classes with additional support has been the most common of the program options in California, particularly in areas where there are few speakers of the heritage language. "Additional and appropriate support" has been variously interpreted to mean peer support, such as classroom buddies, instructional aides, and pullout tutorials.

After the passage of Proposition 227, a five-year study was mandated by the California Department of Education to evaluate the effectiveness of the various programs. Difficulties in evaluating programs were compounded by the fact that implementation of each type of program varied widely. The study found no quantifiable difference among the success rates of the different programs, as reflected by standardized test scores.

The wide variety of implementation among school districts has led some to call for clarification of the terms used in the legislation, such as "overwhelmingly in English." Schools with bilingual immersion programs have claimed that the standardized California tests, such as STAR, do not accurately reflect their students' progress, since the bulk of their learning takes place in the primary language, and there are no standardized non-English assessment tools.

Another problem is that the tests do not reflect student growth. One teacher, for instance, had a seventh-grade English Learner who moved from a second-grade reading level to a fifth-grade level in a single year—a remarkable amount of progress. However, since the student was in seventh grade, he was two full years below grade level, so his achievement was not reflected on his own report card or in the school's yearly progress report. He was simply recorded as FBB—far below basic—the designation used for those who are more than a full year below grade level. This disparity has led some teachers to call for more accurate ways of acknowledging student progress.

California's application for Race to the Top (RTTP) funding for 2010 was unsuccessful. The state finished twenty-seventh out of forty-one states that applied. One of the shortcomings of the application was the state's failure to address individual growth, and one of the commitments for its application for the next round of funding is a promise to consider measures for individual growth.

Skill 14.8   Demonstrate understanding of required program components for English Learners, including:

a. English Language Development (ELD) (as described in the RLA Framework, "Universal Access" section)

The goal of ELD instruction is to provide access to the core curriculum for learners at all stages of English-language ability. California state law mandates that students who test below proficiency on the CELDT test receive thirty to forty-five minutes of daily instruction in English. The focus is on academic English—language that is not likely to be used outside of school. Students are grouped in like-proficiency groupings, or groups that span no more than two of the five CELDT levels. Instruction may center on vocabulary that is specific to a content area such as math or science, or general school vocabulary such as *underline, circle, cross out, check*, etc.

b. Access to core curriculum (primary-language instruction/support, Specially Designed Academic Instruction in English [SDAIE], content-based ELD)

Specially Designed Academic Instruction in English (SDAIE) instruction is a method of turning content instruction into material that is comprehensible to English learners. Teachers trained in SDAIE learn to change the way they speak: not louder, but slower; not with more complexity, but in the simplest language possible. Teachers trained in SDAIE learn to use gestures, illustrations, repetition, pacing, peer support, and many other techniques to make content in all subject areas accessible to students with limited English. They may find themselves acting, pantomiming, or cartooning—always with the thought that the material being taught must be made into comprehensible input (CI).

Primary language instruction/support has been offered in a variety of ways, ranging from newcomer centers, where an English Learner receives instruction in core content areas in the primary language for a maximum of one year, to programs where aides translate for the second-language student, to two-way immersion programs, in which a student is taught in a language other than English for all of kindergarten and then English is gradually introduced during larger portions of the school day as the student moves up the grade levels.

Content-based ELD requires at least an hour of direct English instruction during each school day, and content delivered in English during the balance of the day.

Skill 14.9 **Use assessment to identify appropriate program components for individual English Learners (based on English language proficiency, prior formal schooling, length of time at a given CELDT proficiency level, and current grade level).**

California law mandates various assessments for program placement and redesignation. In 1997, Assembly Bill 748, or AB 748, mandated use of the CELDT as the primary tool for determining program components for individual English Learners. The CELDT test is divided into five levels: beginning, early intermediate, intermediate, early advanced, and advanced. The test must be administered within thirty days of enrollment in a public school and readministered annually until the student is redesignated as a proficient speaker of English.

Under Proposition 227, in 1998, schools are allowed to give structured English instruction (SEI) for a maximum of one year. Under this proposition, bilingual and home-language instruction dropped from 30 percent of English Learners to 8 percent.

Each teacher assumes responsibility for taking into consideration a student's prior school, current age and grade level, CELDT placement, and available programs in developing appropriate program components. Informal assessment can be done by looking at the student's work in comparison with the California English Language Development Standards, found at **www.cde.ca.gov**.

Skill 14.10 **Demonstrate understanding of the similarities and differences between ELD and SDAIE (e.g., compare and contrast the goals, purposes, features, benefits, and limitations of ELD, content-based ELD, and SDAIE) and how they interrelate and work together to provide maximum and continuing language development and achievement of core content standards for English Learners.**

The goal of ELD is to provide access to the core curriculum for learners at all stages of English language ability. The goal of SDAIE instruction is also to provide all students with access to the core curriculum by turning content instruction into material that is comprehensible to English learners, while keeping them in a classroom where instruction is "overwhelmingly" in English.

Taken together, SDAIE and ELD provide a scaffold for a student to improve English comprehension daily without loss of the core curriculum. The direct instruction of the ELD classroom supports and provides a basis for understanding the work being done in the content classroom, while SDAIE reinforces that learning and introduces curriculum content.

Skill 14.11 **Demonstrate knowledge of parent notification rights regarding program options for English Learners (e.g., waiver process) and how to communicate such rights in an appropriate and effective medium (e.g., bilingual phone calls, home visits, primary language materials, videos).**

As a result of the *Williams v. State of California* case (2000), low-performing schools—defined as those in deciles 1-3 on a scale of 1-10—must provide students with adequate textbooks for both home and school, safe facilities, and adequately trained teachers.

Also as a result of this case, parents and guardians must be informed of their right to complain if the materials, facilities, and teachers provided for their student are not adequate. The school must have forms available for complaints. Complaints cannot be turned away as long as they are in writing. (CDE Uniform Complaint Procedures, CA Code of Regulations, Title V, Sections 4600-4687). Complaints may be filed anonymously. Notice must be sent to parents and guardians in their primary language informing them of their right to complain, and notification of those rights must be clearly posted in each classroom.

The **Valenzuela Settlement (AB347)** requires that schools that receive funding for intensive instruction must post a notice in classrooms used for grades 10–12 making parents and guardians aware of the procedures for alleging lack of opportunity if their student has not passed the exit exam by the end of twelfth grade.

California schools have two main types of classroom environments available for language learners:

- In the **mainstream English** class, the assumption is that all students are proficient in English and all instruction is in English.
- In the **sheltered, or structured**, **English** classroom, the "overwhelming majority" of instruction is in English, but the class is specially designed for English learners—usually with an ESL class as part of the instructional day, and core curriculum taught in SDAIE. California law prefers the term SDAIE to the negative connotations of "sheltered" English.

Parents who wish **bilingual or native-language** instruction for their students have the right to sign a waiver and choose the setting they desire (Education Code 52173).

Parents and guardians are encouraged to participate in the English Learners Advisory Committee (ELAC) meetings at their schools, where they will learn the waiver process and understand how to use it. All teachers are accountable for ensuring that the parents of their students are made aware of the waiver process and how to participate in decision making for their students.

COMPETENCY 15.0   FOUNDATIONS OF ENGLISH LANGUAGE LITERACY

Skill 15.1   Demonstrate understanding of links between oral and written language and an ability to use oral language proficiency to promote literacy and vice versa.

For many years, languages were taught by the grammar-translation method in which emphasis was placed on the literary aspects of language and the intellectual growth of the learner. The information age, with its global economy and instant communication, demands that people be able to speak as well as read and write in other languages, especially English.

Research has proven that BICS can be developed in a relatively short period of time, but that CALP takes five years or more (Cummins, 1979). This has caused a rethinking in the teaching of languages. Many educators feel that ELLs cannot wait five or more years to develop proficiency in their academic language—it would only make the divide between native English speakers and minority learners greater. More emphasis is now being placed on integrated skills which interact to develop each other in an attempt to shorten this learning period. As ELLs develop listening skills and learn to speak, they are also taught reading and writing skills. It is believed that integration of all four areas and teaching the skills in context, may decrease the amount of time it takes to acquire CALP.

Skill 15.2   Demonstrate understanding of personal factors affecting English language literacy development (e.g., primary-language literacy level; transfer of primary-language literacy; prior knowledge, education, and background experiences; level of English language proficiency; vocabulary knowledge; motivation).

Many factors affect English-language literacy development. Among these are:

- **Primary-language literacy level:** ELLs who have achieved primary-language literacy have mastered the skills of directionality of print, correspondence of sound-letter, concept of stories related through print, and other emerging literacy skills.
- **Transfer of primary-language literacy:** ELLs who have achieved literacy skills in their primary language are able to transfer many of these skills to ELL. Thus, the saying, "You only learn to read once." Of course, this saying assumes that the ELL is using a language based on phonograms (or letters), based on the Roman alphabet, as is English, and that the language reads from left to right. Learners from countries using an ideographic language, e.g., Chinese, or one that reads from right to left, e.g., Hebrew, will have to learn new skills as they learn to read in English.

- **Prior knowledge, education, and background experiences:** ELLs use their prior knowledge, education, and background experiences to understand concepts being explained to them in the language being learned—English. By building on these concepts, they are able to connect the new schemata with the old ones, increasing their conceptual knowledge.
- **Level of English language proficiency:** ELLs arrive in the U.S. school system with differing levels of academic content knowledge as well as varying English language skills. Some students may be advanced in their academic studies but only beginning to study English. The opposite may also be true.
- **Vocabulary knowledge:** The vocabulary knowledge of ELLs can vary considerably, from students who have limited vocabulary—in both their first language and in English—to those with rich vocabularies. ELLs, like native English speakers, can improve their vocabularies in a text-rich environment, learn new words and concepts in context, and use word-learning strategies (Tompkins, 2009).

MOTIVATION

Researchers Gardner and Lambert (1972) have identified two types of motivation in relation to learning a second language:

- **Instrumental motivation:** acquiring a second language for a specific reason, such as a job
- **Integrative motivation:** acquiring a second language to fulfill a wish to communicate in a different culture

Neither type stands completely alone. Instructors recognize that motivation can be viewed as either a "trait" or a "state." As a trait, motivation is more permanent and culturally acquired. As a state, motivation is considered temporary because it fluctuates, depending on rewards and penalties.

Skill 15.3   Demonstrate understanding of pedagogical practices affecting English language literacy development across the curriculum. For example:

a. Utilizing English Learners' prior knowledge to promote English language development in reading and writing

When teachers are able to active a learner's prior knowledge, the learner is able to learn faster. Students acquire new knowledge and deepen their previous knowledge because the concepts are familiar.

Some methods teachers are able to use to activate prior knowledge are (Unrau, 2008):

- **Double-entry journals:** Students answer questions (approximately 150-250 words) labeled as "Prereading" and "Postreading" in journals or as email assignments. Small groups can discuss the answers.
- **Anticipation guides**: The teacher prepares a list of statements that students react to before reading the text.
- **Directed teading-thinking activity** (Stauffer, 1969): The teacher selects a text and decides on stop points. At each stop point, the teacher asks a question that calls on the students to predict what is happening or what will happen next.
- **Know/want-to-know/learned Strategy** (Ogle, 1986): Students divide a sheet of paper into three columns and label each column with a K, W, or L. They then fill in the paper or write the information on the board. Once the paper is complete, a graphic organizer can be used to consolidate the information.
- **Prereading plan (PreP)** (Langer, 1981, 1982): Students brainstorm associations with the topic to be read. Next, they reflect on the explanations of the associations expressed by their classmates. The final step before reading is to verbalize changes in their concepts or elaborate more on their previous associations.
- **Directed inquiry activity (DIA)** (Thomas, 1986): The teacher prepares several questions using who, what, when, where, why, and how to cover the content mastery goals of the text materials. Students skim the material to locate possible sections that will help formulate the answers. As students skim and make predictions, the teacher asks them how their answer connects with their previous knowledge and skimming. Students then read the text. The teacher continues discussing the text materials so that students will be able to amplify or clarify their predictions.
- **SQ3R** (Robinson, 1946): The basic technique is to:
  - **Survey:** Skim the material to get an idea of its scope
  - Question: Use the titles or headings to ask oneself questions about the text
  - **Read:** Read the material
  - **Recite:** Answer the questions you posed for yourself
  - **Review:** Go back over the material and review it
- **PLAN** (Caverly, 1995): Predict, locate, add, and note. A more recent version of SQ3R:
  - **Predict:** Students draw a graphic representation of the text from the title, headings, graphs, etc., before reading the text.
  - **Locate:** On their representation of the text, students draw a checkmark (√) to represent what they know and a question mark (?) to indicate unfamiliarity with the concept.
  - **Add:** As they read, students add to their diagram.
  - **Note:** Students note new understandings and reconstruct their diagram if necessary. As a follow-up, they can be asked to make a summary of the graphic, a journal entry, or notes and questions for a discussion.

b. Creating a language-rich environment

Teachers can create a language-rich environment by:

- Reading to students in the content areas
- Having students create books in content areas
- Creating opportunities for students to use language
- Supplying a variety of games that use language
- Recording student language on the board
- Supplying resource materials for classroom use, such as:
    - Phone books
    - Dictionaries
    - Menus
    - Recipes
    - Labels
    - Signs
    - Printed directions
    - Student work
    - Alphabet displays
    - Calendars

c. Providing a balanced, comprehensive reading program

Schumm (2006) states that responsible reading programs include:

- Emphasis on the student
- Adequate personnel and material resources
- Models developed and implemented at the school-based level
- A continuum of services
- Service delivery model evaluated on an ongoing basis
- Ongoing professional development
- Teachers and other key personnel who discuss and develop their own philosophy on reading and writing instruction
- Curricula and instruction that meets the needs of all students

d. Planning meaningful and purposeful literacy activities

Teachers of very young children may set up activities for:

- Using literacy materials in dramatic play centers
- Making posters about favorite books
- Labeling classroom items
- Writing morning messages
- Recording questions and information on charts

- Writing notes to parents
- Reading and writing letters to pen pals
- Reading and writing charts and maps

e. Using standards-based thematic unit organization

Tompkins (2009) suggests the following steps to develop a thematic unit:

- Collect a set of textbooks to use in the unit
- Establish a listening center
- Plan learning-log activities to correspond to the unit.
- Identify language arts strategies and skills to be taught
- Plan communicative actives and graphic organizers to use while teaching the unit
- Brainstorm possible projects
- Plan monitoring activities such as checklists and rubrics to be used for assessment

f. Selecting appropriate reading materials

Teachers should collect a wide variety of reading materials including books, poems, stories, and other materials for the classroom library. These materials need to be age-appropriate, geared to students' interests, and at the appropriate reading level.

g. Providing organized, systematic, explicit instruction in key skills

Skills need to be taught in an organized and systematic manner so that students begin to use them unconsciously in their academic work. For reading, these skills include decoding unfamiliar words, noting details, and sequencing events. In writing, these skills include forming contractions, using punctuation marks correctly, and capitalization of proper nouns.

h. Adapting instruction and materials to meet the special needs of English Learners

All materials should be adapted to meet the needs of children with special needs. For example, Braille and textured materials can be used in labels, signs, and other displays for children with visual impairments.

i. Scaffolding literacy activities

O'Malley and Pierce (1996) recommend scaffolding techniques to reduce the language demands on ELLs by:

- **exhibits or projects:** ELLs can be involved in presenting projects or demonstrations that illustrate the concepts or procedures being tested

- **visual displays:** ELLs can use graphic organizers (e.g., diagrams or semantic maps) to illustrate their understanding of vocabulary and concepts
- **organized lists:** ELLs can present lists of concepts or terms and demonstrate understanding by organizing or sequencing them.
- **tables or graphs:** ELLs can complete or construct and label tables and graphs to demonstrate their understanding of how data is organized and interpreted
- **short answers:** ELLs can give short answers or explanations that focus on concepts in the content area

j. Integrating listening, speaking, reading, and writing

In the past, these skills were taught separately. Now, they are taught in an integrated fashion and attempt to mimic real-life communication. The reading of a newspaper article may lead to an oral discussion or an oral discussion may lead to research on a topic and writing about it. Since much of the same vocabulary is being used in each of these communicative incidents, each act reinforces the other and students are able to engage in meaningful learning.

Skill 15.4   Demonstrate knowledge of effective approaches and scaffolding strategies that can be used to develop English Learners' reading and writing proficiency in English across the curriculum (e.g., Language Experience Approach, frontloading vocabulary and language functions, interactive journals, shared reading, learning logs, process writing, graphic organizers, prereading activities).

Language Experience Approach (LEA)

The steps in the Language Experience Approach (LEA) are:

- Provide an experience
- Talk about the experience
- Record the dictation
- Read the text

Sometimes, children are reluctant to "write" their own stories later because their writing is not a "perfect" model as the teacher's was. However, this can be overcome if the teacher alternates with the children when writing the stories.

FRONTLOADING VOCABULARY AND LANGUAGE FUNCTIONS

Frontloading vocabulary and language function is simply preteaching the vocabulary and language functions that might be unfamiliar to the students during a content lesson or reading session. The goal is to increase reading comprehension.

INTERACTIVE JOURNALS

Interactive journals are any type of journal that requires the student to write about classroom content or their feelings. Journals are a low-stakes method of keeping the teacher and the student engaged in a personal dialog.

SHARED READING

In this type of reading exercise, students are given their own copy of a text to follow along in while the teacher reads to them. Unrau (2008) points out some of the benefits of shared reading:

- demonstrates the natural rhythm and beauty of the language
- builds bridges between texts and students lives
- provides practice in strategies that make a text comprehensible
- models fluent reading
- helps students build knowledge of texts and their world

LEARNING LOGS

Learning logs are records of what students have learned or what they are struggling to understand. Students can be asked to summarize what they have learned from a particular text. Teachers give daily feedback of what is expected in a summary. Teachers and students can use learning logs to negotiate a text's meaning.

PROCESS WRITING

Unrau (2008) lists five stages of process writing:

- **Prewriting:** Planning by brainstorming, researching, note taking, listing, clustering, organizing
- **Drafting:** Selecting a format, writing drafts, deciding on an audience
- **Revising:** Reviewing or reflecting on earlier drafts by rethinking, adding, dropping, rearranging, rewriting
- **Proofreading:** Preparing for publication by polishing, correcting spelling, punctuation, and grammatical problems
- **Publishing:** Sharing with an audience by reading, displaying, anthologizing, submitting for publication

GRAPHIC ORGANIZERS

Unrau (2008) lists various types of graphic organizers:

- **Clusters:** also known as mind mapping, semantic mapping, mindscaping, and webbing. A simpler and less-structured form than the formal outline.

- **Characteristics outliner:** similar to a cluster but more structured. Students draw an ellipse or circle in the center and then place arrows or lines between a term and its characteristics.
- **Process organizer or flowchart:** Used to organize each step in a process.
- **Cause-effect organizer:** Causes are connected to their effect by an arrow or line.
- **Problem-solution-evaluation organizer:** Appropriately labeled boxes are filled in with the corresponding information and connected by lines or arrows.
- **Compare/contrast organizer:** A simple Venn diagram or three columns can be used to show similarities and differences. The overlapping circles (or center column) are used to illustrate items that are the same in each concept.

PREREADING ACTIVITIES

Prereading activities are activities that prepare the student for reading (Schumm, 2006):

- Activating or building background knowledge
- Making predictions
- Word maps
- Previewing
- Picture walk (previewing the story using the illustrations)
- Going beyond the printed page (e.g., using globes, films, maps, simulation games, role-playing, and field experiences)
- Setting the mood

COMPETENCY 16.0   INSTRUCTIONAL PLANNING AND ORGANIZATION FOR ELD AND SDAIE

Skill 16.1   Demonstrate understanding of levels of English language development and their significance for instructional planning, organization, and delivery for ELD and SDAIE.

Previously, ELLs were classified as beginning, intermediate, or advanced. These classifications have been replaced and California now uses a system of five levels:

- Beginning
- Early intermediate
- Intermediate
- Early advanced
- Advanced

For the teacher who has multiple levels of English-language proficiency in his/her classroom, planning must take into account the abilities of the students to understand and produce the English language. Undoubtedly, planning will be differentiated to accommodate students' distinct learning abilities. Instruction will have to be modified for students of lower ability, and delivery will have to be modified so that understanding is achieved.

Skill 16.2   Demonstrate an ability to develop lesson objectives and assessments addressing both ELD and content standards appropriate to English Learners' English language proficiency and grade levels.

Regardless of grade level, when dealing with the dual requirements of ELD and content standards, teachers must use careful planning to incorporate both objectives. In California, the ELD standards are organized into the areas of reading, writing, and listening/speaking. The CELDT is aligned with the ELD standards and is used for both placement and achievement.

When developing lesson plans to achieve both goals, the teacher must look at the content standards and decide which items are most important to include in the ELD learning program. Then the teacher determines the language features needed to achieve the content standards. Next, he/she decides how to assess the content and language features being taught. With the three instructional necessities firmly in mind, the teacher can then begin to plan activities, projects, and research needed to achieve the goals.

Skill 16.3   Demonstrate knowledge of how to use different student-grouping strategies for different purposes (e.g., language development, conceptual development, classroom community building) with both individual and group accountability, including using grouping as described in the RLA Framework, "Universal Access" section.

Grouping students solves many instructional needs. ELLs need time to practice **language development** in different settings and with different people. Group work is ideal for this purpose, when all students are working on tasks and helping each other. Native speakers may need to be coached in how to help the ELLs; otherwise, they may step in and do the work, leaving the ELL to sit quietly and do nothing. In terms of **conceptual development**, the students are more likely to be on similar levels. Nevertheless, the ELLs need to feel that they are contributing to the group, so each member of the group should have assigned tasks. To **build classroom communities**, students need to engage in activities that are multicultural, have mixed proficiency levels, and mix different ethnic groups together to achieve a common goal.

Grouping students by their proficiency needs is an efficient way to give them the instruction they need. While grouping is always secondary to quality instruction, the **RLA Framework** suggests that teachers employ flexible grouping strategies according to the students' needs, achievement, and the instructional tasks presented. The following three groupings are recommended when dealing with problems of learning difficulties, based on the severity of the problem (Kame'enui and Simmons, 1998):

- **Benchmark group**: ELLs in this group are generally making good progress but may need help with minor difficulties. A concept may be retaught in a different format.
- **Strategic group**: This group is for students who are one or two standard deviations below the standard mean. Difficulties can be handled by the classroom teacher. A student success team may be indicated. Special education students may need modifications as indicated in their individualized educational plan.
- **Intensive group**: Students are seriously at risk because of extremely and chronically low performance on one or more measures. These students should be referred to a student success team or special education specialist, as indicated.

Skill 16.4   Demonstrate understanding of the importance of organizing daily ELD instruction around meaningful standards-aligned concepts and balancing direct (explicit) instruction with student centered learning.

English-language development happens daily. Standards-based instruction is imperative so all ELLs receive instruction that will help them reach their language goals as soon as possible. Much of the instruction ELLs receive should be **explicit,** with the teacher as a model of expected language and task-production goals.

Student-centered learning focuses on the needs of the student while taking into account his/her abilities, interests and learning styles. The teacher takes on the role of a facilitator, and the students assume active roles and the responsibility for their own learning. In student-centered learning, or active learning, the teacher must plan global goals and help the students achieve them. For example, in a science unit on ecology and the environment, students want to study recycling. It is up to the teacher to incorporate the science unit's objectives and standards in the process, and with the students' help, establish rubrics for evaluation.

Skill 16.5   Demonstrate knowledge of how to create a physical setting that supports student interactions (e.g., through the arrangement of the space), provides a language-rich environment (e.g., through the display and use of a variety of print materials in the primary language and English), and offers stimuli for conversations (e.g., through the display and use of content-related objects such as prints, maps, puzzles, and artifacts).

The physical setting of the classroom supports learning both directly and indirectly. Student interactions are achieved by grouping students at tables in the earlier grades, and by assigning students to work groups in the upper grades. Cooperative group work can be used at all levels. Counting off (all the ones on this side, all the twos on the other side, etc.) or having students draw cards with objects on them and then finding their partners lessens the resistance of students who want to work only with their best friends.

Language-rich environments include posters and charts demonstrating various text styles and word walls for students to check on the spelling of the words they need. Needed language structures can be listed for consultation. Students can be challenged by an arrangement of many foreign language texts using different types of alphabets.

To stimulate conversation, teachers can ask students to bring objects from home related to the content of the lesson. This is especially useful when students are working on multicultural lessons. Have a "Guess what this is used for?" activity (e.g., a *molcajete* for crushing roasted chocolate beans (for a unit on seeds) or a '*tea infuser*' for a unit on leaves) once a week to stimulate interest in different content classes.

Skill 16.6   Demonstrate understanding of how to use team teaching, peer tutoring, educational technologies, and working with bilingual paraprofessionals to support student learning.

No one research-based teaching model has been shown to be more effective than another. The following examples show several models that are currently in use in the classroom (Friend and Bursuck, 2005).

- **One teach, one observe:** One teacher teaches the entire group while one observes and collects data on an individual student, a small group of students or the entire class
- **One teach, one assist:** One teacher instructs the entire group of students while the other professional is circulating among the students providing assistance
- **Parallel teaching:** Two professionals split the group of students in half and simultaneously provide the same instruction
- **Station teaching:** The teachers divide instruction into two, three, or even more nonsequential components, and each is addressed in a separate area of the room, with each student participating at each station

- **Alternative teaching:** A teacher takes a small group of students to the side of the room for instruction
- **Team teaching:** Professionals who have built a strong collaborative relationship and have complementary teaching styles fluidly share the instructional responsibilities of the entire student group

Other teaching models include:

- **Peer tutoring:** Peers are used to tutor students who are weak in certain skills. This approach benefits both students—the tutor reinforces his/her learning and the tutored gains valuable insights into learning.
- **Educational technologies:** Technology has two tremendous advantages over the human element in tutoring students: Students can practice the skills they need in a nonjudgmental environment, and the machine never becomes tired.

Skill 16.7   Apply strategies for involving families and the community and for establishing connections between the school and home to promote student achievement.

Teachers who are culturally responsible use a variety of methods to involve the families and communities in the classroom and school so that student achievement is maximized.

- Plan meetings at hours when working parents can attend
- Maintain a friendly office with translation services when needed
- Invite parents to share their expertise or knowledge with the class
- Invite parents to help out in the classroom
- Call parents or send home handwritten notes (in first language) with good news about their children
- Encourage parent-to-parent communication and hotlines
- Provide school materials in the native/ethnic language
- Provide handouts of parents' rights, per the Bilingual Education Act
- Create a classroom newsletter for parents
- Enter students in artistic or literary venues sponsored by community or professional organizations
- Encourage bilingualism as a badge of honor in school
- Help students achieve remedial aid in a timely manner
- Make meetings a social event with food and performances by students if time permits
- Give recognition to family members at award ceremonies

COMPETENCY 17.0   **COMPONENTS OF EFFECTIVE INSTRUCTIONAL DELIVERY IN ELSD AND SDAIE**

Skill 17.1   **Apply strategies for identifying the difficulty level of the academic language required for a given language or content-area task (e.g., Cummins's four quadrants).**

Cognitive Academic Language Proficiency (CALP) refers to the language skills required for academic achievement, which are usually more difficult to acquire than Basic Interpersonal Skills (BICS). Cummins (1993-2003) states that it takes from five to seven years for students to acquire CALP after initial exposure to a second language.

Cummins recognizes four levels of difficulty in CALP:

- **Level 1:** Cognitive undemanding / Context-embedded
  Examples: Talking with friends; ordering book in the library; playing sports; talking at parties
- **Level 2:** Cognitively undemanding / Context-reduced
  Examples: Ordering book by phone; following instructions from a taped message; reading a letter from a pen pal
- **Level 3:** Cognitively demanding / Context-embedded
  Examples: Solving a math problem using graphs, charts, etc.; doing a hands-on science experiment; playing an interactive computer game
- **Level 4:** Cognitive demanding / Context-reduced
  Examples: Proving math theorems; writing a research report; listening to a lecture on an unfamiliar subject

Academic tasks tend to increase in their cognitive demands as students progress in their schooling, but the context becomes increasingly reduced. ELLs who have not developed CALP need additional teacher support to achieve success. Contextual support in the form of realia, demonstrations, pictures, graphs, etc., provide the ELL with scaffolding and reduce the language-difficulty level of the task.

Skill 17.2   **Apply scaffolding strategies for providing English Learners with support to enable them to successfully complete tasks that require academic language proficiency. For example:**

a. Modifying language without simplification (e.g., modifying vocabulary, speed, stress, intonation), including use of paraphrasing and repetition

- Use synonyms to explain new vocabulary
- Use cognates when known
- Paraphrase and repeat the message
- Use shorter and simplified sentences when explaining new concepts

- Write new vocabulary words, expressions, or idioms on the board as they are explained for further study and review
- Reduce the speed of the spoken language, but retain its natural rhythm and intonation

b. Activating students' prior knowledge

The following activities activate prior knowledge (Unrau, 2008):

See section a, under Skill 15.3

c. Using the primary language to facilitate learning

Scaffolding is a metaphor for supplying support to students as they are learning. The first language can be used to explain concepts or gloss a vocabulary word *when the teacher knows the word(s).*The resource ESOL teacher can use more of the first language in her interactions with the students than the classroom teacher, but both teachers can use the primary language. The trick is not to use the first language excessively, but to use it when lengthy explanations would otherwise be indicated.

d. Contextualizing language (e.g., embedding language in an understandable context)

Teaching language in context makes it easier to grasp. Much of our vocabulary has different meanings in different contexts, making contextualizing language critical to understanding.

Embedded instruction benefits students with the teaching of reading across the curriculum by systematically using reading strategies in the content classrooms and having English-language teachers use content materials in the teaching of English. Literacy is everyone's goal.

e. Using media, technological resources, and other visual supports

Scaffolding using technological resources comes in many forms for language students. There are fluency programs in which students can read and have their pronunciation corrected. There are programs for building background knowledge with videos. There are programs for developing vocabulary. There are word programs for developing writing skills. The Internet can be used for research and emailing assignments. Platforms such as Blackboard or Moodle have multiple functions that can be used in the classroom, including a feature that allows lesson plans to be saved for future use.

f. Using realia, manipulatives, and other hands-on materials that take advantage of other modalities

The use of realia, manipulatives, and other materials serves as indispensible scaffolding in the language classroom. The visual support these items offer reduces complex explanations that L2 students may not fully understand and emphasizes the old adage that a picture is worth a thousand words. At the same time, the teacher is facilitating learning for the visual and kinesthetic learner. An excellent way to initiate a lesson is to show an item that sets the stage for the lesson to come, e.g., a plant or a set of rocks for a science lesson or a sliced pizza for a lesson on fractions.

g. Using formative and summative assessment and reteaching

Formative and summative assessments are necessary to plan the correct scaffolding for each student. Formative assessments are usually informal and frequent and used to observe short-term progress. Summative assessments are more formal and are used to record yearly progress and provide a basis for evaluating the entire school's reading program. Teachers can use these assessments to plan their instruction and the scaffolding each student needs to achieve literacy.

Skill 17.3 **Apply strategies for checking for comprehension during instruction, including monitoring comprehension frequently, checking for different levels (i.e., literal, inferential, and evaluative) of comprehension, and using effective questioning techniques (e.g., providing sufficient wait time, framing questions appropriately, using different question types for students with different linguistic needs).**

Since understanding is critical to reading comprehension, teachers must check frequently to ensure that students have understood. To check for literal meaning, a simple quiz or oral questions are adequate. To check for inferential meaning, teachers can pose questions that require the student to read different sections of the text to answer the questions. Evaluative comprehension involves higher-level skills that require the reader to form an opinion based on his or her experiences or beliefs, to judge an action or request, or to persuade someone of something.

Skill 17.4 **Apply knowledge of how to provide explicit instruction in learning strategies (e.g., cognitive academic language learning approach [CALLA]).**

The cognitive academic language learning approach (CALLA) was designed for advanced beginners to intermediate learners. Teachers instruct in both academic language skills and content. Emphasis is placed on learning strategies, reduced language demands, and content learning. For example, an L2 learner approaching a unit on the Civil War would use the following strategies:

- **metacognitive strategies**
  - **planning:** skimming the text to identify how the text is organized and plan how to complete the learning task posed by the teacher.
  - **monitoring:** clarifying concepts as the unit proceeds
  - **evaluating:** self-evaluation of how well the task was accomplished
- **cognitive strategies:**
  - **activating prior knowledge:** What do I already know about civil wars?
  - **taking notes:** important words and concepts
  - **grouping the notes:** mind map, outline, chart, cause-effect graph
  - **linguistic transfer:** names and cognates from L1
- **socioaffective strategies**
  - **cooperative group work:** group works toward a common goal
  - **self-talk:** encouraging self with a positive attitude

Skill 17.5   Apply knowledge of how to provide explicit instruction in content-specific discourse skills (e.g., procedural and declarative vocabulary, forms/functions, genres, tasks).

PROCEDURAL AND DECLARATIVE VOCABULARY

Vocabulary instruction includes the following types of knowledge about words:

- **procedural vocabulary:** how to use the word, which form to use, and in what context
- **declarative vocabulary:** what a word means
- **conditional knowledge:** when to use a word

Instruction can be supplemented by motivating games and word-play activities. The teacher can provide students with matching sets of pictures and objects on index cards, scrambled words, and other word games. Teams can compete with charades, Pictionary (students draw a word for their classmates to guess), and Bingo.

FORMS/FUNCTIONS

Berman and Slobin (1994) define **form** as a broad range of linguistic/expressive devices. **Function** is the purposes served by the forms used in narrative discourse. Studies suggest that language has specific forms and functions that are used in distinctive discourse. In English narrative discourse, the use of verbs in present tense and past tense is common. In academic discourse, the use of the passive voice and impersonal gender are common. Teachers aware of the distinctions in discourse patterns will guide students in reproducing them.

GENRES

Genres are a combination of communicative purpose, audience, and format. To teach genre-specific discourse skills, teachers instruct students in the components of each genre. In the U.S. classroom, students are expected to be proficient in academic English or demonstrate (CALP). Learning CALPs requires years of academic study, exposure to academic language, feedback, and support in its use (Rico-Diaz, 2008). Teachers must instruct in vocabulary, morphology, syntax, and cognitive strategies for ELLs to learn the needed CALPs. The use of phrases such as "greater than" instead of "bigger" or "Compare these two phases" instead of "How are these alike?" introduces academic language into the everyday classroom.

TASKS

Whole-discourse tasks draw on all levels of context, require real interaction, offer some kind of choice, and can be completed using different strategies. Teachers do not participate in the activities unless necessary and allow their students to run their own activities (Heywood, 2006). Tasks, such as the following, use whole-language texts to encourage students to experiment with language and to interact with the texts.

- **Dictogloss:** The teacher reads a text at a very fast pace. Students are urged to write the parts that they can catch. At the end of the reading, the teacher creates small groups that try to compose the entire text from their notes.
- **Reading graffiti:** The teacher writes a complete text on the board. Students then write questions or comments on the text. Discussion can follow.
- **Floor squares**: Students wander around the classroom looking at questions written on pieces of paper on the floor while music plays in the background. When the music stops, students ask their classmates the question nearest to them.

COMPETENCY 18.0   EFFECTIVE RESOURCE USE IN ELD AND SDAIE

Skill 18.1   **Demonstrate knowledge of how to select and use culturally responsive, age-appropriate, and linguistically accessible materials and resources that are suitable to English Learners' developing language and content-area abilities, including use of materials in the primary language.**

Teachers are responsible for selecting materials that fulfill the needs of their students based on ELA standards and ELD modifications. Certain literary devices, such as repetition and formulaic expressions as well as gestures and facial expressions in the illustrations of texts and reading materials, are helpful to increase comprehension. Materials that reduce the complexity of sentence and paragraph structures, simplify vocabulary, and reduce the length of texts without reducing grade-level content are all appropriate for English Learners.

As with any reading program, teachers must chose books that are culturally responsive and age-appropriate. Fillmore (2001) and Allen (1994) suggest:

- using multicultural texts that present topics of interest to students.
- using international texts and books written by authors outside the students' country that reflect daily concerns, history, social life, art, and customs of various cultures outside the students' country. Some folktales from around the world have been translated into English.
- introducing materials that contain simple language before moving on to books with more complex language and words that are conceptually abstract.
- offering a variety of writing genres.
- using multilevel books/texts to make provision for individual learner differences.
- encouraging children to select their own books.
- using materials with a number of illustrations.
- using content-area textbooks to support curricular areas like science, math, and social studies.
- using real-world print materials to help students discover the values and functions of written language.

By keeping in mind the basic principles of good reading programs, teachers will be able to select appropriate materials for their students.

Skill 18.2 Apply strategies for modifying age- and grade-level appropriate materials and resources to meet the cognitive, linguistic, cultural, and academic needs of English Learners.

Tompkins (2003) defines strategies as problem-solving tactics selected to achieve particular goals. ELLs need help in different areas. Multiple cognitive, linguistic, cultural, and academic strategies are needed for students to achieve the standards of each grade level. Planning and modeling of the strategy to be used by the teacher and the ELLs' peers is necessary for strategies to have the desired effect. It is the combination of metacognitive strategies, linguistic elements, and cultural structures that strengthen the students' learning goals rather than any one "miracle" strategy.

In the area of vocabulary development, the following strategies may be helpful and can be adapted to the grade level as needed:

COGNITIVE STRATEGIES

Blakey and Spence (1990) recommend the following metacognitive strategies for all students:

- Connect new information to old
- Select thinking strategies
- Plan, monitor, and evaluate

These strategies need to be taught so students will internalize them and use them independently (Scruggs, Mastropieri, Monson, and Jorgenson, 1985).

LINGUISTIC STRATEGIES

One strategy that is appropriate for all students and grade levels is to frontload vocabulary and structures used in the content lessons.

Other strategies (e.g., word order, cognates, and elements of language such as prepositions, the use of pronouns, and the mechanics of writing) will have to be taught at appropriate intervals. Teachers can indicate to students which elements transfer positively from the ELL's L1 to the L2 (cognates) and which do not (false cognates); the pronunciation of the vowels, consonants, and diphthongs; and sentence structures, verb tenses, register, and pragmatics of the language. Many of these items will need to be taught to the individual student as he/she indicates the necessity to know the specific language feature.

CULTURAL STRATEGIES

Schools have long been recognized as the primary agents of transmission of culture. Therefore, educators are charged with transmitting the culture of the society in which they work. The United States has a rich cultural heritage, and teachers are also responsible for recognizing and understanding the cultural differences present in their school system and their classroom. Gay (2000) advocates taking the following approach in culturally responsive teaching:

- Developing a cultural diversity knowledge base
- Designing culturally relevant curricula
- Demonstrating cultural caring
- Building a learning community and cross-cultural communication

Grade-level standards can be adapted to relate to the students' lives in numerous ways. **Math problems** can be written to calculate distances to and from specific places in the area, percentages of water to fertilizer, frequency of watering, the taxes on a purchase, or the cost of text messaging. **Science problems** can be used to calculate the impact of earthquakes, the range of tsunamis caused by earthquakes, and methods for cleaning up after oil spills on land and in the oceans.

ACADEMIC STRATEGIES

The academic needs of ELLs must be assessed before planning a program for their specific needs. Once culturally valid assessments have been made, teachers can plan instruction based on these needs by differentiating instruction if necessary or using scaffolding methods to help the ELLs reach their academic goals.

For writing, a teacher might use graphic organizers and learning logs to teach the different writing genres. Scaffolding strategies would include providing models of the desired composition and individual instruction as necessary.

Skill 18.3 **Demonstrate understanding of the importance of using an appropriate variety of multicultural materials for language and content-area learning, including books and other print media, visual aids, props, realia, manipulatives, materials that access other modalities, and human resources.**

Quiocho and Ulanoff (2009) define multicultural children's literature as books that are read to and by children that depict people with diverse cultural, linguistic, socioeconomic, and religious backgrounds. Teachers must read the books they are selecting for the classroom to be sure they avoid bias and stereotypes. The books should also be accurate and authentic.

Teachers rely heavily on books to convey culture, but other visual aids (e.g., realia, props, and other manipulatives) are equally valuable in the classroom. Many cultures have specific ways of dressing (compare the kilt of Scotland with the dhoti of India), cooking (steaming and barbecuing), solving mathematical problems (abacuses), preparing tea (compare the Japanese tea ceremony with the way Russians prepare tea using the samovar). All of these traditions and customs (and others) can be compared and studied in the multicultural classroom to help children learn the deeper cultural significance of these outward demonstrations of cultural differences.

Skill 18.4 **Demonstrate understanding of the appropriate use of technological resources to enhance language and content-area instruction for English Learners (e.g., Web, software, computers, related devices) and apply strategies for using software and Internet resources effectively in ELD and core content-area instruction.**

Technology provides instructors with numerous programs and services that are appropriate for the English-language classroom. The Internet is available 24/7 for research and communication. The advances of smartphones, e-book readers, and tablet computers suggest that these devices are the wave of the future—even in schools.

Various software programs help students by tutoring them in skills from reading comprehension to pronunciation practice. Research in "blended learning" techniques, when teachers use technology to support student learning, shows promise and is a way of keeping technology-savvy students interested in "normal" school learning activities. Blended learning uses teacher-student face-to-face classes for instruction in writing research papers and other school-related materials, followed by emails, blogs, and chat groups to continue the classroom work.

DOMAIN V.   APPROACHES AND METHODS FOR ELD AND CONTENT INSTRUCTION

COMPETENCY 19.0   ELD—APPROACHES AND METHODS

Skill 19.1   Demonstrate knowledge of the current theoretical bases, goals, key features, and effectiveness of research-based ELD approaches.

See Skill 7.1 for information on Immersion Education Models

There is no one program model or approach that is totally successful in all cases. Rather, Rennie (1993) suggests that successful program models are those that develop academic skills and English at the same time. She states that the best programs are tailored to meet the linguistic, academic, and emotional needs of the students; provide ELLs with equitable instruction, allowing them to progress as their native-English-speaking classmates do; and make the best use of district and community resources.

Skill 19.2   Demonstrate understanding of the importance of emphasizing meaningful and purposeful communicative interactions (both oral and written) to promote English Learners' language development and content-area learning and demonstrate knowledge of strategies for promoting communicative interactions (both oral and written) among students.

Communication must be meaningful and purposeful for students to learn. If students see no purpose in the exercises they are given, they may not even make an effort. Teachers can have students engage in real-life activities, both written and oral, to develop communication skills.

Zainuddin (2007) lists the key features of communicative language teaching as described by Nunan (1991):

- Focuses on meaning through interaction in the target language
- Uses materials or texts that reflect authentic or real-world language
- Allows learners to rehearse language used outside the classroom by focusing on language forms or skills and the learning process
- Focuses on previous knowledge, experiences, or skills learners bring into the classroom as important contributors to language learning
- Plans a careful link between classroom language and real-world language

Communication is paramount, even if it contains errors or misstatements. Students need to interact with the teacher and their peers to advance their communication skills.

Here are some suggested oral exercises for students. Ask students to:

- Work on dialogs and create their own
- Hold mock telephone conversations
- Conduct surveys with other classmates or teachers
- Fill-in gap exercises by talking with other classmates
- Give you a word that (dances/runs/is blue/is cold)... (In this exercise, students call out answers to the teacher's question)

For writing, Zainuddin (2007) proposes the following exercises. Ask students to:

- Use labels and captions to explain bulletin board pictures or other displays
- Use order forms for purchasing classroom supplies for classroom activities
- Write checks to pay for classroom book orders
- Write personal letters to share news with a friend
- Write scripts for role-plays or acting out stories
- Write essays using different forms, e.g.:
  o **Enumeration:** to list information in steps or chronologically
  o **Comparison/contrast:** to show how things are different or the same
  o **Problem/solution:** to present a problem and a possible solution
  o **Cause/effect:** to show the relationship
  o **Thesis/proof:** to present an idea and persuade others of its validity

Skill 19.3 **Demonstrate understanding of the importance of using implicit and explicit instruction appropriately with regard to error correction and grammar development (e.g., emphasizing fluency and communication, recognizing when students may benefit from explicit instruction).**

In the communicative language approach, the student is encouraged to communicate regardless of the errors he or she makes. As the student's language develops, teachers should be judicious about correcting errors.

Errors are imperfect language structures that are systematic and part of the learner's developing language system (Diaz-Rico, 2008). Teachers can repeat the message in the correct form without explicitly stating that an error has been made. Should the error interfere with communication or understanding, explicit instruction can be made to demonstrate the correct form(s).

Mistakes are random occurrences caused by memory lapses or carelessness and should not be corrected.

Skill 19.4 **Demonstrate understanding of how to implement content-based ELD (e.g., integrating ELD standards into content teaching; selecting meaningful subject matter; using appropriate grade level content, vocabulary, and discourse skills).**

Content-based ELD is more than having knowledge. It represents skills that are needed to acquire knowledge of content and that make it easier for the student to read and write in the discipline (Diaz-Rico, 2008). The cognitive skills of being able to think clearly, understand key concepts, and express oneself are skills that generally transfer from one content area to another. For content-based instruction to be effective, students, content teachers, and language teachers must work together to achieve the state standards in the content area while developing the English-language skills needed by the ELLs. Planning systematic instruction that covers vocabulary, concepts, and structures is vital to content mastery (Snow, 1993).

COMPETENCY 20.0   ELD–LISTENING AND SPEAKING

Skill 20.1 **Demonstrate understanding of the relationship between the ELD and ELA standards in listening and speaking and how to apply these standards for English Learners at different proficiency levels (i.e., beginning, early intermediate, intermediate, early advanced, and advanced).**

The ELD standards are not intended to replace the ELA standards but to provide scaffolding for students so they can eventually achieve the same performance objectives as native speakers of English.

For example, an ELA standard for middle-school speaking and listening requires the student to participate in a one-to-one conference with a teacher or parent in which the student asks relevant questions and demonstrates understanding by paraphrasing the adult's directions or suggestions.

A beginning ELD student may understand the direction but may need to paraphrase in the primary language or ask questions in the primary language or may demonstrate compliance simply by performing the task rather than verbally rephrasing it. An intermediate ELD student may make errors in both comprehension and expression but can be understood by the teacher. Advanced students may be expected to express themselves with accurate use of language. Thus, the means of fulfilling the standard can be adjusted according to the student's skill level.

Skill 20.2 **Demonstrate conceptual understanding and applied knowledge of strategies for promoting students' knowledge, skills, and abilities related to the ELD and ELA standards in listening and speaking as described in the RLA Framework and emphasized in the CELDT listening and speaking component, including:**

a. Comprehension (e.g., listening to stories and information and responding appropriately using both verbal and nonverbal responses; listening for main ideas, details, and sequences; listening for implied meaning; applying knowledge of vocabulary, idiomatic expressions, discourse markers, organization, and tone)

The teacher must use every possible strategy to make stories and information comprehensible and to make both verbal and nonverbal responses available as a means of demonstrating comprehension. Repetition, gestures, facial expressions, realia, illustrations, slowing the pacing to allow students time to make connections, and tone of voice—all are tools the teacher can use to increase comprehension.

Acceptable responses can vary from the simplest nonverbal response ("Point to the volcano." "Draw a volcano.") to yes/no responses ("Is this the volcano?") to those requiring the expression of the new vocabulary ("What do we call this kind of mountain?") to the sorts of complex assessments that would be required of ELA students ("Using the Internet for research, make a list of currently active volcanoes.")

Students can be shown how to scan unfamiliar material for specific words or phrases, ("What was the *first* thing Elena said?"), to listen for tone ("Does Jack like the giant? How do you know?") and to watch for discourse markers ("Once upon a time," "after a while," "until he got home," "in the end").

b. Comprehension, organization, and delivery of oral communication (e.g., listening and responding appropriately in different contexts; making oneself understood when speaking by using standard English grammatical forms, sounds, intonation, pitch, and modulation; applying strategies for initiating and negotiating conversations; applying strategies for varying speech according to purpose, audience, and subject matter; retelling stories and conversations; restating ideas from oral presentations; participating in conversations with peers and adults; delivering oral presentations)

The teacher must provide multiple opportunities for oral communication. These might include individual teacher conferences, when the student speaks one-on-one with the teacher; group activities such as brainstorming and problem solving, expressing an opinion in group discussion, and role-plays and reenactments; and individual presentations such as recitations, summarizing or retelling stories, and starting conversations with questions. For example, students can practice varying speech according to different purposes, audiences, and subject matter by "translating" a message as it would be delivered to a teacher, a parent, or a friend.

Students can work in pairs to ask and answer questions of each other. Even beginning students can take whole-class surveys, which provide each student with the opportunity to ask the same question many times. Questions for these activities can range from yes/no questions ("Do you like to play basketball?" "Can you make tortillas?") to familiar names ("Who is your favorite singer?" "What is your teacher's name?") to questions for which the interviewee must produce personal information (Beginning: "What time do you usually get up?" Intermediate: "What is your address?" Early advanced: "What do you want to do for a career?")

c. Analysis and evaluation of oral and media communications (e.g., responding orally to questions, identifying types of media)

The teacher should include activities that will allow students to evaluate media communication. There is a wide variety of applicable strategies for teaching about advertisements and commercials, for example:

- Classroom surveys and interviews can be developed by the students that include questions such as, "Do you buy cereal you have seen on TV?" or "Do you buy toys you have seen on TV?"
- Students can create advertisements for their favorite products on posters or give oral presentations.
- Students can determine the target age group for a particular show by observing and recording the products that are advertised. Is the show sponsored by Mattel® toys? By Lexus® cars? What do these things tell you?

Such activities help students define and understand the role of advertising in media presentations.

Students can also learn to determine whether a speaker or writer is credible as a primary or secondary witness to what is being discussed, and to evaluate the credibility of presentations based on other criteria they develop.

Skill 20.3   Demonstrate knowledge of strategies for facilitating English Learners' listening comprehension and speaking skills across the curriculum (e.g., frontloading key vocabulary and language functions, pre-teaching, brainstorming questions prior to a presentation, cooperative learning, whole-class and small-group discussions, role-plays, interviews, debriefing after a presentation).

By teaching the new vocabulary and language functions students need for reading, the teacher encourages his/her students' success The teacher can actively engage students in the learning process by facilitating the definition of new words in context (providing examples or sample statements), designing practice activities, and assessing learning through games or other activities.

Research has demonstrated that one of the most effective strategies for improving student learning is to activate prior knowledge. One of the best ways to do this is through **brainstorming questions**. Students can be asked to predict outcomes and to express opinions about the text to be read.

Discussion activities:

See Skill 4.5

COMPETENCY 21.0   ELD—Reading and Writing

Skill 21.1   Demonstrate understanding of the relationship between the ELD and ELA standards in reading and how to use these standards for English Learners at different proficiency levels.

Approximately 25 percent of school-age children in California enter school with a native or ethnic language other than English. The ELA standards are designed to encourage the highest level of achievement from every student. These standards should not be lowered to accommodate ELD, but rather ELD students should be encouraged to achieve the ELA standards. This will ensure equal opportunities for all children as they become mature adults in a free society. School administrators are charged with delivering the appropriate support to teachers and their students so that this goal can be achieved.

Skill 21.2   Demonstrate conceptual understanding and applied knowledge of strategies for promoting students' knowledge, skills, and abilities related to the ELD and ELA standards in reading as described in the RLA Framework and emphasized in the CELDT reading component, including:

a. Word analysis (e.g., concepts about print; phonemic and morphemic awareness; vocabulary and concept development; decoding; word recognition, including structural analysis, recognition of cognates, and other word identification strategies)

Sound-symbol correspondence is more difficult in English than some other languages because each letter can make a variety of sounds. Recognition of repeating patterns helps students develop decoding skills. Consonant blends such as /ch/, /ph/, and /sh/ are readily recognizable and make the same sound with consistency. Earliest beginners can scan for those language patterns and recognize the sounds they make.

Recognition of cognates and false cognates is very helpful in decoding and can be directly taught. Many words are identical in English and Spanish, with the only difference being pronunciation. Fortunately for students, as they develop skills in content areas such as math and science, the incidence of these cognates increases. Some examples of English-Spanish cognates are:

- *hotel*
- *radio*
- *religion*
- *eclipse*
- *editor*

Many words are the same in English and Spanish, with the addition of a changed vowel at the end of the word. Here are some examples:

- *cost: costo*
- *cause: causa*
- *minute: minute*
- *medicine: medicina*
- *list: lista*
- *map: mapa*

Here are some of the common false cognates between English and Spanish:

- *libreria*—It's not a *library*, but a *bookstore*
- *embarazada*—It doesn't mean *embarrassed*, but *pregnant*
- *asistir*—It doesn't mean *to help*, but *to attend* or *be present*

Prefixes and suffixes can be directly taught to give the student scaffolding in decoding new words. For instance, *-ful* and *-less* can be taught and then combined with known words to make new ones.

- *Help + ful = helpful*
- *Help + less = helpless*
- *Care + ful = careful*
- *Care + less = careless*

b. Fluency (e.g., reading aloud with appropriate pacing, intonation, and expression; applying word recognition skills)

The teacher can utilize a variety of strategies to increase fluency, such as the following:

- Duet reading, when the student reads aloud together with the teacher, helps the student develop proper intonation and pacing.
- Listen/repeat exercises, including short dialogs between teacher and student or between two students.
- Choral reading, when the entire class reads aloud together, starting and stopping and emphasizing at the same points.
- Singing, or language that is sung, which is difficult to forget. Simple common expressions set to familiar tunes, such as "Happy Birthday" or "Are You Sleeping?" can be quickly invented and help develop fluency.

c. Systematic vocabulary development (e.g., applying word recognition skills, using content-related vocabulary, recognizing multiple-meaning words, applying knowledge of text connectors, recognizing common abbreviations, using a dictionary, using morphemes and context to understand unknown words)

The teacher understands that second-language acquisition is a jigsaw process, in which a student acquires comprehension of a word, a phrase, or a concept in ways that may seem random and unmanageable. The imposition of systematic vocabulary development, whether content-related or grouping by phonics or grammatical structures, relieves anxiety and lowers the affective filter.

- Armed with recognizable text connectors (*and, but, because, until, unless,* etc.), a student has a method to help break down text into manageable segments.
- Use of the dictionary, with its many abbreviations, pronunciation symbols, etc., empowers the student to research new words with confidence.
- Recognizing common morphemes such as the prefix *un-* can help students decode *un*-familiar and *un*-known words (without becoming *un*-happy).

d. Reading comprehension (e.g., features, structures, and rhetorical devices of different types of texts; comprehension and analysis of grade-level-appropriate texts; identifying fact and opinion; identifying cause and effect; using a text to draw conclusions and make inferences; describing relationships between a text and one's own experience; evaluating an author's credibility)

The teacher can use a variety of scaffolding techniques to help students recognize features of different types of texts. For instance,

- Students can be taught key words to help differentiate fact from opinion ("I believe"; "it seems to me...").
- Students can draw arrows between listed events in the text to determine what was a cause and what was an effect.

- Students can be directly taught to make inferences ("The old woman was crying. What does that tell us?")
- Students can make text-to-self connections ("Have you ever...?")
- Students can evaluate credibility ("Is the wolf a reliable narrator? Why or why not?")

e. Literary response and analysis (e.g.,, narrative analysis of grade-level-appropriate texts, structural features of literature, literary criticism)

There are many levels of literary response and analysis the teacher can provide for even beginning ELLs to use. Students can develop their own rating systems for books and movies, breaking down the text into elements that they wish to evaluate: setting, plot, characters, etc., and then applying a five-star or ten-star system to arrive at an overall evaluation.

- Students can illustrate a story to demonstrate an interpretive or reflective response to it.
- Students can compare book and movie versions of the same story. They can develop their own versions of the same story with graphic art or poetry.
- Students can use graphics to retell a story. Graphics force the student to decide which story elements are important enough to include in the blank cartoon panels provided.

Skill 21.3   Demonstrate understanding of the relationship between the ELD and ELA standards in writing and how to use these standards for English Learners at different proficiency levels to support achievement of the standards.

Just as all students in California schools must learn to read well, they must also learn to write well. Again, the ELD standards are based on the ELA standards. Standards for ELLs are not lowered; rather all students are expected to achieve the ELA standards in order to be literate and confident communicators. Since the ELA standards state what is expected, but not how to teach, teachers should feel free to adapt the ELD standards to meet their students' needs.

Skill 21.4   Demonstrate understanding of the use of a variety of genres and multicultural texts appropriate to the student's English proficiency level.

Multicultural texts in a variety of genres have often been used to show only positive images of minority cultures. But the most authentic form of multicultural text focuses on a more balanced, complete, and realistic literature that is age-appropriate and asks young readers to grapple with real issues (Nieto, 1992.)

For some, literature is only considered authentic if it has been written by a member of the ethnic group described. Others include authors who have lived within the culture they are describing, regardless of their race. (Barrera, Liguori and Salas, 1992; Howard, 1991; Nieto, 1992). Junko Yokota (1993) defines authentic literature as that which shows evidence that the author is intimately familiar with the nuances of a culture.

Hazel Rochman (1993), in her book *Against Borders*, explains the purpose of multicultural literature in this way:

A good book can help to break down barriers, make a difference in dispelling prejudice and building community, not only with role models and recipes, but with enthralling stories that make us imagine the lives of others. A good story lets you know people as individuals in all their particularity and conflict, and once you see someone as a person—flawed, complex, and striving—you've reached beyond the stereotype. Stories—writing them, telling them, sharing them, transforming them, help us to know each other.

Every student should be accurately represented in the literature used. Negative and inaccurate images can be harmful to students whose ethnicity is being portrayed. Students should be able to see themselves and their lives reflected in the books they read (Aoki, 1992; Slapin and Seale, 1993).

Skill 21.5 Demonstrate conceptual understanding and applied knowledge of strategies for promoting students' knowledge, skills, and abilities related to the ELD and ELA standards in writing as described in the RLA Framework and emphasized in the CELDT writing component, including:

a. Writing strategies and applications (e.g., penmanship development; the writing process, including organization, focus, evaluation, and revision; applying research and technology)

According to the research of Dr. Jill Kerper Mora of San Diego State University, ELD student writing can be expected to lag behind oral language development by one or two levels. The natural progression goes from words to sentences to paragraphs to narratives (Mora, 1993).

An example of an effective strategy for addressing the disparity between oral and written language development is the use of dictations. The ELL dictates as the teacher writes the story or information the learner presents. This helps solidify the correspondence between oral and written language and makes clear that writing is another way to express the same thoughts that are spoken.

Spelling often reflects sound-symbol correspondence, and the syntactical errors present in speech also occur in writing. Evaluation can be done in many ways: teacher modeling, peer modeling, and direct error correction. The English Learner's editing skills will develop along with the learner's ability to compare his/her own work with models. ELLs will learn that their writing needs to be modified in order to be understood by others and learn to reorder text elements to clarify meaning.

Penmanship is one area that has been left behind in the rush to firm up language and math instruction for ELD students. But penmanship is a legitimate part of language instruction because the development of handwriting contributes to the development of other language processes: directionality, graphophonics, and spelling. Students who write with ease are less impeded in their efforts to communicate and more willing to put effort into written communication.

b. Using writing that reflects purpose, speaker, audience, and form across different writing genres (e.g., narrative, expository, persuasive, descriptive)

The teacher knows that the student gradually develops a sense of purpose for writing and understands the difference between writing that has explanation, entertainment, or persuasion as its purpose. The student will also be able to use information gained in research in personal writing and use it within the context of his or her own purpose as writing skills develop.

c. English language conventions (e.g., capitalization, punctuation, sentence structure, grammar, spelling)

Direct instruction in grammar and spelling has had disappointing effects on students' writing. Teachers have not achieved much success with extensive error correction either. The most successful teaching of language conventions has been the presentation of well-written materials. A good reader becomes a good writer as the self-editing process develops and good models are available. A teacher is most likely to be successful if he/she keeps a variety of well-written and easily understood examples of both written and spoken English available to the students.

COMPETENCY 22.0   SPECIALLY DESIGNED ACADEMIC INSTRUCTION IN ENGLISH (SDAIE)

Skill 22.1   Demonstrate understanding of key procedures used in planning SDAIE lessons. For example:

a. Include language objectives and grade-level content objectives in the lesson

It is important that not only teachers but students themselves understand the purposes of classroom activities and the objective of each particular activity.

One way to do this is to be sure that language and content objectives are expressed in the primary language, even if the lesson will be entirely in English. Another method is to post the objectives for each lesson and check back together at the end of the day to see whether the objectives are being met.

It is sometimes helpful to students to rephrase the objective as a question, with "Can you...." or "Can I...." at the beginning. For example, the content objective may be: "The student will compare and contrast two characters within a story." This objective could be rewritten as, "Can you compare and contrast two characters in a story?" Students are able to look at the list of objectives and determine for themselves those that they can or cannot yet do.

b. Determine task complexity and amount of scaffolding required

Scaffolds are structures that are designed to support an effort. When the student is able to achieve a goal, the scaffolding should be withdrawn. For example, a student who has demonstrated the ability to compare and contrast two elements using a Venn diagram no longer needs an example figure on the board. On the other hand, a complex task that requires multiple steps to complete, such as a five-paragraph essay, may require scaffolding (such as charts, glossaries, or examples) to remain available for a longer period of time.

c. Select multiple strategies to access and assess students' prior knowledge

The teacher needs to be aware of a variety of strategies to access and assess students' prior knowledge. Evaluating the students' schema, or prior knowledge of a topic about to be introduced, is critical to effective lesson planning. A social studies lesson about *Cinco de Mayo*, for example, will have less appeal for students who don't understand why the inhabitants of the Western Hemisphere were anxious to avoid invasion by the French army and why the holiday is considered so important in the United States. To give a lesson without an assessment of prior knowledge is to risk presenting material that is already well understood or possibly way beyond students' present level of understanding.

Strategies for assessing prior knowledge can include class discussion in which a simple question is asked, "What do you know about turtles?" A KWL chart can be created that gives students the opportunity to express first what they already know, and second, what they would like to learn. After the lesson, the last third of the chart is completed: What did we learn?

Sometimes students need to be made aware of their background knowledge. "I don't speak Spanish," for example, can be countered with, "What did we have for lunch today?" "Tacos" "What does 'adios' mean?" and similar questions that will demonstrate that the student knows a variety of Spanish words.

d. Identify strategies for creating background knowledge

The teacher should have a variety of strategies for creating background knowledge before a lesson. Before introducing textual subject matter, for example, it is important to create referents for the words that will be encountered. A word bank is one tool. For a lesson on clothing, for example, there are a number of real-life referents in the room because everyone is wearing clothing. Some students will have oral recognition of the words; others will not.

In a multi-level situation, the teacher might say, "I see someone who is wearing black shoes. Who do I see?" The student is not required to use the word *shoes* or the modifier *black*, but only to recognize them and respond with the familiar name of a classmate. If the language seems unfamiliar to everyone, the teacher can demonstrate what shoes are, and what the color black is. Then *black* can be written on the color list and *shoes* on the clothing list in the word bank. Oral recognition then leads directly to recognition of the written word.

At an intermediate level, only words that are potentially unfamiliar need to be frontloaded before the reading. For example, "We are going to read a story about a boy who is tired. Very, very tired. He can't keep his eyes open—even in class!" All of this can be demonstrated and then discussed with questions such as, "Are you ever tired?" (yes/no) "When are you tired?" (a time) "What do you do when you are tired?" (a verb: *sleep, drink coffee, exercise, rest*). After the discussion, the word is put into the word bank on the board.

e. Identify ways to provide students with cognitively engaging input (both oral and written) with contextual support (e.g., visuals, manipulatives, realia, primary-language support, paraphrasing, focus questions)

The teacher understands the following constraints:

- The student is more likely to recall and be able to use words that he/she has spoken or written than those he/she has only heard or read. For this reason, new vocabulary is most effectively taught when the student is required to use it as soon as possible.
- It is important that the affective filter be lowered, which means that the student must not be embarrassed. Otherwise, language use for the ELL becomes a painful experience, one that the student will unconsciously avoid.
- Words are best learned in context rather than isolation.
- Authentic communication is always more effective than made-up or invented situations.

So how is the teacher to develop opportunities for the student to practice contextually embedded, authentic language in a relaxed setting?

Games are always a good option for language interaction. Students may be competing in popping balloons or running to touch items of different colors—but they are not competing in English-language skill. The deflection of attention allows words to be used for authentic communication in context (e.g., *first, second, third, fourth*; *fast, faster, fastest*) in a relaxed way.

Interviews and surveys provide a way for students to interact with each other while gathering real information. For instance, beginners can practice hearing and speaking the numbers from one to ten by collecting each other's phone numbers. They will then have the numbers available for use for asking for rides or help with homework for missed classes, etc. Verbs can be practiced by having each student develop a question: "Can you ride a bicycle?" ("...drive a tractor," "...play golf," etc.) and ask that single question of everyone in the class, recording their answers: "Hong can drive a tractor." "Marissa can't drive a tractor," etc.

f. Identify ways to use modeling and multiple opportunities for guided and independent practice to achieve content and language objectives, including carefully scaffolding interactions (e.g., teacher-student, student-student, student-text)

The teacher needs to have a variety of ways to model and provide opportunities for guided and independent practice to achieve language and content objectives. As an example, teaching the numbers from one to ten to a pre-beginning class could be done in the following way:

- Show the numerals and pronounce the words. Have students repeat the pronunciation.
- Say the numerals in mixed-up order and ask students to hold up the correct number of fingers.
- Dictate the numerals in mixed-up order and ask students to write the numeral they hear.
- Ask selected students to tell the teacher their phone numbers (or a made-up phone number if they don't want to reveal the real one), and the teacher writes the number on the board as it is spoken.
- Using the telephone directory, students dictate five or ten real telephone numbers to each other, working with a partner. The partner watches and corrects what the other student writes.
- After practicing the question, "What's your phone number?" the students ask as many classmates as possible, and write their responses.
- The teacher then asks the class, "What is Carolina's phone number?" and someone who is not Carolina responds while the rest of the students verify the response.

g. Identify ways to promote students' active language use with respect to the lesson's content (e.g., using the primary language, cooperative learning tasks)

The teacher must use a variety of methods to encourage students to use the new language rather than focusing only on comprehension. These can include activities such as the following, in which the objective is to learn the names of classroom objects:

- TPR activities, in which the student obeys a command ("Hold up a pencil") or displays a response on a slate or 3 x 5 card ("Draw a computer mouse").
- Duet reading (the students and teacher read aloud together at the same time).
- Races (each team sends up a runner who must touch whatever classroom object the teacher names before the other team's runner).
- Team drawing on the chalkboard ("Draw a classroom with a flag above the desk. Now draw a wastebasket beside the desk," etc.).
- Singing, rated as the single easiest way to remember new vocabulary.
- Cooperative learning tasks, in which each student has one piece of information and must get other information from classmates as well as share what he/she has with them.

h. Select multiple strategies to assess students' mastery of language objectives and grade-level content objectives (including using authentic assessment) and scaffold assessment tasks when necessary

The teacher must use a variety of strategies to assess students' mastery of language and content objectives. These might include informal assessments such as, "Tell me one thing you learned today that you didn't know before" or "Write a sentence on this card using the word *could* and give it to me on your way out the door."

For example, teaching prepositions of location, the teacher might give a dictation and ask the students to draw what they hear ("Draw a table." " Draw a dog *under* the table." "Draw a chair *next to* the table," etc.)

Games such as "Simon Says" give the teacher a quick opportunity to see who does and who doesn't know the prepositions ("Put your hand on the book." "Simon says, Put your hand inside the book." "Simon says, Put your hand under the book," etc.)

Skill 22.2   Demonstrate understanding of key strategies used in implementing SDAIE lessons. For example, scaffolding strategies that:

a. Access English Learners' prior knowledge (e.g., concepts, vocabulary) related to a lesson, including using an additive cultural approach

Schemata need to be activated to draw upon the ELLs' previous knowledge and learning, especially when they may not have had experiences similar to those of the mainstream culture. The use of graphics to encourage prereading thinking about a topic (e.g., brainstorming, web maps, and organizational charts) activates this knowledge and shows how information is organized in the students' minds. Shumm (2006) states that research has shown:

- More prior knowledge permits a reader to understand and remember more from new materials (Brown, Bransford, Ferrara, and Campione, 1983).
- Prior knowledge must be activated to improve comprehension (Bransford and Johnson, 1972).
- Failure to activate prior knowledge is one cause of poor reading skills (Paris and Lindauer, 1976).
- Good readers accept new information if they are convinced by an author's arguments. Similarly, they may reject ideas that conflict with their prior knowledge (Pressley, 2000).

b. Contextualize a lesson's key concepts and language (e.g., using materials, resources, and activities to support contextualization)

Teachers need to analyze a lesson's key concepts and then contextualize them so that all students understand what the lesson is about. In a lesson on butterflies, for example, a teacher can bring in butterflies (or simply a caterpillar that is ready to change into a chrysalis) at different stages of development. Different resources such as realia, posters, books, and films can be used as resource materials for initiating instruction and activating background knowledge. All of these resources as well as classroom observations can then be used in different learning experiments, projects, and writing activities.

c. Modify and augment State-adopted content-area textbook(s) to address English Learners' language needs, including the incorporation of primary-language resources

Scaffolding an ELL's language needs starts with a careful analysis of the state standards for the grade level. Differentiated instruction is permitted when the ELL does not have grade-level proficiency in the language. Planning of instruction should answer the questions: **What** content will be taught? **Who** is the student (language and cultural background of the student)? **How** will the student be taught (strategies and materials)? and **How well** is the student learning (performance goals and assessment methods)? When available, resource materials in a student's first language are an acceptable scaffolding technique.

d. Demonstrate or model learning tasks

Instructors can bring in papers, projects, mind maps, and posters from previous classes to demonstrate what is expected in a finished project. Modeling a learning task is simply illustrating whatever point or skill is expected from the learners. In Total Physical Response, a teacher would ask students to stand up (teacher stands) or sit down (teacher sits). As instructions become more complicated, the teacher illustrates (or has a student illustrate) the expected action.

e. Use questions to promote critical-thinking skills (e.g., analytical and interpretive questions)

Questions are one of the most frequently used instructional and scaffolding strategies. Teachers should avoid rhetorical questions as many students find them silly or pointless. Questions that call upon students to analyze (e.g., "What are the parts or features of…?", "How would you classify …?", "What evidence do you find …?") or interpret a topic (e.g., "How would you prioritize the facts …?", "Would it be better if…?", "Based on what you know, how would you explain…?") are questions that call on higher-level thinking skills and contribute to learning.

f. Provide English Learners with explicit instruction in metacognitive and cognitive strategies (e.g.,, debriefing, using text features, using self-evaluation and reflection)

METACOGNITIVE STRATEGIES

The ESOL teacher is responsible for helping students become aware of their own individual learning strategies and constantly improve and add to those strategies. Each student should have his/her own toolbox of skills for planning, managing, and evaluating the language-learning process.

Metacognitive strategies for ELL students include:

- **Centering your learning:** Review a key concept or principle and link it to already existing knowledge; make a firm decision to pay attention to the general concept; ignore input that is distracting; and learn skills in the proper order.
- **Arranging and planning your learning:** The following strategies help the learner maximize the learning experience: Take the time to understand how a language is learned; create optimal learning conditions, i.e., regulate noise, lighting and temperature; obtain the appropriate books, etc.; and set reasonable long-term and short-term goals.
- **Evaluate your learning:** The following strategies help learners assess their learning achievements: Keep track of errors that prevent further progress and keep track of progress, e.g.,, reading faster now than the previous month.

COGNITIVE STRATEGIES

Cognitive strategies are vital to second-language acquisition; their most salient feature is the manipulation of the second language. The most basic strategies are: practicing, receiving and sending messages, analyzing and reasoning, and creating structure for input and output, which can be remembered by the acronym PRAC.

- **Practicing:** These strategies promote the learner's grasp of the language: Practice constant repetition, make attempts to imitate a native speaker's accent, concentrate on sounds, and practice in a realistic setting.
- **Receiving and sending messages:** These strategies help the learner quickly locate salient points and then interpret meaning: skim through information to determine "need to know" vs. "nice to know," use available resources (print and nonprint) to interpret messages.
- **Analyzing and reasoning:** Use general rules to understand the meaning and then work into specifics, and break down unfamiliar expressions into parts.
- **Creating structure for input and output:** Choose a format for taking meaningful notes, practice summarizing long passages, use highlighters as a way to focus on main ideas or important specific details.

g. Develop English Learners' academic language (e.g.,, frontloading vocabulary)

Frontloading vocabulary is a strong method of assuring reading success. When students are given explanations of new vocabulary they need for upcoming reading or content classes, they are better able to handle the academic demands placed upon them. By using examples of a word in its context, asking students to decide if the word is used correctly, and asking them to draw pictures of the word, teachers are actively engaging students in the learning process.

h. Provide clear models of expected performance outcomes

Using rubrics to explain what is expected is an excellent way to clarify any misconceptions students may have about an assignment. Another excellent method is to show papers or projects from previous classes.

i. Transform text from one genre to another genre

Examples are: Students can be asked to take a text and create a skit out of it. Skits could be changed into a short story.

j. Provide opportunities for English Learners to engage in analysis and interpretation of text, both oral and written

Students can analyze and interpret texts with graphic organizers, journals, note taking, and summaries. For beginners, teachers can provide graphics with sample entries filled in and as the students become more familiar with them, provide fewer and fewer clues.

Oral discourse can also be analyzed. Teachers can ask students how they felt about a dialog, how people in their culture would respond in a similar situation, what the main idea of the speech was, and why they believe or disbelieve this particular speaker.

k. Provide English Learners with opportunities to learn and use forms of English language necessary to express content-specific academic language functions (e.g., analyzing, comparing, persuading, citing evidence, making hypotheses)

ELLs need opportunities to debate, write written reports, make hypotheses, etc., but in most cases, these structures will have to be taught. Citing evidence and making hypotheses are academic skills used throughout an academic's life and need to be taught, beginning with simplified reports or research papers.

Teachers need to provide models of the language activity/structure they are teaching and demonstrate it to the students. The teacher can list the specific vocabulary and rhetorical structures used on the board for illustration. These forms can be copied and distributed to the class.

l. Provide authentic opportunities for English Learners to use the English language for content-related communicative purposes with both native and nonnative speakers of English

ELLs need the opportunity to practice English regardless of their level. Grouping ELL students with native speakers and other nonnative speakers of English gives them an opportunity to practice the language and the social elements of communication. Many ELLs have content knowledge but have difficulty expressing it, whereas many native speakers may not have the content knowledge necessary to complete a task. Both native speakers and ELL students benefit when working in small groups on assigned tasks.

In addition to research projects, students enjoy working on skits, role-plays, drama, and singing. Games such as Pictionary and charades can be adapted to content for encouraging vocabulary learning.

m. Assess attainment of lesson content using multiple modalities (e.g., verbal, nonverbal)

For mini-assessments of lessons, the teacher can ask students to give a "thumbs up" or "thumbs down" to questions about content. Teachers can use observation to determine if students understand and are progressing or if they do not understand and need help. Useful techniques with beginners include asking students to do something like make the sound of a monkey, draw a monkey, or move like a monkey.

For more advanced learners, verbal assessment may be more appropriate. Students can be evaluated on rubrics, written work, answering structured and unstructured questions, free recall, completing graphic illustrations of text, and word associations. Formal assessments include end-of-chapter tests and teacher-made tests.

n. Provide comprehensible and meaningful corrective and positive feedback to English Learners

Feedback is valuable only if the student understands it. Teachers can illustrate the correct response, go over the test with the students, providing the correct answers and illustrating the most common errors, and even use mime or translators if necessary.

Skill 22.3   Apply knowledge of procedures and strategies used in SDAIE to plan, implement, and evaluate SDAIE lessons that are effective in developing English Learners' academic language and content-area knowledge and skills and in leading them to full English language proficiency.

Each lesson given to ELL students must be considered in terms of SDAIE principles. Teachers should ask themselves the following types of questions:

- Am I using every tool possible to make the content of this lesson comprehensible?
- Is all new vocabulary contextualized?
- Am I creating a variety of ways to access the new content?
- Do my assessment methods accurately gather data about whether this material is understood by my students?

SUBAREA III.   CULTURE AND INCLUSION

DOMAIN VI.   CULTURE AND CULTURAL DIVERSITY AND THEIR
                RELATIONSHIP TO ACADEMIC ACHIEVEMENT

COMPETENCY 23.0   CULTURAL CONCEPTS AND PERSPECTIVES

Skill 23.1   Demonstrate understanding of concepts and perspectives used in
              defining culture (e.g., cultural universals, cultural relativism,
              ethnocentrism, cultural pluralism, cultural congruence, impact of
              geography on cultural forms and practices, intragroup and
              intergroup differences).

Cultural universalism is defined as the elements, patterns, traits, or institutions that
are common to all human cultures worldwide. Some anthropologists and sociologists
minimize the importance of cultural universals, claiming that many so-called cultural
elements are, in fact, biologically inherited behaviors, leading to the "nature vs. nurture"
controversy.

Cultural relativism refers to the principle that a person's beliefs and activities should
be understood in the context of his/her society. This concept is based on the work of
the anthropologist Franz Boas (1887), who wrote: "civilization is not something absolute,
but ... is relative, and ... our ideas and conceptions are true only so far as our civilization
goes."

Ethnocentrism: Ethnocentrism usually focuses on one's own community and the belief
that it is superior to all others.

Cultural pluralism: Cultural pluralism concerns the existence of groups with different
ethnic, religious, or political backgrounds within one society.

Cultural congruence: Cultural congruence concerns the way people develop
expectations about their society that are congruent with their views of their society
because it allows them to maintain stable identities. Having stable identities tells the
members of the society how to behave and gives them a sense of psychological
coherence that reinforces their conviction that they know what to do and the
consequences of doing it.

Groups benefit from cultural congruence because it permits individuals to concentrate
on the tasks at hand and not worry about who they are. The sub-fields of cultural
geography indicate the extent to which modern life has been affected by cultural
geography (e.g., globalization, westernization, modernization, Americanization,
Islamization, colonialism, post-colonialism, internationalism, immigration, emigration,
and ecotourism).

Impact of geography on cultural forms and practice: Cultural geography is the study of cultural products and norms and their variations across and relation to spaces and places. It focuses on describing and analyzing the ways language, religion, economy, government, and other cultural phenomena vary or remain constant from one place to another, and on explaining how humans function spatially.

Intragroup and intergroup differences: Crosscultural studies focus on intracultural issues, when members of the same culture are involved, and intercultural issues, which involve members of different cultures. Examples of interculture include the classroom culture, youth culture, company culture, or disciplinary culture. Even within these limited cultures, there are differences in the intraculture of their members.

Skill 23.2   Demonstrate understanding of external and internal elements of culture and how they exemplify cultural perspectives. For example:

a. External elements of culture (e.g., shelter, clothing, food, arts and literature, religious structures, government, technology, language)

There are many different ways students are affected by the cultural differences between their native culture and the culture they are acquiring through schooling and daily life in a foreign culture.

The following points, based on work by Peregoy and Boyle (2008), illustrate some of the many different ways external culture affects students in their participation, learning, and adjustment to a different society and its schools.

- **Shelter:** What types of shelters are used? Are they fixed or movable? Large or small? Are they primitive or constructed using modern materials? Individual family structures or communal? Who may enter the shelter? What is the role of the individual—men, women, and children—in maintaining the shelter?
- **Clothing:** What type of clothing is used? Does the climate dictate seasonal changes in clothing? Does the religion of the culture pose restrictions on clothing? Are women subjected to specific clothing requirements?
- **Arts and literature:** How are art and literature represented in the culture? Does the culture have a long, distinguished history? How is religion represented in the arts and literature? Who creates the art and literature: men or women? Are artisans honored by the culture?
- **Religious structures:** Have the religious structures revered by the culture been present for centuries or are they more recent? Are they man-made or natural sites? Are the structures minimalistic or are they filled with precious metals and stones?

- **Government:** Is the government a monarchy, dynasty, or democracy? Have the rulers taken over the government in a coup? Are the true leaders of the country in exile? What position does the government take toward its citizens? Have the students and their families had to flee their country or were they allowed to leave peacefully?
- **Technology:** Is the culture technologically advanced or primitive? Is technology available to all or only the elite? Is technology available for personal use or only for governmental necessities? If the culture is technologically advanced, does it create technology or simply consume it?
- **Language:** What language (or languages) is spoken by members of the culture? Is the culture a mono- or multilingual society? What is the official language? Has the official language been imposed by colonialism or adapted naturally?
- **Food:** What foods are eaten? In what order and how often is food eaten? Which foods are restricted? Which foods are typical? What social obligations are there with regard to food giving, reciprocity, and honoring people? What restrictions or proscriptions are associated with handling, offering, or discarding food?

b. Internal elements of culture (e.g., values, customs, worldview, mores, beliefs and expectations, rites and rituals, patterns of nonverbal communication, social roles and status, gender roles, family structure, patterns of work and leisure)

The following points, adapted from Peregoy and Boyle (2008), illustrate some of the many different ways internal culture affects students in their participation, learning, and adjustment to a different society and its schools.

- **Family structures:** What constitutes a family? What are the rights and responsibilities of each family member? What is the hierarchy of authority within the family?
- **Life cycles:** What are the criteria for defining stages, periods, or transitions in life? What rites of passage are there? What behaviors are considered appropriate for children of different ages? How might these conflict with behaviors taught or encouraged in school?
- **Roles and interpersonal relationships:** How do the roles of girls and women differ from those of boys and men? How do people greet each other? Do girls work and interact with boys? Is deference shown to anyone, and if so, to whom and by whom?
- **Discipline:** What is discipline? Which behaviors are considered socially acceptable for boys versus girls at different ages? Who or what is considered responsible if a child misbehaves? The child? Parents? Older siblings? The environment? Is blame even ascribed? Who has authority over whom? How is behavior traditionally controlled? To what extent and in what domains?
- **Time and space:** How important is punctuality? How important is speed in completing a task? How much space are people accustomed to? What significance is associated with different cultural locations or directions, including north, south, east, and west?

- **Religion:** What restrictions are there on topics discussed in school? Are there dietary restrictions to be observed, including fasting? What restrictions are associated with death and the dead?
- **Health and hygiene:** How are illnesses treated, and by whom? What is considered the cause of illness? If a student were involved in an accident at school, would any of the common first-aid practices be unacceptable?
- **History, traditions, and holidays:** Which events and people are sources of pride for this culture? To what extent does the culture in the United States identify with the history and traditions of the country of origin? What holidays and celebrations are considered appropriate for observing in school? Which ones are appropriate for private observance?

Skill 23.3   Apply strategies for analyzing the significance of and responding to student diversity in relation to external and internal elements of culture.

It is often difficult to understand all of the cultural nuances that are used in multicultural classrooms. Obviously, teachers try to understand the each different culture's ways of expressing approval and disapproval, the roles of the sexes, reactions to authorities, etc. Nevertheless, it is challenging to provide appropriate academic instruction when students do not respond to activities appropriately.

To overcome these difficulties, teachers may choose to keep a journal in which they record their observations of who interacts with whom, under what circumstances certain students seem most comfortable, and which activities seem to have the most positive responses from the class. Based on careful observation of the class, teachers can adapt their activities to better suit their students.

Skill 23.4   Demonstrate understanding of historical and contemporary perspectives on cultural diversity and multicultural education with a focus on how student interaction and grouping patterns are affected by:

a. Issues of power and status

Power and status have been major factors in human interaction for centuries. Power is usually attributed to the "superior culture and language." Members of different societies achieve power when they are able to speak, read, and write in a foreign language. Those who are monolingual or illiterate have a lesser status. Consider the following examples: French used in diplomatic circles, English as a colonial language in India and other countries, and the eradication of native languages through contact with other cultures all over the world.

b. Impact and interplay of demographic trends

Consider these facts about the world's population:

- It is expected to be 9.1 billion by 2050 and most of this growth will occur in less developed countries (Rosenberg, 2006). During the period 1990-2000, the developed countries have received nearly 2.6 million immigrants annually, with nearly half arriving in the United States from Asia, Latin America, and the Caribbean.
- The median age is 40. Birth rates are decreasing, but increased life expectancy is creating an aging population.
- It is moving to urban areas. Between 2000 and 2030, the urban population is expected to grow by 1.8 percent a year.

These changing demographics have had and will continue to have a significant impact on the classroom. The magnitude of cultural differences and the idea of cultural pluralism will continue to create challenges for most teachers.

c. Bias and discrimination with regard to inter- and intragroup differences, including social class, age, gender, occupation, education level, geographic isolation, race, U.S.-born versus immigrant status, sexual orientation, and handicapping condition:

Cultural bias is interpreting and judging other cultures by one's own. Discrimination refers to actual behavior toward another group. According to the United Nations, "Discriminatory behaviors take many forms, but they all involve some form of exclusion or rejection."

- **Social class:** In India, there are approximately 160 million "untouchables." the majority of whom live in deplorable conditions and bonded servitude.
- **Age:** Age discrimination can be against youths (15-25), adults 40 and older, or the elderly. In theUnited States, the Discrimination in Employment Act has attempted to address discrimination against age in the workplace.
- **Gender:** Gender discrimination takes many forms. In the workplace, gender discrimination occurs when a person is hired, promoted, or fired based on gender. Salary differences between the sexes is discriminatory. In an educational context, students may claim to have been excluded from programs or student groups or denied loans or scholarships because of gender.
- **Occupation:** Many occupations are seen as traditional for one sex or another. For example, childcare is traditionally a female role, while construction is typically male. Occupational discrimination may be against male as well as female members of society.
- **Education level:** Despite gains made against discrimination in education, many societies still limit the access of women and certain sectors of their populations to education. In 1960, the United Nations Educational, Scientific and Cultural Organization (UNESCO) issued a statement against discrimination in education.

One section of the document recommends free and compulsory primary education. However, secondary and higher education should be accessible to all, based on individual capacity.

- **Geographic isolation:** Minorities may suffer bias and discrimination in education because of their geographic isolation (e.g., Alaskan natives). Isolated locations may draw teachers who are not as well qualified as those in urban areas where access to universities and modern technology are easier to obtain.

- **Race:** Racial discrimination has been banned in the United States since the middle of the twentieth century. Yet racism continues to be an issue in some schools where discrimination against Native Americans, African Americans, Latin Americans, Jews, and Muslims occurs when these cultures come into conflict with each other and the dominant white society.

- **U.S.-born versus immigrant status:** Being born in the United States is considered by some to be superior to being an immigrant. All too often, children of recent immigrants who were born in the United States claim superiority to recent arrivals of the same ethnic group.

- **Sexual orientation:** Approximately 75 percent of U.S. students have no state laws to protect them from bullying and harassment based on their sexual orientation. There have been several court cases recently regarding the right of same-sex couples to marry and a female student to attend her senior prom with her girlfriend. Worldwide, more than eighty countries continue to view homosexuality as illegal.

- **Disabilities:** In many situations, the disabled are discriminated against regardless of their ability to perform as productive members of society. The Americans with Disabilities Act is an attempt to address discrimination of this kind in public institutions.

Skill 23.5 **Demonstrate understanding of political and socioeconomic factors affecting English Learners and their families (e.g., parents'/guardians' voting and citizenship status, family income and employment, housing, health care availability, parents'/guardians' level of educational attainment).**

- **Parents'/guardians' voting and citizenship status:** Parents and guardians may or may not have citizenship status and be voters. Often the adults in the ELL's family enjoy full citizenship status and advocate for the rights of other family members. In many cases, the opposite is true. When parents or guardians are undocumented, the entire family may be living in fear of being discovered and deported. Living with this anxiety for ELLs can be especially hard. The United States may be the only country they have ever really known. If sent back to their "native" land, they would undoubtedly feel displaced and become resentful of the United States.

- **Family income and employment:** Frequently, immigration to the United States—the land of opportunity—is the result of a dream. Some immigrants live in a "honeymoon"-like state and are willing to work at almost anything to better themselves. Others may have been forced to leave their native land because of religious or political persecution, threats of extortion, or business reasons. These immigrants may have led productive lives as political leaders, businessmen/women, or professionals such as lawyers or doctors. They may have found their financial circumstances reversed in a matter of hours or days. Such conditions cause feelings of resentment and stress for all members of the family—the youngest of whom may be the ELLs who really do not understand why all of this has happened to them.

- **Housing:** Immigrants may find the housing in the United States completely different from that in their native country. It may be more luxurious or it may be considerably inferior to what they had before. Children who previously had their own rooms may now have to share with one or more family members. Families who lived in warm climates where homes never had to be heated or cooled may find central heating and air conditioning difficult to adjust to. Trying to acquire the necessary conveniences of the typical American home may be difficult for low-income families struggling to make ends meet.

- **Health care availability:** Unless family members have good jobs that provide health care as part of the benefits package, English Learners and their families will probably use the emergency rooms of hospitals or free clinics in their neighborhoods, which often involve long waiting periods. While these services try to provide adequate health care, there may be little opportunity for prevention and early diagnosis.

- **Parents'/guardians' level of educational attainment**: Many ELLs' parents or guardians may have university degrees with corresponding positions of responsibility. Other ELLs' family members may have never had the opportunity to go to school and will find it difficult to accommodate the needs of the ELL. It is not unusual to find illiterate parents who want their children to have the opportunities they never had and to work very hard to see that their children succeed in school.

Skill 23.6 Demonstrate knowledge of practical applications of current research and research-based theories related to cultural factors that influence the achievement of English Learners.

Teaching and learning depend on accurate, clear communication between a teacher and his/her students. At first, language differences may cause poor communication. However, there are other factors that interfere with communication in the classroom:

- Research has shown that culture may restrict communication if the student is from a culture in which the teacher is seen as an authority figure. In some cultures the student may not speak unless addressed directly.
- Another problem may be a reluctance to "show off" at the expense of other classmates.
- A third problem may be the amount of "wait time" before continuing with the lesson. Wait time varies considerably among different cultures.
- Still another problem is the "known-answer" question. Some students may find this type of question odd or even silly and may be reluctant to answer them. The teacher should look at his/her questioning style or even introduce the questions and their purpose before beginning the session.

COMPETENCY 24.0   CULTURAL CONTACT

Skill 24.1   Demonstrate understanding of differences among various processes of cultural contact (e.g., assimilation, acculturation, biculturalism, accommodation).

At its most basic level, cultural adaptation is generally considered to be assimilation, acculturation, and accommodation, though social anthropologists have many more definitions with which to describe the complex phenomena of cultures coming together.

ASSIMILATION

Assimilation is the integration of immigrants or minorities into the predominant culture. This implies a loss of the immigrants' native culture through changes in language, customs, ethnicity, and self-identity.

The melting pot theory was an attempt to explain the assimilation process in the United States when it was considered correct to assume that the United States was a homogeneous society, and cultural differences, except physical differences such as skin color, were ignored.

Social scientists use four benchmarks to evaluate the degree of social assimilation:

- socioeconomic status
- geographic distribution
- second-language attainment
- intermarriage

The degree to which the immigrants or minorities achieve socioeconomic status through education, jobs, and income mark the degree of assimilation. As the immigrant culture becomes assimilated by increased socioeconomic attainment, longer residency in the United States, and higher generational status, it tends to spread out geographically. Language assimilation is considered to be a three-generation process. The first generation tries to learn the "new" language but the native tongue remains dominant, the second generation is bilingual, and the third generation loses their "native" language, speaking only the language of the new country. High rates of intermarriage are presumed to be strong indicators of social integration because intermarriage reduces the capacity of families to pass on one consistent culture.

See Skill 10.1 for information on Acculturation and Accommodation

Skill 24.2   Demonstrate understanding of psychological and social-emotional issues involved in experiencing different cultures (e.g., culture shock, psychological distance).

Culture shock occurs when people encounter other cultures and are "shocked" by the differences they encounter. Feelings of isolation, confusion, anxiety, and rejection can occur when a person is suddenly exposed to another culture. For children, this may be as simple as differences in schooling and as complex as dealing with the loss of friends, family, and their native environment. They may try to cope by engaging in psychological distancing.

Culture is part of the systematic organization of human psychological functions. Thus it takes time for immigrants to adapt to a new setting. People may be able to distance themselves from the new culture yet they remain part of the setting in which they find themselves. The duality of closeness to and distance from a new culture is referred to as **psychological distancing.** Research suggests that we fear things we see in ourselves and try to distance ourselves from them (Schimel, 2000).

Skill 24.3   Demonstrate understanding of stages or phases of acculturation (e.g., honeymoon, culture fatigue/shock, adjustment/adaptation, acceptance) and the features associated with each phase.

Culture refers to the shared beliefs, values, and rule-governed patterns of behavior, including language, that define a group and are required for group membership (Goodenough, 1981; Saville-Troike, 1978). Cultural adjustment occurs when people from different cultures are subjected to changes in these beliefs, habits, and customs. These changes may occur because a person has fled his/her country or left it permanently in an effort to seek better educational, financial, or cultural opportunities. Or a person may choose to leave his/her native country and become part of a foreign culture.

There are four generally recognized stages of acculturation:

- **Honeymoon:** Everything looks bright and positive. The individual or family has arrived in the new country and is ready to begin a new life. Everyone is eager to please, ready to interact, and happy to be in their new home.
- **Hostility:** Frustration begins to occur as reality strikes. The new language, the new survival tasks (dealing with subways or buses), new foods, and new ways of doing things at work or school are unfamiliar and viewed as problems with the new society. Depression, anger, anxiety, and homesickness are felt during this phase.
- **Humor:** Accomplishments bring on a triumphant feeling that the new society might not be so bad. As individuals or families experience success and adjust to life's new demands, they are able to laugh at themselves and their previous frustrations.
- **Home:** Patriotism for the native country is retained while the new country is accepted as the new home. A transition from the old to the new norms has occurred and the new location is seen as home.

The length of time each stage lasts depends on the individual and may be shortened by positive experiences in the individual's circle of contacts.

Skill 24.4 Demonstrate understanding of factors that promote or impede adjustment to different cultures.

While there is a continuous effort to establish a "standard English" to be taught to ELLs, English learning and acquisition depends on the cultural and linguistic background of the ELL, as well as preconceived perceptions of English Learner cultural influences. These factors can act as a filter, creating confusion and inhibiting learning. Since language by definition is an attempt to share knowledge, the cultural, ethnic, and linguistic diversity of learners influences both their own history as well as how they approach and learn a new language.

Teachers must assess the ELL to determine how cultural, ethnic, and linguistic experience can affect the student's learning. This evaluation should take into account many factors, including:

- the cultural background and educational sophistication of the ELL
- the exposure of the ELL to various English-language variants and cultural beliefs

No single approach, program, or set of practices fits all students' needs, backgrounds, and experiences. The ideal program for a Native American teenager attending an isolated tribal school may fail to reach a Hispanic youth enrolled in an inner-city or suburban district.

Culture encompasses the sum of human activity and symbolic structures that have significance and importance for a particular group of people. Culture is manifested in language, customs, history, arts, beliefs, institutions, and other representative characteristics, and is a means of understanding the lives and actions of people.

Customs play an important part in language learning because they directly affect interpersonal exchanges. What is polite in one culture might be offensive in another. For example, in the United States making direct eye contact is considered polite, and not to make eye contact connotes deviousness, inattention, or rudeness. However, in many Asian cultures exactly the opposite is true. Teachers who are unaware of this cultural difference can easily offend an Asian ELL and unwittingly cause a barrier to learning. Teachers who are familiar with this cultural difference can make an effort not to offend the learner, and can teach the difference between the two customs so that the ELL can learn how to interact appropriately in the classroom.

Beliefs and institutions have a strong emotional influence on ELLs and should always be respected. While customs should be adaptable, like switching registers when speaking, no effort should be made to change the beliefs or values of an ELL. Presenting new ideas is a part of growing, learning, and understanding. Even though the beliefs and values of different cultures often have irreconcilable differences, they should be addressed. In these instances teachers must respect alternative attitudes and adopt an "agree to disagree" attitude. Presenting new, contrasting points of view should not be avoided because new ideas can strengthen original thinking as well as change it. All presentations should be neutral, however, and no effort should be made to alter a learner's thinking. While addressing individual cultural differences, teachers should also teach tolerance of all cultures. This is especially important in a culturally diverse classroom, and will serve all students well in their future interactions.

Studying the history and various art forms of a culture reveals a lot about it and offers opportunities to tap into the interests and talents of ELLs. Comparing the history and art of different cultures encourages critical thinking and often reveals commonalities as well as differences, leading to greater understanding among people.

See Skill 9.2 for information regarding culture.

Skill 24.5   Analyze English Learners' experiences in relation to concepts of cultural contact and apply related knowledge to educational contexts (e.g., problem solving, student interactions, conflict resolution).

Teachers are both participants and observers in their classrooms. They are in a unique position to observe what makes their students uncomfortable. By recording their observations in a journal, the teacher can begin to note which activities and topics make the students in his/her classroom uncomfortable. Does this discomfort come from multicultural insensitivity?

Cooperative group work is based on the premise that many cultures are more comfortable working in collaborative groups. However, while this is true, many students may feel that the teacher is the only academic authority in the classroom and, as such, should be the one to answer questions rather than their peers. Different students feel more comfortable with different instructional formats, due to both cultural and individual preferences. By balancing group work with teacher-directed instruction, both preferences can be accommodated.

Literacy and reading instruction are areas where multicultural sensitivity can be increased in the classroom regardless of the level of the students. Many immigrant children arrive in the classroom with few, if any, literacy skills. They may not have had the opportunity to go to school. Others may be fully literate, with substantial prior education. In both cases, culturally sensitive reading materials are important for all students, both native English speakers and ELLs, so that they all have the opportunity to discuss the ways in which different cultures are alike and different. Oral discussion of books will provide opportunities for comprehensible input and negotiation of meaning.

Many researchers believe that the key to any reading program is extensive reading (Day and Bamford, 1998; Krashen, 1993). Advantages include building vocabulary and background knowledge, interest in reading, and improved comprehension. For the multicultural classroom, it is important to provide culturally sensitive materials. All materials should be of high literary quality. Avoid materials that distort or omit certain historical events; include stereotyping; contain loaded words; use speech that is culturally offensive; portray gender roles, elders, and family inaccurately; or that might distort or offend a student's self-image.

Show and tell is another strategy for increasing multicultural sensitivity. Students of all ages can bring in objects from their home cultures and tell the class about their uses, where they are from, how they are made, and so on.

Misunderstandings can be worked into the classroom by asking students to share an incident that involved cultural misunderstanding. Questions can be asked about the nature of the misunderstanding—about what was involved: words, body language, social customs, or stereotypes.

Visual/holistic versus verbal/linear-sequential: Not all learners learn in the same manner. Some students learn best visually—through seeing information whether it be written text, charts, pictures, or flowcharts. Other students prefer to hear the message spoken by a teacher or other students. Still others learn best through tactile experiences, e.g., manipulating objects or equipment, creating models, or presenting material through art or drama.

According to Cassidy (2004), the holistic-analytical dimension refers to the way in which individuals tend to process information, either as a whole (holistic) or broken down into parts (analytic). Riding and Cheema (1991, in Cassidy, 2004) determined that the holistic-analytical learner is commonly associated with the following terms: analytic-deductive, rigorous, constrained, convergent, formal, critical, and synthetic. The verbalizer-imager refers to individuals who tend to represent information either as words or images (Cassidy, 2004).

Teachers need to be aware of the different ways students learn so they can prepare classroom experiences and material that encompass different learning styles. By presenting materials through different multisensory channels, all students have an opportunity to learn material through their preferred learning style and to have it reinforced in other ways.

COMPETENCY 25.0   CULTURAL DIVERSITY IN CALIFORNIA AND THE UNITED STATES

Skill 25.1   Demonstrate knowledge of major demographic trends related to the cultural and linguistic diversity of California and the United States (e.g., primary languages spoken by English Learners).

California is considered to be one of the most linguistically diverse areas in the world. Since the passage of Proposition 63 in 1986, English has been the official language of California. According to the census of 2005, 57.59 percent of the state spoke English as a first language in the home; 28.21 percent spoke Spanish. Other languages frequently spoken as first languages are Filipino, Chinese, Vietnamese, and Korean.

Skill 25.2   Demonstrate understanding of current trends and features of migration and immigration in California and the United States. For example:

a. Contemporary causes of migration and immigration (e.g., push/pull factors), both voluntary and forced

One theory of migration is **push/pull migration**. This refers to factors that cause emigration (the push factor) and immigration (the pull factor). Often the push/pull occurs because of economic reasons. Emigrants are able to secure work and working conditions superior to those in their native land and thus seek better opportunities in other countries.

Large-scale migrations have caused world governments to carefully consider what is culture and cultural identity. For many ELLs entering U.S. schools, their cultural identity has been challenged by migration. Political unrest and wars, natural disasters, the need for improved living conditions—all contribute to the desire of populations and individuals to migrate to other countries and cultures. In recent U.S. history, one of the most notable periods of immigration was the third period of migrations from Cuba, from December 1965 to April 1973, known as the "freedom flights," which resulted from the fall of Batista (Beebe and Mackey, 1990). Many of these refugees were wealthy, well-educated professionals or businesspeople, who as time went on and their hopes of an early return to Cuba diminished, were forced to start or purchase modest businesses. Those without resources were forced into more menial jobs.

The fall of Saigon in April of 1975 led to a wave of immigration from Vietnam. According to Singer and Wilson (2007) between 1983 and 2004, over 387,741 people immigrated to the United States from Vietnam, making Vietnamese the seventh most commonly spoken language in the U.S. Because of strong U.S. government support of Vietnamese immigration, President Gerald Ford signed the Indochina Migration and Refugee Assistance Act in 1975 and Congress passed the Refugee Act of 1980. These acts permitted the early entry of refugees to the United States in response to the Vietnamese government's establishment of the Orderly Departure Program (ODP) under the United Nations High Commissioner for Refugees in response to world protest of the former enemy combatants.

These two comparatively recent historical events illustrate not only changes in our recent cultural history, but in the lives of those who are forced to make decisions that drastically affect their futures and their children. In modern society, relationships are defined by the family, the school, the workplace, professional organizations, and the church. Each organization has its own power hierarchy, its expected roles and statuses, its characteristic values and beliefs, attitudes and ideologies (Kramsch, 1998). Geographic mobility, professional change, and life experiences may cause people to experience internal conflict with their multiple social identities.

b. Characteristics of contemporary migrants and immigrants (e.g., countries of origin, destinations, levels of education, socioeconomic status, native languages, secondary migration)

Contemporary migrants and immigrants can be those seeking better economic conditions. However, there are a multitude of other factors in contemporary migration. **Natural disasters** (e.g., the earthquake in Haiti in 2009) may cause migration. Religious missionaries and employees of transnational corporations, NGOs, and the diplomatic service are expected to work overseas as a condition of employment.

The **destinations** of emigrants may vary. While Europe has long attracted immigrants from poorer countries, British citizens may retire to Spain or Italy and Canadians to Florida or Texas. Both are examples of older citizens seeking lower living expenses and warmer climates.

Many countries put up barriers to immigration because of the influx of poorly educated immigrants, e.g., Spain has attempted to stem the flow of immigrants from Africa. Other countries, such as Japan, are rethinking their immigration policies because of internal problems, e.g., an aging workforce and low birthrates. **Educational opportunities** are certainly a reason for immigrating to another country, but generally students are not considered immigrants.

The **socioeconomic status** of many immigrants is better than what it was in their native country even for those who are unskilled laborers. It is for this reason that they seek better opportunities elsewhere. Some immigrants, however, who leave their native lands because of political unrest, oppression, ethnic cleansing, and genocide, are more concerned with personal safety than with economic opportunities.

Native languages: The United States is a pluralistic society with a multitude of native languages being spoken at any one time within its borders. English is the *de facto* official language of the country, but it is not officially recognized by federal law as such. Hawaii recognizes English and Hawaiian as the official languages of the state. Other states provide for the use of English and another language, such as French (in Louisiana) or Spanish (in New Mexico). In 2006, approximately 12 percent of the country spoke Spanish (including Creole) at home, followed by Chinese, French, Tagalog, Vietnamese, German, and Korean. Native languages are generally used by immigrants in familiar circles while in most cases the family struggles to learn the language of the country to which they have immigrated.

Secondary migration occurs when one or more family members leave their native country in search of work, leaving other family members behind. When the other family members join the first individual or group, it is referred to as secondary migration.

Skill 25.3   Demonstrate understanding of important issues and challenges faced by culturally and linguistically diverse groups in California and the United States. For example:

a. Challenges associated with primary language maintenance and loss

For parents of children immigrating to the United States, use of the primary language is natural and part of the culture. When children begin using English in the school environment and in the community at large, a small part of their culture is being replaced. The loss of the primary language may or may not become an issue within the family and the family's cultural society.

- **Additive bilingualism** refers to cases when a second language is learned without causing adverse effects on the first language. Canada is frequently cited as a country where the second language does not pose a threat to the acquisition of the first language.

- **Subtractive bilingualism** occurs when the child from a minority group learns a second language and is not provided with the opportunity to fully develop his/her first language. It is believed to have negative effects on the mental development of the child. This is common among the Maori of New Zealand and the Hispanics in the United States.

b. Challenges associated with various stages or phases of acculturation

For ELLs, acculturation occurs primarily in the school setting. Schools are agents of cultural transmission, reflecting the culture of those having the power to run the school, i.e., community members and the school faculty (Unrau, 2000). Different schools have different norms, regulations, academic requirements, traditions, and beliefs. As ELLs become familiar with the school setting, they may engage because they have no choice, or they may disengage if they do not feel sufficiently challenged or held accountable.

c. Issues related to an individual's legal status (e.g., documented, undocumented, refugee), including the relationship of individuals to their nation of origin and types/availability of support networks and services

For some undocumented immigrants, escaping a homeland of insecurity, injustice, poverty, and political strife is reason enough to take the risks involved in immigrating to a new country. Undocumented immigrants may suffer physical and verbal harassment because they cannot appeal to authorities for support. In the workplace, they are subject to underpayment or no payment for work done. Emergency room treatment and public education for the children of undocumented immigrants is not always available. Certain support groups such as the Catholic Legal Immigration Network and Americans for Legal Immigration work to overcome these injustices.

d. Societal and intragroup challenges to culturally and linguistically diverse groups (e.g., prejudice and discrimination, economic challenges, interactions between newcomers and U.S.-born members of the same cultural group)

Prejudices and discrimination are examples of negative power forces that push people apart. Kenneth Boulding referred to this as "**disintegrative power**—the integration that is achieved through hatred, fear, and the threat of a common enemy." (Boulding,1989). When one group creates negative stereotypes of another group and discriminates against them, it can lead to violence.

Most immigrants face **economic challenges**. Most have made tremendous sacrifices to arrive in a new country. Some are forced to do so, others have lost everything because of natural disasters, and still others chose to save and immigrate in the hopes of a better life. Whatever the reasons, most immigrants are faced with the challenge of earning a living. For unskilled workers, with few or no language skills, this often means doing manual labor. Immigrants with professional training, e.g., doctors, may still have to undergo extensive retraining or validation of their credentials. As the U.S. laws become tighter on the requirements for legally working, it is more and more difficult for undocumented immigrants to support themselves and their families adequately.

Interactions between newcomers and U.S.-born members of the same cultural group may become **polarized** as each group tries to build up its power base. Newcomers stick together with the goal of helping each other overcome the difficulties of arriving in a new place. Many former immigrants help their fellow countrymen and -women—they may be family members, but others may feel superior if they have achieved some degree of success. They may be able to speak the language well, they may have purchased a house or car, they may have seen their children through school and on to college, and therefore, they may look down on the recently arrived with their traditional clothing, bad accents, and poverty. Over a period of years, these differences may polarize a community into two large and opposing groups.

e. Challenges associated with group stereotypes and individual variation

Teachers and administrators should work to reduce stereotyping before it becomes a problem. Most individuals do not realize the depth and strength of their own cultural patterns until they have the opportunity to experience a cross-cultural interaction that is threatening or that challenges or violates their cultural values (Zainuddin, 2007). Encouraging students to look at the common traits among all human beings will give them insight into the differences and similarities among us all. For example, studying the family and the societal group offers windows into different cultures. The trappings may be different, but most families have tremendous love for each other and will try to protect other members from harm.

Based on Bennett's (1995) work, a strong school program would include the following elements:

- a learning environment that supports positive interracial contact
- a multicultural curriculum
- positive teacher expectations from all students
- administrative support
- teacher-training workshops on identifying and combating stereotyping

Skill 25.4 **Use knowledge of issues and challenges faced by culturally and linguistically diverse groups to provide effective instruction and equitable access to English Learners.**

ELLs often feel as if they lose a part of themselves when faced with the complexities of learning a new language and culture. To lessen these feelings of alienation and isolation and enhance learning in the English classroom, the teacher should incorporate elements of the ELL's culture and previous knowledge into his/her teaching. Including culture study in the classroom can be achieved by having each student do a research project on his or her culture and report back to the class. Culture studies of this nature promote reading, writing, speaking, learning to give presentations, and creating visuals. Should there be more than one student from the same culture, pairs or small groups could be organized. Alternative types of assessment could be used to evaluate the process.

COMPETENCY 26.0 **CROSS-CULTURAL INTERACTION**

Skill 26.1 **Demonstrate understanding of cultural differences in patterns of nonverbal communication (e.g., distance between speakers; eye contact; gestures; touching; facial expressions, including smiles).**

Communication in a culture involves not only the language but also gestures, facial expressions, and body stance, among other elements. For the nonverbal elements, the teacher or students can model them. Next, ask the ELLs how to communicate the same message in their culture. For example, the distance between different speakers and the way to indicate the height of a person may be different in different cultures.

Skill 26.2 **Demonstrate understanding of cultural differences in oral discourse patterns and practices (e.g., ways conversations open and close, timing of responses, turn-taking practices, volume of voice, use/role of silence) and cultural differences in written discourse (e.g., style of argumentation, use of voice, formality level, organizational structure).**

ORAL DISCOURSE

- **Ways conversations open and close:** Kramsch (1998) notes that in a classroom discussion, American students begin with whomever takes the initiative. Japanese students begin with one female member of the group, followed by another female, then the youngest male, and finally the oldest male member of the group. To begin in this way indicates to the Japanese participants the social position of the first speaker. In this way, the other members of the group determine what language style and vocabulary to use. The first speaker has no knowledge of the position of the other speakers and takes the greatest chance in losing face. For other cultures, such face-saving devices may dictate the social norm used when beginning conversations.

- **Timing of responses:** "Wait time" varies considerably in different cultures. Teachers can observe their students to see how long the wait time varies in the cultures in their classroom. In many cultures, children do not speak until called upon; in other cultures, children may shout out an answer as soon as the question is asked. Students who are struggling to formulate their answers may need more time than the teacher normally gives for responding. Also, if the questions are rhetorical, students may be reluctant to answer them, as they see no point to such questions.

- **Turn-taking practices:** The turn-taking order of the Japanese speakers above indicates that inferiors and juniors go first because for them to save face is not as important as for superiors or elders. Teaching turn-taking in speaking, the use of materials, and other classroom procedures may be a yearlong task.

- **Volume of voice:** When listening to speeches, there are several important keys (including voice volume or quality, intonation, or dialect) that may signal that the speaker wishes to be interpreted literally, ironically, seriously, or playfully. Careful consideration of the contextualization cues are necessary to interpret participant speech (Gumperz 1977, 1981). In many Asian cultures people speak softly—to speak loudly is considered rude. Native Americans may speak so softly that they are inaudible.

- **Use/role of silence:** North Americans value small talk, but many Asians (and other cultures) value silence. Many cultures believe Americans talk too much. In the classroom, Asians may need more time to process a question, prepare an adequate answer, and choose an appropriate style in which to answer. Teachers must allow extra wait time in order to accommodate the cultural differences in the use of silence. Native Americans may use silence as a power issue.

WRITTEN DISCOURSE

- **Style of argumentation:** African American students may look away from speakers and freely state their opinions to the teacher. These behaviors may be seen as disrespectful or not paying attention in the first instance and challenging the teacher's authority in the second. Students are actually observing correct protocol in their culture and taking pride in their opinions.

- **Use of voice:** In English texts, voice is the sound of the story or the narrator. In other cultures, voice may reflect the oral traditions of the culture and be quite different from English voice and texts. Both voice and genre have to be taught to ELLs.

- **Formality level:** Written language is more formal than spoken language in most cases. For beginning writers, it is difficult to separate written language with its more formal structures from the daily oral language they hear. Teachers need to instruct ELLs and native speakers alike in the degree of formality and the conventions expected in written work.

- **Organizational structure:** Gee (1985) and Michaels (1981) claim that teachers prefer linear, single-topic story telling like the story telling used in reading and writing activities. Children from oral cultures often prefer narrative-style stories and assume a shared knowledge with their audience. Such children may be interrupted more often and erroneously referred for psychological assessments or placed in special education classes.

Skill 26.3   **Apply strategies for providing authentic opportunities for English Learners to use the English language for communicative purposes with both native and nonnative speakers of English in both social and academic settings and demonstrate conceptual understanding and applied knowledge of how to facilitate positive interactions among culturally diverse students. For example, explicitly teaching about:**

a. Cultural differences in communication styles

Native speakers have to be taught about the cultural differences in the communication styles of immigrants as well as immigrants being taught the American cultural differences in communication styles. Role-plays with students of different cultures acting out a real-life situation can be used to initiate discussion of these differences.

b. Intercultural communication strategies

Some cultures (e.g., the North American culture) believe in coming "straight to the point." In other cultures, the participants need time to warm up (e.g., the Japanese). When intermediaries (e.g., the teacher or ESOL expert) understand these differences, they can explain the cultural differences and encourage each party to be more tolerant of the other's cultural norms.

c. Strategies for resolving cultural conflicts (e.g., conflict resolution strategies)

Encouraging students to suspend judgment, investigate the situation, and try to understand it is a key position to take when confronted with difficult situations where cultural conflicts are involved.

d. Strategies that enable students to appreciate and analyze multiple perspectives

SDAIE emphasizes that every student brings a unique perspective to each learning situation. The teacher as the model and facilitator for the lesson needs to encourage all students to contribute and expand everyone's knowledge.

e. Strategies for helping students become aware of the concepts of ethnocentrism and cultural relativism

Ethnocentrism and cultural relativism are two extremes on opposite ends of a philosophical debate. In a multicultural society, the responsibility for teaching tolerance and openness often falls to the classroom teacher, using the strategies of debate, cooperative group learning, multicultural literature, and library/Internet research. Students can engage in show-and-tell expositions about cultural norms from different cultures.

Skill 26.4   Demonstrate an ability to analyze schools' and classrooms' implicit cultural values and preferences and their differential impact on students from diverse cultural groups.

A school's culture—positive or negative—stems from its vision and its established values. Schools need to have a system of values in place that emphasizes staff and students working toward goals together. Schools need to establish clear norms and expectations for each student in an atmosphere of trust. Trusting relationships between the staff and the students need time to develop and be sustained but are imperative to a high-performing school.

High-performing schools have a positive core ideology that includes a core purpose and a set of fundamental values and beliefs. When evaluating a school or classroom, ask yourself, "Are the talks about values and beliefs followed up on or left at the talking stage?"

High-performing schools engage in reinforcing behaviors through rituals, hero making, storytelling, symbolic display, and rules. They use phrases such as "a hunger for improvement," "promoting excellence," and "pushing the boundaries of achievement" to define their commitment to students—all students.

DOMAIN VII.   CULTURALLY INCLUSIVE INSTRUCTION

COMPETENCY 27.0   THE ROLE OF CULTURE IN THE CLASSROOM AND SCHOOL

Skill 27.1   Demonstrate understanding of the important role culture plays in the classroom and the school and how the degree of congruence between the school/classroom culture and a student's home culture can affect the student's learning and achievement.

People know what is expected of them in their own cultures, but when different cultures come together, they may not know what they are expected to do or how to react to different situations. Teachers should be able to bridge these situations by being culturally aware and respectful of all cultures.

Teachers who are culturally aware avoid using cultural elements that cause students' embarrassment. Not only are many cultural elements of the mainstream American culture completely opposite to those of other cultures, some are offensive. To avoid these problems, teachers must actively study other cultures.

By encouraging an open dialog with parents, teachers become aware of cultural differences and things such as which cultures limit the role of women in society, or encourage education and learning, permit touching or reject it, respect time or disregard it completely, are deeply religious, etc. As teachers become familiar with the cultures present in the classroom, they are more equipped to address cultural differences. In extreme cases, students may come to school seeking a "safe haven" from problems at home or the problems that caused them to become refugees. It is up to teachers to provide this safe haven.

Skill 27.2   Demonstrate conceptual understanding and applied knowledge of the importance of examining how a teacher's own cultural beliefs, values, attitudes, and assumptions impact learning and achievement among students from diverse cultural backgrounds (e.g., classroom management style, teaching style, interactions with students and parents).

Teachers raised in the North American culture are considered field-independent. In general, this means that the teacher is independent, competitive, emphasizes details of concepts, emphasizes facts and principles, etc. (Zainuddin, 2007). Students from Asian or Hispanic cultures are more field-sensitive. Field-sensitive cultures value assisting others, are sensitive to others' feelings, seek guidance and demonstration from the teacher, and teachers instruct primarily by modeling. When the classroom teacher is insensitive to these cultural differences, communication problems may occur in the classroom.

Skill 27.3 **Apply strategies to acquire in-depth knowledge of English Learners' home cultures and cultural experiences (e.g., using observations, community resources, home visits, interviews, informal conversations, written and oral histories).**

Many teachers and school districts set up visits to the homes of their students to acquire in-depth knowledge of English Learners' home cultures and cultural experiences. When this is not possible, parents and/or guardians can be invited to the school for interviews. Teachers need to observe students carefully in the classroom and conduct informal conversations with them. Encouraging students to participate in activities such as telling oral histories and/or writing about the family and their experiences helps the teacher gain valuable information about students' home cultures. When the information is available, lessons can be planned around activities that are meaningful to the students.

COMPETENCY 28.0 **CULTURALLY INCLUSIVE LEARNING ENVIRONMENT**

Skill 28.1 **Demonstrate understanding of characteristics of classroom and school environments that facilitate culturally responsive accommodations to diverse communities.**

Teachers have their own learning styles, which are so ingrained they are probably unaware of them. So do students. Many of the factors affecting learning styles are culturally ingrained. It is important to explain to students, especially older learners, your reasons for choosing one style over the other. Many cultures use and value group work. Other cultures (e.g., Haitian) see the teacher as the authority for academic matters and may feel the teacher is not teaching when students are assigned to group work. If the teacher briefly explains to students (and their parents in PTA meetings) the reasons behind certain decisions, students may learn to expand their learning styles and become more open to other types of learning activities.

Skill 28.2 **Demonstrate understanding of factors that contribute to classroom and school environments that support cultural diversity and student achievement. For example:**

a. High expectations for all students

For many years, immigrants were not encouraged to strive for high levels of achievement. The No Child Left Behind Act (NCLB) has challenged schools on this issue. As schools are evaluated on disaggregated data, more schools are encouraging all students to reach higher goals. Also, TESOL has developed standards to be used as the starting point from which ESOL students can acquire the same education as all other students.

b. High level of respect for cultural and linguistic diversity, including valuing and validating the primary language and its use

TESOL standards state that the goal of using English to communicate in social settings does not in any way suggest that students should lose their native-language proficiency.

c. High level of interaction among students with different backgrounds (e.g., cooperative group work)

Cooperative group work is based on the premise that many cultures are more comfortable working in collaborative groups. However, while this is true, many students may feel that the teacher is the only academic authority in the classroom and, as such, should be the one to answer questions rather than their peers. Different students feel more comfortable with different instructional formats, due to both cultural and individual preferences. By balancing group work with teacher-directed instruction, both points of view can be accommodated.

d. Multicultural perspectives infused throughout the curriculum

To ensure multicultural perspectives throughout the curriculum, teachers can look at different themes through multicultural perspectives using the myths, narratives, and literature of different cultures to set the stage for a topic. Teachers who foster an atmosphere of multiculturalism and openness to different points of view earn the trust of their students.

e. Use of proactive approach to cultural conflict (e.g., by openly discussing topics such as prejudice, discrimination, racism, stereotypes, and intergroup and intra-group relations)

Racism, stereotyping, and discrimination are difficult social issues to address in the classroom. Even so, teachers are charged with addressing them. Encouraging an all-inclusive classroom climate where everyone is equal is a start. This is fairly easy when dealing with young children, but with older students, the movie *The Ron Clark Story* (2006) could be used to initiate a discussion of these themes. The movie shows how an idealistic young teacher from North Carolina deals with the problems of racism, stereotyping, and discrimination in his New York City classroom.

f. Zero tolerance for culturally insensitive behavior

In California, teachers are expected to be aware of the cultural differences among their students and to create an atmosphere of zero tolerance for cultural insensitivity. For example, members of a minority group may call one another by names that would give offense if used by those who are not members of the group. This distinction is often confusing to children and needs to be directly taught. One example to help clarify this is to compare it to arguments between brothers and sisters, who would be insulted if a nonsibling joined in on one side or the other.

English-speaking high school students whose sports teams were called "Braves" had difficulty understanding why Native Americans were offended by the team's name. One Native American girl explained that it upset her to see Native Americans hung in effigy or scalped on posters. The teacher emphasized to the class that it didn't matter whether the larger community found it offensive. If the minority group was offended, the behavior was unacceptable.

To create an atmosphere of zero tolerance, a teacher needs to be keenly aware of cultural insensitivity in his or her own presentations and in the classroom. The teacher should take a proactive approach to potential conflicts by actively discussing prejudice, discrimination, racism, stereotypes, and intergroup and intragroup relations. The teacher should strive to create a high level of cooperative interaction in the class.

g. Strong parent/guardian and community involvement in class and school activities and in school organizations and programs

Parents and other family members often delight in being part of the educational community when encouraged to do so. Schools that encourage all stakeholders in the community to participate in the school system have strong community resources upon which to draw when (and if) problems occur.

Some benefits of outreach programs include:

- Older members of the community can be encouraged to mentor at-risk students
- Parents and grandparents can serve as tutors for students with academic difficulties
- Room parents provide support for the many classroom events throughout the school year
- PTA groups provide family members with organizational and financial skills opportunities to serve the school community
- Invitations to relatives of ELL students to talk about their homelands and cultures are an excellent way to encourage otherwise reticent parents to get involved with the school

Skill 28.3 Apply knowledge of attitudes, practices, and strategies for creating culturally inclusive classroom and school environments and for promoting all students' achievement.

A culturally inclusive classroom and school environment is achieved only by those who study the culture of their students. By observing the following suggestions, teachers can ensure a culturally aware classroom:

- Review the textbooks used in your classroom. Observe the roles of the males, females, people of color, and ethnic minorities. Do the roles seem just? Comment on inequities.

- Analyze the nonverbal communication you use and focus on teaching your students what it means.
- Communicate respect and sincere interest in your students and their cultures.
- Make sure your classroom sends a positive, welcoming message.
- Encourage home/school interaction. Attend cultural celebrations in your students' communities.
- Make sure you are assessing content and not merely language ability.
- Avoid using children as interpreters for their parents. (This may invert the normal parental hierarchy, robbing parents of their authority.)
- Understand the cultural conflict between the dominant school culture and the minority home culture.
- Encourage parents to continue speaking their native language in the home.

(Adapted from Zainuddin, 2007)

COMPETENCY 29.0 FAMILY AND COMMUNITY INVOLVEMENT

Skill 29.1 Demonstrate understanding of family and community involvement with regard to culturally inclusive curriculum and instruction (e.g., rationale for and outcomes of family and community involvement, roles of family and community members in planning and implementing culturally inclusive curriculum and instruction).

Often in schools, parents, grandparents, and other people involved in children's lives want to take an active role in the educational process. They also all seem to have an opinion on the appropriate method for teaching students how to read. Sometimes this can lead to controversy and misunderstandings.

It is important to provide opportunities for the public to come into the school and participate in activities. During these fun programs, it is also important to share tidbits of information about the methodologies and strategies being implemented. In this way, the public can begin to understand the differences between ESOL instruction today and what it may have been like in their native cultures when they attended school. This comparison addresses what is often the biggest concern expressed by adults concerning current educational trends.

Taking the time to educate parents and other family members not only helps to enhance understanding and open communication, it can also provide more support for students than the school alone would ever be able to provide.

Some strategies for educating parents and family members include:

- Bingo games in which the correct answer on the Bingo board is a fact about English-language instruction
- small parent workshops offered on various topics
- newsletter articles or paragraphs

- individual parent meetings
- inviting parents to observe lessons
- small tidbits of information shared during other social times when parents are invited into the school

Communicating general information about English and appropriate English-language instruction is important. It is just as important to share specific information about students with parents, other school personnel, and the community. Once the teacher has gathered sufficient information on the students, he/she must find appropriate methods to share this information with those who need it. Again, depending on the audience, the amount and type of information shared may vary.

Some ways to share information with parents/guardians include:

- individual parent meetings
- small group meetings
- regular parent updates through phone calls
- charts and graphs of progress sent home
- notes sent home

By establishing communication with parents and other family members, the school staff and classroom teachers can gain insight into parents' concerns and facilitate the implementation of a culturally inclusive curriculum.

Skill 29.2   Demonstrate understanding and apply knowledge of culturally responsive strategies for communicating with family members (e.g., knowledge of potential site resources for translating communications to the home) and for involving family members in their children's learning.

Parents and other family members often delight in being part of the educational community when encouraged to do so. Schools which encourage all the stakeholders in the community to participate in the school system have strong community resources upon which to draw when (and if) problems occur. For this reason, it is important to be sure family members understand the communications sent home. When this is a school wide goal, translators can be provided and the communications translated into the students' home language.

Many parents enjoy sharing their expertise when invited to participate through outreach programs such as the following:

- older members of the community can be encouraged to mentor at-risk students.
- parents and grandparents can serve as tutors for students with academic difficulties.

- room mothers and fathers provide support for the many classroom events throughout the school year.
- the PTA groups are an excellent place for family members with organizational and financial skills to serve the school community.
- Invitations to relatives of ELL students to talk about their homelands and cultures are an excellent way to encourage otherwise reticent parents to get involved in their school.

Skill 29.3 Demonstrate understanding and apply knowledge of strategies for involving community members in the classroom and school (e.g., providing insight about different cultural, religious, and linguistic traditions; sharing content expertise).

Encouraging parents, guardians, and other valued members of the community to share their expertise allows each culture the opportunity to examine various aspects of their culture and those of others. Parents, guardians, and community leaders are stakeholders in the school and community, and smooth relationships among different cultures need to be established early on and maintained through dialog. Depending on the cultural makeup of the school and outside community, individual classes or the entire school might hold a festival, a picnic, or fair to celebrate a cultural holidays or custom. For example, Cinco de Mayo and the Chinese New Year are two holidays widely celebrated in many communities.

Skill 29.4 Demonstrate understanding of and plan strategies for involving language minority parents/guardians and community members in school governance and decision-making processes (e.g., serving on district and school committees).

Each school and school district has a multitude of school advisory committees for the parents of the children involved. These committees welcome parental involvement, and it is the legal obligation of the teacher and the school staff to provide information to all parents of all children in the school about serving on committees to improve academic achievement, formulate policies on multilingual and multicultural issues, and provide the best education possible for special needs students.

Some of the committees that welcome parental involvement are:

- Autism Advisory Committee (AAC)
- Community Advisory Committee of Special Education (CACSE)
- District English Learners Advisory Committee (DELAC)
- GATE Parent Advisory Committee (GAC)
- Migrant Education Parent Advisory Committee
- Parent Education/Involvement Task Force
- Parent Teacher Association/Parent Teacher Student Association Council

- School English Learners Advisory Committee (SELAC)

Skill 29.5   Demonstrate understanding and apply knowledge of strategies for addressing conflicts related to differences in cultural values among students, teachers, parents/guardians, and/or the community.

Educational institutions have always attempted to redress racial conflict and its underlying themes of bias, prejudice, and injustice (Mitchell, 1990). Mitchell suggests three methods for reducing racial conflict through the schools:

- **Multicultural education:** Usually discusses social differences and ignores the topics of racism or ethnic differences
- **Antiracist education**: Cole (1990) provides a manual to use so individuals can reflect on racism
- **Conflict resolution:** Agencies such as School Mediation Associates of Cambridge, Massachusetts, work with schools and communities to plan, set goals, and mediate when conflicts arise because of race, ethnicity, class, or gender

Policies explicitly outlining multicultural education, antiracist education, and conflict resolution must be well publicized and enforced throughout the schools and districts. Mitchell suggests policies should include the following:

- Racial and cultural diversity among members of the administration, faculty, and staff
- Services for victims of bias-motivated violence
- Reporting and monitoring of trends in racial attitudes
- Committees on human relations that include students, faculty, and staff

COMPETENCY 30.0   CULTURALLY INCLUSIVE CURRICULUM AND INSTRUCTION

Skill 30.1   Demonstrate understanding of features, goals, and outcomes of different approaches to multicultural curriculum reform, from additive to transformative.

Characteristics of the **additive approach** to multicultural curriculum reform:

- **Features**: Adds ethnic content without restructuring the curriculum
- **Goals:** Increase the linguistic abilities of students without diminishing L1 ability
- **Outcomes:** A resource for bilingual peoples to draw upon

Characteristics of the **transformative approach**:

- **Features:** Tries to infuse various perspectives, frames of reference, and content from various groups
- **Goals:** Extend students' understanding of the complexity of U.S. society
- **Outcomes:** Deeper understanding of cultural issues and the United States as a society with multicultural input from many cultures based on a common language

Skill 30.2 Demonstrate knowledge of content included in an effective multicultural curriculum and resources for multicultural curriculum development

The additive curriculum would encourage students to take a look at leaders, sports figures, writers, and politicians from various countries. The library would be a starting place for this type of curriculum as would the regular classroom textbooks, many of which strive to include cultural diversity. Technological resources can be as simple as a PC with a word processor program and translation dictionaries. Web sites such as online dictionaries and Wikipedia, are excellent resources for the classroom teacher.

The transformative curriculum encourages teachers to use action research, service learning projects, and personal reflection to deepen their knowledge of the topics being discussed. Students are urged to use higher-order thinking skills. The Web site www.web.goddard.edu/~tla/interestweb.htm provides a list of Web sites dedicated to transformative language arts.

Skill 30.3 Demonstrate conceptual understanding and applied knowledge of attitudes and instructional practices and strategies that reflect an inclusive approach with regard to students' cultural and language backgrounds.

A multicultural curriculum should include equal opportunities for all students. The classroom reflects an atmosphere of multiculturalism and opportunities for each and every student regardless of background and culture. The classroom should be a nonthreatening place where students can learn, be creative, and succeed. Each student is encouraged to respect the culture of everyone in the class and become more knowledgeable about culture in general.

The curriculum should reflect recognition of deep cultural values (e.g., family structures and male/female roles) instead of surface ones. The teachers and administrators need to explore ways to amplify the understanding of these values throughout the school. By sequencing such core values in each school year, the school demonstrates the welcoming, nonthreatening atmosphere ELLs need for learning.

Skill 30.4   Apply knowledge of cultural influences (e.g., different attitudes toward conformity and individuality, different values regarding cooperation and competition, different expectations and preferences with regard to teacher-student interactions and instructional formats) when planning and implementing instruction.

Students who have teachers from their own culture will have less difficulty in understanding the teacher's instructions than those from different cultures. When addressing a multicultural classroom, the teacher will want to plan activities that further academic and linguistic knowledge in such a way that the students will respond positively. Thus, teachers need to be aware of their teaching style and provide a variety of activities in different modes so that students from all cultures have the opportunity to experience education in ways they are familiar with. For example, Hispanics are generally auditory learners, Asians are highly visual learners, and students from non-Western cultures learn through tactile and kinesthetic modes (Zainuddin, 2007).

In the multicultural classroom, different cultures react differently with respect to conformity and individuality. The teacher can accommodate various styles by arranging group work in such a way that each member is held accountable for a specific task within the group (Unrau, 2008).

Different cultures respond differently to cooperation and competition. For example, Muslims, Native Americans, and Asians value cooperation and loyalty to the group. They prefer not competing with others. Activities emphasizing noncompetitive group results will probably work better with these students.

In many cultures, teachers are the absolute authority. In others, children are expected to respect their elders and not to disagree with them. These cultural mores may cause problems in a classroom if the teacher uses activities such as debates or asks a student to defend his/her position on a topic.

Over the course of the school year, teachers can introduce particular activities that students have refused to participate in previously by focusing on the reward, the materials, the situation, or the task requirements (Zainuddin, 2007). In this way, the student is gradually introduced to a wider array of learning experiences while having support from previously successful activities.

Skill 30.5 **Demonstrate understanding of how to apply knowledge of English Learners' cultural backgrounds and experiences to instruction (e.g., to help contextualize language and content for students, to help students access prior knowledge).**

Teachers can use parents' working environments to extend the learning experiences of their students by inviting parents in to the classroom to speak about their professions. For example, if many of the parents work in landscaping, nurseries, or agriculture, field trips could be arranged and students could conduct research on topics related to these industries. Using examples of cash crops, fruits, or ornamental plants, mathematical problems and science projects could be created.

REFERENCES

Alderson, J. 1992. Guidelines for the evaluation of language education. In: Ellis, R. 1997. The empirical evaluation of language teaching materials. *ELT Journal.* 51 (1) Jan.

Allen, V. G. 1994. Selecting materials for the instruction of ESL children. In: Zainuddin (2007).

Alliance for Excellent Education. 2007. Policy Brief. June. Washington, DC www.all4ed.org

Lawsuit Against NCLB Renewed. 2008. Education Matters. News from Washington, D.C. February. www.aaeteachers.org

Au, K. H. 1993. *Literacy instruction in multicultural settings.* Orlando, FL.: Harcourt Brace.

———. 2002. Multicultural factors and effective instruction of students of diverse backgrounds. In: Farstrup, A., and S. J. Samuels, eds. *What research says about reading instruction.* Newark, DE: International Reading Assn. Coral Gables: Univ. of Miami. 392-413.

Banks, J. A. 1988. *Multicultural Leader.* 1 (2). Educational Materials and Services Center. Spring.

Bebe, V. N., and Mackey, W. F. 1990. *Bilingual schooling and the Miami experience.* Coral Gables, FL: University of Miami. Institute of Interamerican Studies. Graduate School of International Studies.

Bennett, C. 1995. *Comprehensive multicultural education: Theory and practice.* 3rd ed.. Boston: Allyn & Bacon.

Berko Gleason, J. 1993. *The development of language.* 3rd ed. New York: Macmillan.

Bialystok, E.. ed.. 1991. *Language processing in bilingual children.* Cambridge: Cambridge University Press.

Blakey, E., and S. Spence, 1990. Developing metacognition (ED327218). Syracuse, NY: ERIC Clearinghouse on Information Resources..

Burstall, C., M. Jamieson, S. Cohen, and M. Hargreaves. 1974. *Primary French in the balance.* Slough: NFER.

California Department of Education. Testing and Accountability. CELDT Questions and Answers. Rev. 11/03/09. http://www.cde.ca.gov/ta/tg/el/celdtfaq.asp

Candlin, C. 1987. In Batstone, R. 1994. *Grammar.* Oxford: Oxford University Press.

Chamot, A. U., and J. M. O'Malley. 1994. *The calla handbook.* Reading, MA: Addison-Wesley.

Cloud, J. 2007. Are We Failing Our Geniuses? Time. August 16. http://www.time.com/magazine/article/0,9171,1653653,00.html

Collier, V. P. 1989. How long? A synthesis of research on academic achievement in second language. *TESOL Quarterly.* 23: 509-31.

————. 1992. A synthesis of studies examining long-term language minority student data on academic achievement. *Bilingual Research Journal.* 16 (1-2): 187-212.

————. 1995. Acquiring a second language for school. *Directions in Language and Education.* Washington, DC: NCBE. 1(4): 1-10.

Conflict Research Consortium. Online training program on intractable conflict (OTPIC) conflict management and constructive confrontation: A guide to the theory and practice. University of Colorado. Revised July 20, 1999. http://conflict.colorado.edu/

Criteria for evaluating instructional materials: Kindergarten through grade eight. reading/kanguage arts framework for California public schools. California Department of Education. 2007.

Cummins, J. 1981. *Bilingualism and minority language children.* Toronto: Institute for Studies in Education.

Diaz-Rico, L. T. 2004. *Strategies for teaching english learners.* 2nd ed. Boston: Pearson.

Diaz-Rico, L. T., and K. Z. Weed. 1995. *Language and academic development handbook: A complete k-12 reference guide.* Needham Heights, MA: Allyn & Bacon.

Dulay, H., and M. Burt. 1974. You can't learn without goofing. In: J. Richards, ed. *Error analysis, perspectives on second-language acquisition.* New York: Longman.

Ellis, R. 1985. *Understanding second-language acquisition.* Oxford: Oxford University Press.

————. 1994. *The study of second-language acquisition.* Oxford: OUP.

Entwhistle, N. J., and D. Entwhistle. 1970. The relationships between personality, study methods and academic performance. *British Journal of Educational Psychology.* 40(2): 132-43. doi.apa.org

Fillmore, L. W. 2001. Scott, Foresman ESL: Accelerating english language learning. In Zainuddin (2007).

Friend, M., and W. D. Bursuck. 2005. *Models of coteaching: Including students with special needs: A practical guide for classroom teachers.* 3rd ed. Boston: Allyn & Bacon.

Garcia, E. 1994. *Understanding and meeting the challenge of student cultural diversity.* Boston: Houghton Mifflin.

Garinger, D. 2002. Textbook evaluation. *TESL Web Journal.* 1(3).

Genesee, F. 1987. *Learning through two languages: Studies of immersion and bilingual education.* Cambridge, MA: Newbury House.

————, ed. 1994. *Educating second-language children: The whole child, the whole curriculum, the whole community.* Cambridge: Cambridge University Press.

Grellet, F. 1981. *Developing reading skills.* Cambridge: Cambridge University Press.

Harris, M., and P. McCann. 1994. *Assessment.* Oxford: Heinemann.

Heywood, D. 2006. Using whole-discourse tasks for language teaching. www.jalt-publications.org/tlt/chaprep/ Jan 2006.

Hoff, D.J. 2009. National Standards Gain Steam. Education Matters. September. www.aaeteachers.org

Jerald, C. D. 2006. School culture: "The hidden curriculum." The Center for Comprehensive School Reform and Improvement. Issue Brief. December 2006. www.centerforcsri.org

Kramsch, C. 1998. *Language and culture.* Oxford: Oxford University Press.

Krashen, S. 1985. The Input Hypothesis. New York: Longman.

———— .1982. *Principles and practice in second language acquisition.* Oxford: Pergamon Press.

_____ . 1981. *Second-language acquisition and second-language learning.* Oxford: Pergamon Press.

Lambert, W., and O. Klineberg 1967. *Children's views of foreign peoples: A crossnational study.* New York: Appleton. (Review in Shumann, J. 1975. Affective factors and the problem of age in second language acquisition. *Language Learning.* 25/2: 209-35).

Larsen, D., and W. Smalley 1972. *Becoming bilingual: A guide to language learning.* New Canadian, CT: Practical Anthropology.

Larsen-Freeman, D. 1997. Chaos/complexity science and second language acquisition. *Applied Linguistics.*18(2): 141-65.

Long, M. 1990. The lease a second language acquisition theory needs to explain. *TESOL Quarterly.* 24(4): 649-66.

The Map of Standards for ELS. 2002. 3rd ed. West Education.

McArthur, T., ed. 1992. *The oxford companion to the english language.* Oxford: Oxford University Press. 571-73.

McClelland, D., J. Atkinson, R. Clark, and E. Lowell 1953. *The achievement motive.* New York: Appleton, Century, Crofts.

McDonough, J., and S. Shaw 1993. *Materials and methods in ELT: A teacher's guide.* Blackwell.

McKay, S. L. 1987. *Teaching grammar: Form, function, and technique.* New York: Prentice Hall.

McLaughlin, B. 1990. The development of bilingualism: Myth and reality. In Barona, A., and E. Garcia, eds. *Children at risk: poverty, minority status and other issues in educational equity.* Washington, DC: National Association of School Psychologists.

Menken, K. 2006. *Teaching to the Test: How No Child Left Behind Impacts Language Policy, Curriculum, and Instruction for English Language Learners.* Bilingual Research Journal, 30:2 Summer. pp. 521-546.

Mitchell, V. 1990. *Curriculum and instruction to reduce racial conflict.* (ED322274). New York: ERIC Clearinghouse on Urban Education.

Naiman, N., M. Frolich, H. Stern, and A. Todesco. 1978. *The good language learner.* Toronto: The Modern Language Centre, Ontario Institute for Studies in Education.

National Center on Education and the Economy. 2001. California performance standards.

National Education Center. 2010. *Provide Students with Multiple Ways to Show What They Have Learned.* Backgrounder. March. www.nea.org

Nieto, S. 1992. We have stories to tell: A case study of puerto ricans in children's books." In Harris, V.J., ed. *Teaching multicultural literature in grades K-8.* Norwood, MA: Christopher-Gordon Publishers.

No Child Left Behind Act. Criticisms. Wikipedia. Page last updated on 11 July 2010.

Nunan, D. 1989. *Designing tasks for the communicative classroom.* Cambridge: Cambridge University Press.

O'Malley, J. M., and L. V. Pierce. 1996. *Authentic Assessment for English Language Learners.* New York: Longman.

Ovando, C. J., M. C. Coombs, and V. P. Collier, eds. 2006. *Bilingual and ESL classrooms: Teaching in multicultural contexts.* 4th ed. Boston: McGraw-Hill.

Penfield, W., and L. Roberts. 1959. *Speech and brain mechanisms.* New York: Atheneum Press. (reviewed in Ellis, R. 1985).

Peregoy, S. F., and O. F. Boyle. 2008. *Reading, writing, and learning in ESL.* 5th ed. Boston: Pearson.

Prabhu, N. S. 1987. *Second language Ppdagogy: A perspective.* London: Oxford University Press.

Quiocho, A., and S. H. Ulanoff. 2009. *Differentiated literacy instruction for english language learners.* Boston: Allyn & Bacon.

Reading/Language Arts Framework for California Public Schools. Kindergarten through Grade Twelve. 1999. Sacramento: California Department of Education.

Reid, J. The learning style preferences of ESL students. *TESOL Quarterly.* 21(1): 86-103.

Rennie, J. 1993. ESL and bilingual program models. Eric Digest. http://www.cal.org/resources/Digest/rennie01.html

Richards, Platt, and Weber. 1985. Quoted by Ellis, R. The evaluation of communicative tasks. In Tomlinson, B., ed. 1998. *Materials development in language teaching.* Cambridge: Cambridge University Press.

Rinvolucri, M. 1984. Grammar games: Cognitive, affective and movement activities for EFLstudents. Cambridge: Cambridge University Press.

Rinvolucri, M., and P. Davis. 1995. *More grammar games: Cognitive, affective and movement activities for EFL students.* Cambridge: Cambridge University Press.

Rochman, H. 1993. *Against borders: Promoting books for a multicultural world.* Chicago: American Library Association.

Rosansky, E. 1975. The critical period for the acquisition of language: Some cognitive developmental considerations. In: *Working Papers on Bilingualism.* 6: 92-102.

Rosenberg, L. 2006. Global Demographic Trends. *Finance and Development.* (Sept) 43(3).

Schiffrin, D., D. Tannen, and H. Hamilton., eds. 2003. *The handbook of discourse analysis.* New York: John Wiley & Sons.

Schimel, J. et al. 2000. Running from the shadow: Psychological distancing from others to characteristics people fear in themselves. *Journal of Personality and Social Psychology.* 78(3): 446-62.

Schmidt, R. W. 1990. The role of consciousness in second language acquisition. *Applied Linguistics.* 11(2): 129-58.

Schumm, J. S. 2006. *Reading assessment and instruction for all learners.* New York: The Guilford Press.

Sinclair, J., and M. Coulthard. 1975. *Towards an analysis of discourse.* Oxford: Oxford University Press.

Singer, A., and Wilson, J.H. (2007) Refugee Resettlement in Metropolitan America. Migration Policy Institute. 2010. Washington, D.C. www.migrationinformation.org

Slavin, R. E., and Cheung, A.. 2003. *Effective reading programs for English language learners: A best-evidence synthesis.* U.S. Dept. of Education. Institute of Education Sciences.

Snow, C., and M. Hoefnagel-Hohle. 1978. Age differences in second language learning. In: Hatch, ed. *Second language acquisition.* Rowley, MA.: Newbury House.

Taylor, O. L. 1990. *Cross-cultural communication: An essential dimension of effective education.* Rev. ed. hevy Chase, MD: Mid-Atlantic Equity Center.

Teachers of English to Speakers of Other Languages. 1997. *ESL standards for pre-k–12 students.* Alexandria, VA: TESOL.

Teaching Tolerance. n.d. *Anti-gay discrimination in schools.* Southern Poverty Law Center, http://www.tolerance.org.

Thomas, W. P., and V. P. Collier. 1995. Language minority student achievement and program effectiveness. Manuscript in preparation. (in Collier, V.P. 1995).

Tollefsen, J. 1991. *Planning language, planning inequality.* New York: Longman.

Tompkins, G. 2009. *Language arts: patterns of practice*. 7th ed. Upper Saddle River, NJ: Pearson.

Traugott, E. C., and M. L. Pratt. 1980. *Linguistics for students of literature*. San Diego: Harcourt Brace Jovanovich.

2008-2009 Adequate Yearly Progress (AYP) Results: Many More Schools Fail in Most States. 2008. National Education Association. www.nea.org

United Nations Cyberschoolbus. 1996. *Understanding discrimination*. www.cyberschoolbus.un.org

Unrau, N. 2008. *Content area reading and writing*. 2nd ed. Upper Saddle River, NJ: Pearson.

Ur, P. 1996. *A Course in language teaching*. Cambridge: Cambridge University Press.

Valsiner, J. 2003. Culture and Its transfer: Ways of creating general knowledge through the study of cultural particulars. In Lonner, W. J., D. L. Dinnel, S. A. Hayes, and D. N. Sattler, eds. *Online readings in psychology and culture* (Unit 2, Chapter 12),http://www.wwu.edu/~culture, Center for Cross-Cultural Research, Western Washington University, Bellingham, WA.

Weir, C. 1993. *Understanding and developing language tests*. Hemel Hempstead: Prentice Hall International.

Willing, K. 1988. Learning strategies as information management: Some definitions for a theory of learning strategies. *Prospect*. 3/2: 139-55.

Yokota, J. 1993. Issues in selecting multicultural children's literature. *Language Arts*. 70: 156-67.

Zainuddin, H. et al. 2007. *Fundamentals of teaching english to speakers of other languages in k-12 mainstream classrooms*. 2nd ed. Dubuque: Kendall/Hunt.

Zwiers, J. 2007. *Building academic language: Essential practices for content classrooms, grades 5-12*. San Francisco: Jossey-Bass.

Sample Test

1. **If you are studying phonology, then you are studying:**
   (Easy) (Skill 1.1)

   A. The smallest unit within a language system to which meaning is attached.

   B. The way in which speech sounds form patterns.

   C. Individual letters and letter combinations.

   D. The definition of individual words.

2. **Speakers can change sentences to questions by changing the:**
   (Easy) (Skill 1.1)

   A. Pitch

   B. Morphemes

   C. Root words

   D. Stress

3. **"Bite" and "byte' are examples of which phonographemic differences?**
   (Average) (Skill 1.2)

   A. Homonyms

   B. Homographs

   C. Homophones

   D. Heteronyms

4. **Words which have the same spelling or pronunciation, but different meanings are:**
   (Easy) (Skill 1.2)

   A. Homonyms

   B. Homographs

   C. Homophones

   D. Heteronyms

5. **Which word in the following contains the schwa sound?**
   (Average) (Skill 1.2)

   A. Few

   B. Legmen

   C. Sanity

   D. Berry

6. **If you are studying "morphemic analysis", then you are studying:**
   (Easy) (Skill 1.3)

   A. The smallest unit within a language system to which meaning is attached.

   B. The root word and the suffix and/or prefix

   C. The way in which speech sounds form patterns

   D. Answers A and B only

7. **The study of morphemes may provide the student with:**
    (Average) (Skill 1.3)

    A. The meaning of the root word

    B. The meaning of the phonemes

    C. Grammatical information

    D. All of the above

8. **Which of the following items is NOT a morpheme?**
    (Average) (Skill 1.3)

    A. fatal

    B. –s

    C. too

    D. mist

9. **Which of the following phonological pre-reading skills promotes fluent reading and writing?**
    (Rigorous) (Skill 1.5)

    A. Instruction in the Roman alphabet

    B. Recognizing and creating rhymes

    C. Syntax instruction

    D. Study of cognates

10. **Which of the following is an example of eliciting prior knowledge from a student's first language?**
    (Average) (Skill 1.6)

    A. Point to the ball.

    B. Raise your hand if you see something red in the picture.

    C. Is Mr. Brown riding a bicycle or riding a car?

    D. How do you say "mother" in French? In Vietnamese?

11. **If you are studying "syntax", then you are studying:**
    (Easy) (Skill 2.1)

    A. Intonation and accent when conveying a message

    B. The rules for correct sentence structure.

    C. The definition of individual words and meanings.

    D. The subject-verb-object order of the English sentence

12. **Language learners seem to acquire syntax:**
    (Average) (Skill 2.1)

    A. At the same rate in L1 and L2.

    B. Faster in L2 than L1.

    C. In the same order regardless of whether it is in L1 or L2

    D. In different order for L1

13. **Arrange the following sentences, written by ELLs, to show the order of acquisition of negation, ranging from least to most.**

    Sentence 1: Kim didn't went to school.
    Sentence 2: No school. No like.
    Sentence 3: Kim doesn't like to go to school.

    (Average) (Skill 2.1)

    A. Sentence 1, Sentence 2, Sentence 3.

    B. Sentence 3, Sentence 2, Sentence 1.

    C. Sentence 1, Sentence 3, Sentence 2.

    D. Sentence 2, Sentence 1, Sentence 3.

14. **How can teachers provide accurate examples of syntax to their students? (Average) (Skill 2.2)**

    A. Modeling

    B. Using guests from other countries.

    C. Show and Tell by ELL's parents.

    D. Using CDs and videos from England and other nations of the United Kingdom

15. **Which of the following is one reason why non-native speakers do less and less well as they move through the U.S. education system? (Rigorous) (Skill 2.3)**

    A. Undeveloped language skills in L2.

    B. Less cognitive maturity in L1.

    C. High level of literacy in L1.

    D. Use of L2 in the home.

16. **Which one of the following is NOT included in the study of semantics? (Average) (Skill 2.4)**

    A. Grasping the meaning of words from the context

    B. Studying the same word in a variety of contexts.

    C. Translating difficult terms.

    D. Register.

17. **Idioms are particularly difficult for ELLs because: (Average) (Skill 1.5)**

    A. Idioms frequently rely on hyperbole or metaphors.

    B. They can't be translated.
    C. They are in context.

    D. The language is old fashioned.

18. **Which one of the following items is an informative function of language?**
    (Average) (Skill 3.1)

    A. Describing the concept behind a science project.

    B. Creating a poem.

    C. Explaining a personal experience.

    D. Asking how something works.

19. **The vocabulary word "ain't" has been used for hundreds of years instead of /am not/, /is not/, and /has not/. It is an example of**

    _____.
    (Rigorous) (Skill 3.3)

    A. A dialect.

    B. How language evolves.

    C. Socio-economic effects on language.

    D. A southern drawl.

20. **English has grown as a language primarily because of:**
    (Easy) (Skill 3.3)

    A. Wars/technology and science

    B. Text messaging/immigrants

    C. Immigrants/technology and science

    D. Contemporary culture/wars

21. **Identify the major factor in the spread of English.**
    (Easy) (Skill 3.3)

    A. The invasion of the Germanic tribes in England.

    B. The pronunciation changes in Middle English.

    C. The extension of the British Empire.

    D. The introduction of new words from different cultures.

22. **Which of the following registers reflects the "manner of discourse" between an employer and a high school student employee at a fast food restaurant?**
(Average) (Skill 3.4)

   A. Bro, I need a burger, fries, and a Coke?

   B. I need a burger without onions.

   C. Hey, man. Let me get that for you.

   D. Let me take that order to your table, sir.

23. **Which one of the following items is a CALP?**
(Rigorous) (Skill 4.3)

   A. Where is the passage that supports your argument?

   B. Raise your hand if you know the answer.

   C. Let's get some pizzas and cokes for after the game.

   D. Can you give me five ones and a five, please?

24. **Which one of the following would promote an ELL's ability to develop discourse competence?**
(Rigorous) (Skill 4.5)

   A. Show and Tell.

   B. Reading a text, and answering questions.

   C. Playing Bingo.

   D. Listing to a radio program.

25. **Which of the following items illustrates pragmatics in different cultures?**
(Rigorous) (Skill 5.2)

   A. Eyes closed, sleeping on a plane.

   B. Children jumping rope or playing hopscotch.

   C. Indicating the height of a friend by holding the hand vertical to the floor.

   D. Soccer players greeting each other in the dressing room.

26. The researcher most identified with the impact of social influences on language learning is _____.
(Average) (Skill 6.1)

   A. Chomsky.

   B. Krashen.

   C. Piaget.

   D. Vygotsky.

27. Match the theorists with the elements of their explanations.
(Place the number after the letter.)
(Rigorous) (Skill 6.1)

   A. _____ Chomsky
   B. _____ Piaget
   C. _____ Vygotsky
   D. _____ Collier

   1. Children are active learners who construct their worlds.

   2. Social communication which promotes language and cognition.

   3. Nature is more important than nurture.

   4. Language is a reflection of thought.

28. Brain research has affirmed the importance of _____ in language learning.
(Average) (Skill 6.1)

   A. puberty

   B. maturity

   C. aphasia

   D. the brain's size

29. Which of the following is a metacognitive strategy?
(Rigorous) (Skill 6.2)

   A. Encouraging yourself.

   B. Evaluating your learning.

   C. Asking questions.

   D. Analyzing and reasoning.

30. Place the number in front of the phrase to order the stages in the language acquisition process, from Beginning (1) to Proficiency (5).
(Rigorous) (Skill 6.3)

   A. _____ Experimental or simplified speech

   B. _____ Lexical chunks

   C. _____ Private speech

   D. _____ Formulaic speech

   E. _____ Silent period

31. **According to its goal, Communication Based ESL emphasizes: (Rigorous) (Skill 7.1)**

    A. language rules

    B. comprehensible language

    C. language with emphasis on content, vocabulary, and basic concepts

    D. immersion

32. **Which of the following cognitive strategies is helpful to ELLs learning the language? (Rigorous) (Skill 7.2)**

    A. taking risks

    B. mumbling

    C. using formulaic expressions

    D. requesting retesting when the ELL feels ready to move on

33. **Which of the following reasons supports the idea of language being an interactive process? (Rigorous) (Skill 7.3)**

    A. Reading in a language develops its oral skills.

    B. Reading improves listening skills.

    C. Reading is a pleasure of its own.

    D. Reading different genres is unnecessary to improve language.

34. **Carrell and Eisterhold used _____ to explain their theory of language learning. (Average) (Skill 8.1)**

    A. left brain-right brain

    B. LAD

    C. age

    D. schemata

35. **Which one of the following is a learning style according to Willing (1988)? (Rigorous) (Skill 8.1)**

    A. Kinesthetic

    B. Analytic

    C. Visual

    D. Auditory

36. According to Ellis (1985), _____ does not affect the _____ of Second Language Acquisition. (Rigorous) (Skill 8.1)

    A. sex/process

    B. youth/importance of comprehensible input

    C. social context/stages

    D. age/route

37. To avoid "dumping" ELLs in special education classes, which of the following measures can be used to assure reliability in tests/testing? (Average) (Skill 8.1)

    A. subjective tests

    B. home language survey

    C. timed tests

    D. multiple raters

38. Which one of the following factors might cause an ELL from Argentina difficulties when faced with learning English? (Average) (Skill 8.1)

    A. the writing system

    B. multiple vowel sounds

    C. rhetorical questions

    D. directionality in reading materials

39. When an ESOL teacher is helping an ELL to understand material that is difficult for them, which of the following theorist's principals is the teacher implementing? (Rigorous) (Skill 8.2)

    A. Cummins.

    B. Vygotsky.

    C. Tompkins.

    D. Krashen.

40. Which one of the following is the best way to provide constructive feedback? (Rigorous) (Skill 8.2)

    A. Give specific information on what is wrong.

    B. Give feedback on papers returned a week later.

    C. Mark the errors without comments on a written paper.

    D. Give feedback during an evaluation.

41. **Which one of the following is an example of "integrative motivation" in learning a new language?**
(Rigorous) (Skill 9.1)

   A. A State Department officer who will travel to a foreign country.

   B. Foreign university students who plan to return to their country.

   C. Translators.

   D. Children who are new to a culture.

42. **The term "affective domain" includes all of the following except?**
(Average) (Skill 9.1)

   A. Inhibition.

   B. Reflection.

   C. Teacher expectations.

   D. Classroom culture.

43. **Which one of the following is NOT an acceptable way to give feedback in the language classroom?**
(Average) (Skill 9.2)

   A. Saying, "I don't understand."

   B. Writing, "Explain this in more detail" on a paper.

   C. Writing, "Good job" on a paper.

   D. Saying, "What on earth were you thinking?"

44. **Inter-language is best described as:**
(Easy) (Skill 9.2)

   A. A language characterized by overgeneralization.

   B. Bilingualism.

   C. A language learning strategy.

   D. A strategy characterized by poor grammar

45. According to the acculturation theory, which event occurs with new immigrants arriving in the United States?
(Rigorous) (Skill 10.1)

A. Two cultures collide; both are displaced

B. The dominant culture replaces the weaker culture

C. Biculturalism occurs.

D. Transculturation occurs.

46. Which of the following statements is NOT a tenet of Ong's (1982) theory of culture? Oral cultures were:
(Rigorous) (Skill 10.1)

A. highly socialized

B. subordinate

C. closer to the real world

D. more situational

47. Which of the following concepts by the ELL may reflect the negative feelings of the ELL's family and friends?
(Average) (Skill 10.1)

A. Ignoring time rules and constraints.

B. Acting out in class.

C. Shouting out answers.

D. Failing to sit quietly when requested to do desk work.

48. Which one of the following statements about culture and its manifestation is most likely to cause learning difficulties for the ELL?
(Average) (Skill 10.2)

A. Lengthening wait time.

B. ELLs may not understand the new culture and its differences.

C. Teachers may offend the ELLs when they are unaware of cultural differences.

D. Involving parents and guardians in the educational process.

49. **Which of the following is NOT an acceptable strategy for involving parents in the educational process?**
(Easy) (Skill 10.2)

   A. A newsletter in the L1 when possible.

   B. Group meeting with parents.

   C. Criticizing the ELL's performance during social events.

   D. Calling the ELL's home.

50. **Which of the following statements does NOT illustrate Collier & Thomas's (1999-2000) principles for high academic standards?**
(Easy) (Skill 10.2)

   A. Set high goals for all students.

   B. Including relevant life experiences in classroom content.

   C. Appealing to parents for help raising ELL's low results in academics.

   D. Talking with students.

51. **How are California's ELA Standards supported by the ELD standards?**
(Average) (Skill 11.1)

   A. By using videos games designed for academic learning.

   B. Through meaningful and comprehensible activities.

   C. Activities designed to support language study through cultural studies.

   D. By using L1

52. **When employing group work on projects, accurate assessments for ELLs may be achieved using _____.**
(Rigorous) (Skill 11.2)

   A. individual assessment and assessment as a part of the group

   B. assessment as a part of the group

   C. assessment of the process only

   D. individual assessment only

53. **What technique is being applied in the following situation? (Rigorous) (Skill 11.2)**

> Ms. Jones has decided each ELL must know the planets in the solar system in order of their relationship to the sun. She decides that the acceptable standard will be 6 out of 8. Next, she assigns each of the ELL's to a group to investigate the planets and report back to the other members of the class. After the reports a skill will be given to the parents. A final evaluation will be given after all the activities.

A. Curriculum mapping.

B. Curriculum calibration.

C. Backwards lesson planning.

D. Differentiated instruction.

54. **All of the following are criteria to be considered when reclassifying ELLs except _____. (Average) (Skill 12.1)**

A. CELDT

B. parent or guardian opinion

C. Teacher evaluation

D. IQ exams

55. **Which of the following statements about tests is NOT accurate? (Average) (Skill 12.2)**

A. Language proficiency tests are fairly accurate.

B. Unit tests and final exams are examples of language achievement tests.

C. Language tests test all areas of language learning.

D. The TOEFL is widely used by college admission officers for evaluating foreign candidates.

56. **Translation bias affects which testing criteria? (Rigorous) (Skill 12.3)**

A. Validity

B. Reliability.

C. Practicality.

D. None of the above.

57. **To eliminate linguistic bias in tests, ELLs may be tested _____. (Rigorous) (Skill 12.4)**

   A. in English only

   B. in their first language

   C. in both their first language and in English

   D. using a translator

58. **Identify the most appropriate test for the employment of a court translator. (Rigorous) (Skill 12.5)**

   A. An achievement test.

   B. A placement test.

   C. A proficiency test.

   D. A diagnostic test.

59. **Teachers with heavy class loads who wish to assess their ELLs writing abilities may decide to use which of the following testing formats because of practicality? (Average) (Skill 12.5)**

   A. Research papers.

   B. One-page essays.

   C. Journals.

   D. Quick writes.

60. **District benchmarks are valuable to teachers because _____ . (Easy) (Skill 12.6)**

   A. Schools can be compared to each other.

   B. Students can be compared with grade level standards.

   C. Low performing schools can be compared with high performing schools in the district.

   D. One ELL's performance can be compared with other ELLs.

61. **The following are all alternative assessments except ____. (Easy) (Skill 13.1)**

   A. portfolios

   B. teacher assessments

   C. interviews with students

   D. seeking parents' opinions

62. **An ELL's progress may be documented by all of the following except _____. (Average) (Skill 13.1)**

   A. achievement tests

   B. story or text retelling

   C. diagnostic tests

   D. language placement tests

63. **To be eligible for the GATE program, a student must _____. (Average) (Skill 13.1)**

   A. demonstrate English fluency

   B. score high on standardized tests

   C. be referred by his/her teacher

   D. have an IQ $\geq$ 132

64. **Which one of the follow is NOT a criterion for recommending students to Special Education? (Easy) (Skill 13.2)**

   A. have one of 13 recognized disabilities

   B. already have an IEP from another school

   C. have limitations related to language learning

   D. be at least 4 years old.

65. **Which one of the following is NOT a reason for reteaching a skill? (Rigorous) (Skill 13.3)**

   A. the material was too complex

   B. the skill will be recycled in later units

   C. background knowledge was lacking

   D. the student has failed several standards

66. **The Civil Rights Act of 1964 established that _____ could not discriminate against English Language Learners. (Easy) (Skill 14.1)**

   A. Any program receiving federal financial assistance.

   B. Any landlord or restaurant owner.

   C. Any public or private school.

   D. Any employer operating under government regulations.

67. **The May 25 Memorandum of 1970 established that school districts with English Language Learners who were excluded from effective participation must: (Average) (Skill 14.1)**

   A. Provide special education classes for those students.

   B. Provide curriculum in the primary language.

   C. Take affirmative steps to rectify the language deficiency.

   D. Provide teachers familiar with the primary language and culture.

68. A Language Assessment Committee and program criteria for ELL student assessment and monitoring became requirements for schools under:
(Rigorous) (Skill 14.1)

A. *Castaneda v. Pickard.*

B. *Lau v. Nichols.*

C. *Williams v. State of California.*

D. Proposition 227.

69. The Valenzuela Settlement requires that schools receiving funding for intensive instruction take what action to ensure that parents and guardians are aware of the procedure for alleging lack of opportunity if their student has not passed the high school exit exam by the end of 12th grade?
(Easy) (Skill 14.11)

A. Send a letter home.

B. Post a notice in the classroom.

C. Conduct administrative home visits.

D. Ensure personal contact by telephone.

70. Under the Williams verdict, low performing schools must provide students with what three things?
(Rigorous) (Skill 14.11)

A. Textbooks in the primary language, trained teachers, and after-school tutoring.

B. Trained teachers, safe facilities, and adequate textbooks for home and school.

C. Bilingual aides, bilingual teachers, and textbooks in the primary languagA.

D. Safe facilities, bilingual teachers, and textbooks for home and school.

71. Under the Williams Act, a complaint from parents cannot be turned away if it is:
(Average) (Skill 14.11)

A. Legitimate.

B. Expressed in English.

C. Written.

D. Delivered to the school board.

72. **When must the CELDT test be administered to English Language Learners? (Average) (Skill 14.9)**

   A. At the conclusion of each school year.

   B. Within 30 days of enrollment and annually until redesignation.

   C. Within 90 days of enrollment.

   D. Immediately upon enrollment.

73. **State law mandates how many minutes of daily instruction in English for students who test below proficiency on CELDT? (Rigorous) (Skill 14.8)**

   A. 10-15.

   B. 20-30.

   C. 30-45.

   D. 45-60.

74. **Which has been the most common program option for English Learners in California public schools? (Average) (Skill 14.7)**

   A. Mainstream programs with additional support.

   B. Dual-language immersion programs.

   C. Structured English Immersion classes.

   D. Newcomer Centers.

75. **What is instrumental motivation for learning a second language? (Rigorous) (Skill 15.2)**

   A. A specific goal, such as a job.

   B. A wish to communicate within the culture.

   C. A permanent, culturally acquired motivation.

   D. A permanent motivation based on rewards and penalties.

76. **What defining instructional goal is shared by both ELD and SDAIE instruction? Rigorous) (Skill 14.10)**

   A. Achieving English mastery as rapidly as possible.

   B. Providing ESL instruction during the regular school day.

   C. Accurately assessing student proficiency levels.

   D. Providing access to the core curriculum for all students.

77. **How are students grouped in ELD classrooms?**
(Rigorous) (Skill 14.8)

   A. In heterogeneous groups to benefit less proficient students.

   B. In mixed groups of all CELDT levels.

   C. In groups separated into each CELDT level.

   D. In groups that span no more than two CELDT levels.

78. **Why was California's 2010 application for Race to the Top funding unsuccessful?**
(Rigorous) (Skill 14.7)

   A. The plan failed to establish a need for additional funding.

   B. The plan failed to show an adequate population of English Language Learners.

   C. The plan failed to show measures for individual achievement.

   D. The plan failed to show measures for assessing the training of teachers.

79. **What is SARC?**
(Easy) (Skill 14.1)

   A. School Acceleration Rate Credit.

   B. Standard Area Recognition Cooperative.

   C. School Accountability Report Card.

   D. Standards Accelerated Rate Credit.

80. **Under Proposition 227, parents may sign a waiver if they want their student to receive:**
(Rigorous) (Skill 14.2)

   A. Total Immersion Language Instruction

   B. Sheltered English Instruction

   C. Bilingual Education

   D. Special Education Designation

81. **According to CDOC figures, what is the likelihood of an EL student reclassifying to English proficient status after 10 years in California schools?**
(Average) (Skill 14.2)

   A. More than 90%.

   B. More than 50%.

   C. Less than 70%.

   D. Less than 40%.

82. **What challenge is common to a two-way immersion school? (Average) (Skill 14.3)**

    A. Cultural and economic differences among the students.

    B. Differences in ability levels among the students.

    C. Differences in motivation among the students.

    D. Differences in skill levels among the teachers.

83. **Why are there no centralized government records for heritage language schools? (Rigorous) (Skill 14.3)**

    A. They are private schools, and not required to keep government records.

    B. They are after-school programs, and not required to keep government records.

    C. Their records are in other languages.

    D. They have been discouraged by the Department of Education.

84. **What did the 5-year CDOE study of California schools show about the effectiveness of various instructional methods for ELL students? (Rigorous) (Skill 14.5)**

    A. Students in Newcomer Centers for a year do significantly better over time.

    B. Students in pull-out programs do significantly better over time.

    C. Students in SDAIE classrooms do significantly better over time.

    D. No method was shown to be better than the others.

85. **What three elements make a teacher "highly qualified?" (Average) (Skill 14.5)**

    A. B.A. degree, state credential, demonstrated subject matter mastery.

    B. M.A. degree, state credential, demonstrated subject matter mastery.

    C. State credential or waiver, B.A. degree, completion of student teaching.

    D. 160 completed credits, state credential or waiver, completion of student teaching.

86. What is the result of legislative language such as "overwhelmingly in English" and "appropriate additional support?"
(Rigorous) (Skill 14.6)

   A. Districts have wide latitude in interpretation.

   B. Best practices are difficult to identify and disseminate.

   C. There is a wide variance in the quality of services statewide.

   D. All of the above.

87. If a student is bilingual and biliterate by third grade, he is likely to be attending:
(Average) (Skill 14.7)

   A. A heritage language school.

   B. A dual language school.

   C. A Structured English Immersion school.

   D. A newcomer center.

88. If the teacher is speaking only English, but uses pantomime, cartooning, and acting to make his meaning comprehensible, the classroom is probably:
(Average) (Skill 14.8)

   A. An ELD class.

   B. A SDAIE class.

   C. A dual-immersion class.

   D. A heritage language class.

89. A Prereading Plan is one method to:
(Rigorous) (Skill 15.3)

   A. Separate the students into skill levels.

   B. Focus attention on a topic.

   C. Activate a student's prior knowledge.

   D. Record student progress.

90. Posters, exhibits, and organized lists are examples of what kind of literacy activities?
(Average)(Skill 15.3)

   A. Prereading.

   B. Extended.

   C. Scaffolded.

   D. Enriched.

91. **A pull-out program that teaches English learners about the language is:**
(Easy) (Skill 19.1)

A. Grammar-based.

B. Communication-based.

C. Content-based.

D. Needs-based.

92. **Mock telephone conversations, student surveys, and student-developed dialogs are examples of:**
(Average) (Skill 19.2)

A. Structured English immersion.

B. Content-based ESL.

C. Communicative language activities.

D. Grammar-based language instruction.

93. **Imperfect language structures that are occasional results of carelessness or memory laps and should not be corrected by the instructor are:**
(Easy) (Skill 19.3)

A. Mistakes.

B. Errors.

C. Developmental.

D. Implicit.

94. **Key words and phrases such as "In the first place," "Until," or "Therefore," that help students make sense of text are called:**
(Average) (Skill 20.2)

A. Idioms.

B. Verbal responses.

C. Details.

D. Discourse markers.

95. **The main purpose of brainstorming is to:**
(Easy) (Skill 20.3)

A. Assess students' prior knowledge.

B. Activate students' prior knowledge.

C. Increase students' prior knowledge.

D. Compare students' prior knowledge.

96. **The main purpose of role plays and creative drama activities are to:**
(Easy) (Skill 20.3)

   A. Facilitate receptive language skills.

   B. Facilitate productive language skills.

   C. Facilitate both productive and receptive language skills.

   D. Facilitate neither productive nor receptive language skills.

97. **ELD language standards are designed to:**
(Rigorous) (Skill 21.1)

   A. Take the place of ELA standards for ELL students.

   B. Bring ELA standards into line with ELL students' language abilities.

   C. Provide more realistic standards for ELL students.

   D. Provide a scaffolding for ELL students to achieve ELA standards.

98. **Duet reading and choral reading are methods for improving:**
(Average) (Skill 21.2)

   A. Confidence.

   B. Comprehension.

   C. Fluency.

   D. Word recognition.

99. **Multicultural texts are most helpful if they:**
(Rigorous) (Skill 21.4)

   A. Present a positive picture of a minority culture.

   B. Present a realistic picture of a minority culture.

   C. Present an idealistic picture of a minority culture.

   D. Present a negative picture of a minority culture.

100. **ELL students' written language will typically lag behind their oral language by:**
(Rigorous) (Skill 21.5)

   A. A full year.

   B. One-two years.

   C. Five years.

   D. More than five years.

101. The most successful teaching of language conventions such as spelling, grammar, and punctuation is done by:
(Rigorous) (Skill 21.5)

   A. Direct instruction.

   B. Practice drills.

   C. The presentation of well-written materials.

   D. The presentation of poorly written materials.

102. Front-loading vocabulary by creating a word bank before confronting a text is one way to:
(Easy) (Skill 22.1)

   A. Create background knowledge.

   B. Provide cognitively engaging input.

   C. Assess students' prior knowledge.

   D. Clarify objectives.

103. Scaffolded interactions typically follow which pattern of progression?
(Rigorous) (Skill 22.1)

   A. Student-text, student-student, student-teacher.

   B. Student-teacher, student-text, student-student.

   C. Student-student, student-teacher, student-text.

   D. Student-teacher, student-student, student-text.

104. Resources such as realia, posters, films, and primary-source guests can all be used to:
(Rigorous) (Skill 22.2)

   A. Analyze a text.

   B. Extend a text.

   C. Contextualize a text.

   D. Take the place of a text.

105. Understanding one's own learning patterns is part of:
(Easy) (Skill 22.2)

   A. Cognition.

   B. Metacognition.

   C. Recognition.

   D. Ignition.

106. **In building vocabulary, visuals, manipulatives, and realia are examples of: (Average) (Skill 22.1)**

    A. Contextual support.

    B. Metacognitive support.

    C. The affective filter.

    D. Distractions.

107. **What activity is rated by many teachers as the single easiest way to learn new vocabulary? (Average) (Skill 22.1)**

    A. Learned dialogs.

    B. Invented role plays.

    C. Singing.

    D. Playing games.

108. **Asking students to demonstrate mastery of language objectives by writing a single sentence on an index card as they leave class is an example of: (Rigorous) (Skill 22.1)**

    A. Informal assessment.

    B. Standardized assessment.

    C. Formative assessment.

    D. Formal assessment.

109. **English Language Learners are more likely to readily accept new information if it does not conflict with their: (Rigorous) (Skill 22.2)**

    A. Politics.

    B. Religion.

    C. Prior knowledge.

    D. Plans.

110. **Teacher feedback is valuable only if: (Average) (Skill 22.2)**

    A. It doesn't cause embarrassment.

    B. It is understood.

    C. It is timely.

    D. All of the above.

111. **The study of the cultural differences between the southwestern culture and the southern culture in the United States is called _____. (Easy) (Skill 23.1)**

    A. cultural relativism

    B. cultural pluralism

    C. ethnocentrism

    D. cross-cultural studies

112. **Which of the following is NOT an element of external culture?**
(Easy) (Skill 23.2)

A. Shelter

B. Literature

C. Clothing

D. Rites and rituals

113. **All of the following are ways a teacher can observe culture in the classroom and overcome the difficulties associated with cultural nuances except:**
(Average) (Skill 23.3)

A. maintaining a journal of classroom interactions.

B. using a journal to note which activities seem to have the most positive effect on the class.

C. use only U. S. cultural mores in the classroom.

D. inviting parents to visit the classroom and talk about their culture.

114. **Why has culture become such an important issue in the classroom?**
(Average) (Skill 23.4)

A. people moving to urban areas

B. more and more immigrants from Asia, Latin America, and the Caribbean

C. an aging population

D. All of the above.

115. **Which one of the following is NOT an example of discrimination?**
(Average) (Skill 23.4)

A. Attacking a woman because she is wearing a burka.

B. Stating that the custom of not looking someone in the eye is devious.

C. Native born immigrant children feeling superior to non-native born immigrants.

D. Minority teachers who are not well trained teaching in remote regions.

116. **Which of the following illustrates the hardships of immigrants? (Average) (Skill 23.5)**

    A. long waiting periods to receive basic medical services.

    B. difficulty adjusting to climate changes

    C. retraining to secure professional status

    D. All of the above.

117. **When Ms. Jones notices that Yuki is NOT participating in group discussions, she believes that Yuki sees her as _____. (Average) (Skill 23.6)**

    A. an enemy.

    B. someone not giving her sufficient time to answer.

    C. silly, for asking stupid questions.

    D. an authority figure who has not asked her a question.

118. **Which of the following terms is the correct one for the situation below? (Rigorous) (Skill 24.1)**

> Ursula has lived in the U.S. for nearly five years. She rarely talks about her homeland and tries to imitate her classmates' speech and behavior. She is striving to be accepted by the culture surrounding her.

    A. Acculturation.

    B. Assimilation.

    C. Accommodation.

    D. Transculturation.

119. **Which of the following items would cause culture shock to newly arrived immigrants? (Rigorous) (Skill 24.2)**

    A. kissing in public.

    B. using a drive-in bank teller

    C. bathing daily with hot, running water

    D. All of the above.

120. Based on the example below, in which stage of assimilation is Pierre?
(Average) (Skill 24.3)

Pierre arrived in the U. S. in 2003 at the age of 12. He has been living with his uncle and aunt, who are well assimilated into the U.S. culture. Pierre misses his parents and brothers. He finds his high school studies fairly easy and his classmates lazy. He is worried about his goal of becoming a professional soccer player and doesn't understand why he can't have wine with his meals when he eats out with his aunt and uncle.

A. Honeymoon stage.

B. Hostility stage.

C. Humor stage.

D. Home stage.

121. When faced with cultural habits or beliefs that are completely different from the teacher's beliefs, what is the best way for the teacher to address this issue in the classroom?
(Rigorous) (Skill 24.4)

A. Politely correct the ELL in private.

B. Address the issue with the ELL's parents.

C. Ask for administrative assistance in resolving the issue.

D. Agree to disagree.

122. How can teachers resolve the issue of students who see her as an authority figure and disdain group work?
(Rigorous) (Skill 24.5)

A. Accept their feelings and permit them to work alone.

B. Give lectures on the content and assign individual work.

C. Balance group work with individual work.

D. Assign group work and use teacher-directed instruction when necessary

123. Which of the following types of reading materials should be avoided?
(Average) (Skill 24.6)

A. Culturally inclusive.

B. Culturally sensitive.

C. Inaccurate gender roles.

D. Distinct genres.

124. The second most spoken language in California is:
(Easy) (Skill 25.1)

A. Chinese

B. Japanese

C. Spanish

D. Vietnamese

125. Which event led to the Freedom Flights from Cuba?
(Rigorous) (Skill 25.2)

    A. the Bay of Pigs invasion

    B. death of Che Guevara

    C. overthrow of Fulgencio Batista

    D. release of Guantanamo Bay detainees

126. _____ is the term used when a father leaves his native country, comes to the U.S., gets a job, and sends for his wife.
(Easy) (Skill 25.2)

    A. Assimilation

    B. Socioeconomic improvement

    C. Secondary migration

    D. Accommodation

127. When children arriving in the U.S. begin using English in a natural way, what cultural phenomenon occurs?
(Rigorous) (Skill 25.3)

    A. additive bilingualism

    B. subtractive bilingualism

    C. cultural loss

    D. Transculturation

128. When newcomers and U. S. born members from the same culture group become opposed, this is referred to as _____.
(Easy) (Skill 25.3)

    A. polarization

    B. discrimination

    C. intra-cultural division

    D. acculturation

129. Identify the way in which oral cultures differ from the U. S. culture.
(Rigorous) (Skill 26.2)

    A. Use of linear, single topic stories when narrating

    B. Assume shared knowledge of their audience.

    C. Interrupt and challenge teacher's authority.

    D. Use silence as a power tool.

130. To teach non-native speakers of English, the cultural differences in communication styles, _____ is appropriate.
(Rigorous) (Skill 26.3)

    A. the use of role-plays

    B. debating

    C. holding classroom discussions

    D. extra wait time

131. An open dialogue with parents helps teachers to:
(Average) (Skill 27.1)

A. Explain their standards.

B. Discipline their students.

C. Understand cultural differences.

D. Teach parents as well as students.

132. A student who assists others, is sensitive to others' feelings, and seeks guidance is:
(Rigorous) (Skill 27.2)

A. Field independent.

B. Field sensitive.

C. Field dependent.

D. Field insensitive.

133. Teachers reared in North America are typically:
(Rigorous) (Skill 27.2)

A. Field independent.

B. Field sensitive.

C. Field dependent.

D. Field insensitive.

134. Home visits, interviews, and oral histories are ways for a teacher to:
(Easy) (Skill 27.3)

A. Learn about students' home cultures.

B. Teach about the students' new culture.

C. Learn about debilitating or abusive conditions.

D. Change the way students think.

135. A student who believes the teacher is shirking his duty by assigning group work instead of lecturing is probably:
(Average) (Skill 28.1)

A. Uneducated.

B. Rude.

C. Lazy.

D. From a different cultural background.

136. **No Child Left Behind encourages schools to raise expectations for all students by:**
(Rigorous) (Skill 28.2)

A. Penalizing low scores.

B. Rewarding high scores.

C. Disaggregating data.

D. Allocating funds based on improvement.

137. **Open discussion of sensitive topics such as racism and discrimination is part of:**
(Average) (Skill 28.2)

A. A reactive approach.

B. An inactive approach.

C. An active approach.

D. A proactive approach.

138. **Zero tolerance for culturally insensitive behavior requires:**
(Average) (Skill 28.2)

A. Keen awareness of potential conflicts.

B. In-depth study of world history.

C. Constant questioning of students.

D. Strict control of conversations.

139. **An advantage of strong community involvement in school activities is:**
(Easy) (Skill 28.2)

A. Parents learn along with their students.

B. Teachers can share the work load.

C. The community becomes a resource if problems occur.

D. Classroom utility is maximized.

140. **Encouraging parents to continue speaking the first language at home is:**
(Rigorous) (Skill 28.3)

A. Counterproductive.

B. Harmful.

C. Useless.

D. Advantageous.

141. **The most frequent statement of concern made by adults about their children's schooling is:**
(Average) (Skill 29.1)

A. I wish I had had these opportunities.

B. They don't do things the way they used to.

C. Kids today have it too easy.

D. Kids today have it too hard.

142. **Open communication with parents can help teachers understand:**
(Rigorous) (Skill 29.1)

    A. Why students perform poorly.

    B. Why students perform well.

    C. Elements of native culture parents want to preserve.

    D. Elements of native culture parents want to eliminate.

143. **Mentoring and tutoring are ways to get involved for:**
(Easy) (Skill 29.2)

    A. Teachers.

    B. Peers.

    C. Parents and grandparents.

    D. Administrators.

144. **Teachers have a legal obligation to inform parents about their opportunity to participate in:**
(Average) (Skill 29.4)

    A. Classroom visits.

    B. Tutoring.

    C. After-school activities.

    D. Policy-making committees.

145. **Bias-motivated injustice and violence can be reduced by:**
(Average) (Skill 29.5)

    A. School security guards.

    B. Police visits.

    C. Anti-racist education.

    D. Stronger punishments.

146. **Adding ethnic content to the curriculum without restructuring is:**
(Rigorous) (Skill 30.1)

    A. The transformative approach.

    B. The additive approach.

    C. The reductive approach.

    D. The simplest approach.

147. **Extending student understanding of the complexity of U.S. society is a goal of:**
(Easy) (Skill 30.1)

    A. The transformative approach.

    B. The additive approach.

    C. The reductive approach.

    D. The simplest approach.

148. Service learning projects and personal reflection are part of:
(Average) (Skill 30.2)

A. Additive curriculum.

B. Transformative curriculum.

C. Bilingual curriculum.

D. Cross-cultural curriculum.

149. The learning style of Hispanic students is more likely to be:
(Rigorous) (Skill 30.4)

A. Auditory.

B. Visual.

C. Kinesthetic.

D. Any of these.

150. American Indians and Asians are more likely to succeed in an environment that is:
(Rigorous) (Skill 30.4)

A. Cooperative.

B. Competitive.

C. Individualized.

D. Rigidly structured

ANSWER KEY

1. B	39. D	82. A	125. C
2. A	40. A	83. A	126. C
3. C	41. D	84. D	127. C
4. B	42. B	85. A	128. A
5. C	43. D	86. D	129. B
6. D	44. C	87. B	130. A
7. C	45. B	88. B	131. C
8. A	46. B	89. C	132. B
9. B	47. B	90. C	133. A
10. D	48. C	91. A	134. A
11. B	49. C	92. C	135. D
12. C	50. C	93. A	136. C
13. D	51. B	94. D	137. D
14. A	52. A	95. B	138. A
15. B	53. C	96. C	139. C
16. D	54. D	97. D	140. D
17. A	55. C	98. C	141. B
18. A	56. A	99. B	142. C
19. B	57. C	100. B	143. C
20. C	58. C	101. C	144. D
21. C	59. B	102. A	145. C
22. B	60. B	103. D	146. B
23. A	61. D	104. C	147. A
24. A	62. C	105. B	148. B
25. C	63. A	106. A	149. A
26. D	64. C	107. C	150. A
27. A-3, B-4, C-2, D-1	65. D	108. A	
	66. A	109. C	
	67. C	110. D	
28. A	68. B	111. D	
29. B	69. B	112. D	
30. A-5, B-3, C-2, D-4, E-1	70. B	113. C	
	71. C	114. D	
	72. B	115. B	
	73. C	116. D	
31. B	74. A	117. D	
32. C	75. A	118. B.	
33. B	76. D	119. D	
34. D	77. D	120. B	
35. B	78. C	121. D	
36. D	79. C	122. D	
37. D	80. C	123. C	
38. B	81. D	124. C	

Rigor Table

Easy	Average	Rigorous
1, 2, 4, 6, 11, 20, 21, 44, 49, 50, 60, 61, 64, 66, 72, 79, 91, 93, 95, 96, 102, 105, 111, 112, 124, 126, 134, 139, 143, 147	3, 5, 7, 8, 10, 12, 13, 14, 15, 16, 17, 18, 22, 26, 28, 34, 37, 38, 42, 43, 48, 51, 54, 55, 62, 63, 67, 69, 70, 71, 74, 82, 83, 84, 85, 87, 88, 90, 92, 94, 98, 106, 107, 110, 113, 114, 115, 116, 117, 120, 123, 128, 129, 131, 135, 137, 138, 141, 144, 145, 148	9, 19, 23, 24, 25, 27, 29, 30, 31, 32, 33, 35, 36, 39, 40, 41, 45, 46, 47, 52, 53, 56, 57, 58, 59, 65, 68, 73, 75, 76, 77, 78, 80, 81, 86, 89, 97, 99, 100, 101, 103, 104, 108, 109, 118, 119, 121, 122, 125, 127, 130, 132, 133, 136, 140, 142, 146, 149, 150

RATIONALES

1. **If you are studying phonology, then you are studying:**
(Easy) (Skill 1.1)

  A. The smallest unit within a language system to which meaning is attached.
  B. The way in which speech sounds form patterns.
  C. Individual letters and letter combinations.
  D. The definition of individual words.

Answer: B. The way in which speech sounds form patterns.
The smallest unit within a language system to which meaning is attached is a morpheme. The term phonographemic refers to the study of individual letters and letter combinations. The definition of individual words is known as making the meaning of a word explicit. The way in which speech sounds form patterns is phonology, so option B the best answer.

2. **Speakers can change sentences to questions by changing the:**
(Easy) (Skill 1.1)

  A. Pitch
  B. Morphemes
  C. Root words
  D. Stress

Answer: A. Pitch.
The smallest unit within a language system to which meaning is attached is a morpheme. Root words are one type of morphemes and the key to understanding a word because this is where the actual meaning is determined. Stress occurs at the sentence or word level and can modify meaning. Pitch determines the context or meaning of words in communication and is therefore, the correct answer.

3. **"Bite" and "byte' are examples of which phonographemic differences? (Average) (Skill 1.2)**

   A. Homonyms
   B. Homographs
   C. Homophones
   D. Heteronyms

Answer: C. Homophones.
'Homonyms' is a general term for words with two or more meanings. Homographs are two or more words with the same spelling or pronunciation, but have different meanings. Heteronyms are two or more words that have the same spelling but different meanings and spellings. Homophones are words that have the same pronunciation, but different meanings and spellings and the correct response.

4. **Words which have the same spelling or pronunciation, but different meanings are: (Easy) (Skill 1.2)**

   A. Homonyms
   B. Homographs
   C. Homophones
   D. Heteronyms

Answer: B. Homographs.
See explanation given after question 3.

5. **Which word in the following contains the schwa sound? (Average) (Skill 1.2)**

   A. Few
   B. Legmen
   C. Sanity
   D. Berry

Answer: C. Sanity.
All of the words contain the letter /e/ with its various forms of pronunciation. Only the /i/ in C. sanity is pronounced as a schwa.

6. If you are studying "morphemic analysis", then you are studying:
(Easy) (Skill 1.3)

A. The smallest unit within a language system to which meaning is attached.
B. The root word and the suffix and/or prefix.
C. The way in which speech sounds form patterns.
D. Answers A and B only.

Answer: D. Answers A and B only.
The study of the way in which speech sounds form patters is called phonology. The smallest unit within a language system to which meaning is attached is a morpheme. The root word and the suffix and/or prefix are components of morphemes and basic to the analysis of a word. Therefore, both A and B are necessary for the study of morphemic analysis so the correct answer is D.

7. The study of morphemes may provide the student with:
(Average) (Skill 1.3)

A. The meaning of the root word.
B. The meaning of the phonemes.
C. Grammatical information.
D. All of the above.

Answer: C. Grammatical information.
The meaning of the root word comes from its source or origin, and the meaning of phonemes relates to its sound. The correct answer is C which gives grammatical information to the student rather than (e.g. prepositions or articles)

8. Which of the following items is NOT a morpheme?
(Average) (Skill 1.3)

A. fatal
B. –s
C. too
D. mist

Answer: A. fatal
B, C, and D contain one morpheme. Morphemes are the smallest unit of language to which meaning is attached. Generally, they are the root word, a prefix and a suffix. Answer A consists of two morphemes combined to make a word: the root word fate and the suffix /al/.

9. **Which of the following phonological pre-reading skills promotes fluent reading and writing?**
   (Rigorous) (Skill 1.5)

   A. Instruction in the Roman alphabet
   B. Recognizing and creating rhymes
   C. Syntax instruction
   D. Study of cognates

Answer: B. Recognizing and creating rhymes.
Instruction in the Roman alphabet is necessary only for those students who come from countries (such as China or Saudi Arabia) or a Jewish culture (which uses Hebrew) and use different alphabets for reading and writing. Syntactic instruction and the study of cognates are on-going language skills studied well into high school (even college) and would not be phonological skills or pre-reading skills. Therefore, answer B Recognizing and creating rhymes is the most appropriate answer for a pre-reading and writing skill.

10. **Which of the following is an example of eliciting prior knowledge from a student's first language?**
    (Average) (Skill 1.6)

    A. Point to the ball.
    B. Raise your hand if you see something red in the picture.
    C. Is Mr. Brown riding a bicycle or riding a car?
    D. How do you say "mother" in French? In Vietnamese?

Answer: D. How do you say "mother" in French? In Vietnamese?
Answers A, B, and C require the student to use knowledge of the target language vocabulary. Only D is requesting vocabulary information from the primary language.

11. If you are studying "syntax", then you are studying:
   (Easy) (Skill 2.1)

   A. Intonation and accent when conveying a message
   B. The rules for correct sentence structure.
   C. The definition of individual words and meanings.
   D. The subject-verb-object order of the English sentence.

Answer: B. The rules for correct sentence structure.
The intonation and accent used when conveying a message refer to pitch and stress. The definition of individual words and meanings is semantics. The subject-verb-object order of the English sentence refers to is the correct order for most English sentences, but the rules for correct sentence structure refers to syntax, so B is the best option.

12. Language learners seem to acquire syntax:
   (Average) (Skill 2.1)

   A. At the same rate in L1 and L2.
   B. Faster in L2 than L1.
   C. In the same order regardless of whether it is in L1 or L2
   D. In different order for L1

Answer: C. In the same order regardless of whether it is in L1 or L2.
All language learners must progress through the same hierarchical steps in their language learning process. They go from the least to the most complicated stages regardless of whether it is in the L1 or L2.

13. Arrange the following sentences, written by ELLs, to show the order of acquisition of negation, ranging from least to most.

   Sentence 1: Kim didn't went to school.
   Sentence 2: No school. No like.
   Sentence 3: Kim doesn't like to go to school.

(Average) (Skill 2.1)

   A. Sentence 1, Sentence 2, Sentence 3.
   B. Sentence 3, Sentence 2, Sentence 1.
   C. Sentence 1, Sentence 3, Sentence 2.
   D. Sentence 2, Sentence 1, Sentence 3.

Answer: D. Sentence 2, Sentence 1, Sentence 3.
The correct order is D.

14. How can teachers provide accurate examples of syntax to their students? (Average) (Skill 2.2)

    A. Modeling

    B. Using guests from other countries.

    C. Show and Tell by ELL's parents.

    D. Using CDs and videos from England and other nations of the United Kingdom.

Answer: A. Modeling.
Answers B, C, and D may provide accurate syntax to the students and it may not. Many of these sources may have good language skills, but the accents will probably be very different from the classroom teacher's. Therefore, assuming the teacher has good language skills, she is the best source of syntax for her students. As students develop their language skills, they should be exposed to English from non-native speakers and from other English speaking countries.

15. Which of the following is one reason why non-native speakers do less and less well as they move through the U.S. education system? (Rigorous) (Skill 2.3)

    A. Undeveloped language skills in L2.

    B. Less cognitive maturity in L1.

    C. High level of literacy in L1.

    D. Use of L2 in the home.

Answer: B. Less cognitive maturity in L1.
As ELLs move through the U.S. educational system, they continue to develop their L2. Thus, this is not a factor in their limited development in education. A high level of literacy in L1 has a positive effect on language learning and education. Many skills learned in L1 can be transferred to L2, so students continue to learn and should do well in school. Parents who use L2 in the home with their children may be doing them a disservice as both the parents and children are working below their actual cognitive level. The correct answer is B. Children who have less cognitive maturity in L1are always playing catch-up with others of their same age because they have not fully developed their cognitive skills. Development of these skills has been interrupted.

16. Which one of the following is NOT included in the study of semantics? (Average) (Skill 2.4)

A. Grasping the meaning of words from the context
B. Studying the same word in a variety of contexts.
C. Translating difficult terms.
D. Register.

Answer: D. Register.
The only skill not studied in semantics is D. Register. Register is studied in sociolinguistics and is the variety of language used in a specific social context.

17. Idioms are particularly difficult for ELLs because: (Average) (Skill 1.5)

A. Idioms frequently rely on hyperbole or metaphors.
B. They can't be translated.
C. They are in context.
D. The language is old fashioned.

Answer: A. Idioms frequently rely on hyperbole or metaphors.
Idioms are translated, and usually literally which prevents the ELL from understanding what is being implied. Idioms may not be in context which makes them more difficult to be understood. The language may be old fashioned, but others are part of today's pop culture and are difficult for many adults to understand. The correct option is A because idioms frequently rely on hyperbole or metaphors.

18. Which one of the following items is an informative function of language? (Average) (Skill 3.1)

A. Describing the concept behind a science project.
B. Creating a poem.
C. Explaining a personal experience.
D. Asking how something works.

Answer: A. Describing the concept behind a science project.
According to Halliday (1985) language can be classified according to its function. Creating a poem is an imaginative function, explaining a personal experience is a personal function, asking how something works is a heuristic function, and describing a concept is an informative function.

19. The vocabulary word "ain't" has been used for hundreds of years instead of /am not/, /is not/, and /has not/. It is an example of _____. (Rigorous) (Skill 3.3)

    A. A dialect.
    B. How language evolves.
    C. Socio-economic effects on language.
    D. A southern drawl.

Answer: B. How language evolves.
The word "ain't" first came into usage in the 17th century when many different contracted forms of speech began to appear. For reasons unknown, in the U.S. it became unacceptable (as did many other contracted forms) but remains in regular usage in rural, working class, and inner city people's speech. In the 17th century it was used instead of has not/have not (*an't/ain't*), in the 18th century */an't/* was used for *am not, are not,* and *is not*. It is an excellent example of B--how language evolves.

20. English has grown as a language primarily because of: (Easy) (Skill 3.3)

    A. Wars/technology and science
    B. Text messaging/immigrants
    C. Immigrants/technology and science
    D. Contemporary culture/wars

Answer: C. Immigration/technology and science.
While all of the options have influenced the growth of English, new immigrants continually adding new words to the language is the most influential factor. The second largest body of new words comes from technology and science making Option C the best option.

21. Identify the major factor in the spread of English.
(Easy) (Skill 3.3)

    A. The invasion of the Germanic tribes in England.
    B. The pronunciation changes in Middle English.
    C. The extension of the British Empire.
    D. The introduction of new words from different cultures.

Answer: C. The extension of the British Empire.
The sun never set on the British Empire during the 19th century causing English to spread all over the world. (The predominance of English in data banks—an estimated 80-90 percent of the world's data banks are in English—helps keep English as the foremost language in the world today.) Thus, Option C is the correct one.

22. Which of the following registers reflects the "manner of discourse" between an employer and a high school student employee at a fast food restaurant?
(Average) (Skill 3.4)

    A. Bro, I need a burger, fries, and a Coke?
    B. I need a burger without onions.
    C. Hey, man. Let me get that for you.
    D. Let me take that order to your table, sir.

Answer: B. I need a burger without onions.
Answer A sounds like two equals speaking. Answer C is probably someone trying to be of service to an equal. Answer D is a restaurant employee trying to help a customer. It could be the manager or the waiter. Only in Option B is the register that of an employer speaking to an employee—formal, but not excessively so.

23. Which one of the following items is a CALP?
(Rigorous) (Skill 4.3)

A. Where is the passage that supports your argument?
B. Raise your hand if you know the answer.
C. Let's get some pizzas and cokes for after the game.
D. Can you give me five ones and a five, please?

Answer: A. Where is the passage that supports your argument?
BICS are basic interpersonal conversational skills such as normal classroom language (e.g. Answer B), speaking on the phone, language for interacting with peers (e.g. Answer C), and arriving at meaning with adults (e.g. Answer D). CALPS are cognitive academic language proficiency. These are defined as the formal language needed to succeed in the academic world. Answer A is the best option since the teacher is asking for proof of an academic position.

24. Which one of the following would promote an ELL's ability to develop discourse competence?
(Rigorous) (Skill 4.5)

A. Show and Tell.
B. Reading a text, and answering questions.
C. Playing Bingo.
D. Listing to a radio program.

Answer: A. Show and Tell.
Discourse come from the French and is used in linguistics as a term for a unit or piece of connected speech or writing that is longer than a conventional sentence. The only answer which complies with the linguistic definition is A. Show and Tell where the student must present an object or event in a short speech or talk.

25. Which of the following items illustrates pragmatics in different cultures?
(Rigorous) (Skill 5.2)

A. Eyes closed, sleeping on a plane.
B. Children jumping rope or playing hopscotch.
C. Indicating the height of a friend by holding the hand vertical to the floor.
D. Soccer players greeting each other in the dressing room.

Answer: C. Indicating the height of a friend by holding the hand vertical to the floor.
Answers A, B, and D are fairly universal examples of appropriate behaviors in cultures over the world. However, Answer C illustrates the method of demonstrating height in some Latin American cultures. In the U.S., height is indicated by holding the hand palm down.

26. The researcher most identified with the impact of social influences on language learning is _____.
(Average) (Skill 6.1)

A. Chomsky.
B. Krashen.
C. Piaget.
D. Vygotsky.

Answer: D. Vygotsky.

27. Match the theorists with the elements of their explanations. (Place the number after the letter.)
(Rigorous) (Skill 6.1)

A. _____ Chomsky
B. _____ Piaget
C. _____ Vygotsky
D. _____ Collier

1. Children are active learners who construct their worlds.
2. Social communication which promotes language and cognition.
3. Nature is more important than nurture.
4. Language is a reflection of thought.

Answers: A-3, B-4, C-2, D-1.

28. Brain research has affirmed the importance of _____ in language learning.
(Average) (Skill 6.1)

A. puberty
B. maturity
C. aphasia
D. the brain's size

Answer: A. puberty
Answer C aphasia can be discarded as it refers to brain-damage. Neither answer B maturity nor Answer D the size of the brain are defining factors in the study of languages. Very young children to older adults often study languages with varying degrees of success. Many studies argue that brain's size has relatively little impact on intelligence or language capabilities. However, puberty does affect language study. Different theories have been used to explain the effect of puberty on language learning. One theory suggests that at puberty, the brain changes areas of the brain for processing language. Another theory is the critical-age hypothesis which suggests that the ability to learn the native language develops from birth to puberty. This is a fixed period after which children cannot acquire more syntax (arrangement of the words) or morphology (construction of the word). Thus, the brain is accepting a second language on the same terms as a first language and accent is not affected in young children, but not after puberty.

29. Which of the following is a metacognitive strategy?
(Rigorous) (Skill 6.2)

A. Encouraging yourself.
B. Evaluating your learning.
C. Asking questions.
D. Analyzing and reasoning.

Answer: B. Evaluating your learning.
Answer A encouraging yourself is an affective strategy. Answer C asking questions is a social strategy. Answer D analyzing and reasoning is a cognitive strategy. Only Answer B is a metacognitive strategy—becoming aware of an individual's learning strategies.

30. **Place the number in front of the phrase to order the stages in the language acquisition process, from Beginning (1) to Proficiency (5).**
(Rigorous) (Skill 6.3)

   A. _____ Experimental or simplified speech
   B. _____ Lexical chunks
   C. _____ Private speech
   D. _____ Formulaic speech
   E. _____ Silent period

Answers: A-5, B-3, C-2, D-4, E-1.

31. **According to its goal, Communication Based ESL emphasizes:**
(Rigorous) (Skill 7.1)

   A. language rules
   B. comprehensible language
   C. language with emphasis on content, vocabulary, and basic concepts
   D. immersion

Answer: B. comprehensible language.
A, language rules, are associated with a grammar-based ESL language model. C, is associated with Content-based ESL. D, immersion, is a form of bilingualism whether it be indigenous language immersion or the Canadian French immersion model. The goal of communication based ESL is comprehensible or understandable language and little care is given to errors or mistakes. Thus, choice B is correct.

32. **Which of the following cognitive strategies is helpful to ELLs learning the language?**
(Rigorous) (Skill 7.2)

   A. taking risks
   B. mumbling
   C. using formulaic expressions
   D. requesting retesting when the ELL feels ready to move on

Answer: C. using formulaic expressions
Answer A is an affective strategy used when encouraging oneself. Answer B is an avoidance strategy—maybe the teacher won't call on me if I don't answer. D is a way for the ELL to take charge of their learning and is a metacognitive strategy. C, using formulaic expressions, is the correct response. It is a cognitive strategy that permits the LL to establish social discourse without really requesting or giving out information.

33. Which of the following reasons supports the idea of language being an interactive process?
(Rigorous) (Skill 7.3)

A. Reading in a language develops its oral skills.
B. Reading improves listening skills.
C. Reading is a pleasure of its own.
D. Reading different genres is unnecessary to improve language.

Answer: B. Reading improves listening skills.
Answer C is universally recognized truth but says nothing of the supposed negotiation between reader and author. Answer D is generally considered false as reading in different genres is necessary to develop academic language skills. It is questionable as to whether reading, Answer A, unless being done aloud, would improve listening skills. The correct Answer then is B since reading does improve other language skills, especially in the areas of syntax and semantics.

34. Carrell and Eisterhold used _____ to explain their theory of language learning.
(Average) (Skill 8.1)

A. left brain-right brain
B. LAD
C. age
D. schemata

Answer: D. schemata
Answer A refers to the left brain-right brain is an attempt to explain the lateralization of the brain. Language is one area where the clear delineations of language functions can be seen in each area of the brain. However, most functions of the brain are more bilateral. Answer B refers to Chomsky's theory of a language acquisition device (LAD). Answer C, age, is more closely associated with Ellis and his theory of route (order) of language acquisition. Thus, the correct answer is D.

35. Which one of the following is a learning style according to Willing (1988)? (Rigorous) (Skill 8.1)

    A. Kinesthetic
    B. Analytic
    C. Visual
    D. Auditory

Answer: B. Analytic
Reid (1987) identified four perceptual learning tendencies: visual, auditory, kinesthetic and tactile. Willing proposed four main learning styles: concrete, analytic, and communicative, and authority-oriented. Therefore, B is the correct answer.

36. According to Ellis (1985), _____ does not affect the _____ of Second Language Acquisition. (Rigorous) (Skill 8.1)

    A. sex/process
    B. youth/importance of comprehensible input
    C. social context/stages
    D. age/route

Answer: D. age/route
Ellis's theory concerns the age and route (order) of language learning. His research suggests that both native speakers and second language learners will go through the same stages when learning a language regardless of their age. D is the correct answer.

37. **To avoid "dumping" ELLs in special education classes, which of the following measures can be used to assure reliability in tests/testing? (Average) (Skill 8.1)**

    A. subjective tests
    B. home language survey
    C. timed tests
    D. multiple raters

Answer: D. multiple raters
The question references the types of tests and testing situations that should be used to assure ELLs of reliable and valid tests. Answer B home language survey offers insights into the family structure and life, but it does not give information on the academic ability of the ELL. Timed tests can skew the testing results as many ELLs are unfamiliar with this testing criterion. Subjective tests (A) are not appropriate, objective tests should be employed. The correct answer is D. By using multiple raters factors such as bias in tests can be avoided. Too, multiple raters see the ELLs from different perspectives, ensuring a more complete picture of the ELL's abilities.

38. **Which one of the following factors might cause an ELL from Argentina difficulties when faced with learning English? (Average) (Skill 8.1)**

    A. the writing system
    B. multiple vowel sounds
    C. rhetorical questions
    D. directionality in reading materials

Answer: B. multiple vowel sounds
The writing system used by Latin American's is the Roman alphabet, so this Answer A can be discarded. Rhetorical questions may annoy some students, but they should not cause great learning difficulties, so Answer C can be discarded. Reading materials in Latin America read from left to right, so Answer D can be discarded. Answer B, multiple vowel sounds, may cause difficulty for Spanish speakers because Spanish has a one-to-one correspondence with the vowel sound whereas English has over 26 and most do not directly correspond to the vowel.

39. **When an ESOL teacher is helping an ELL to understand material that is difficult for them, which of the following theorist's principals is the teacher implementing?**
(Rigorous) (Skill 8.2)

A. Cummins.
B. Vygotsky.
C. Tompkins.
D. Krashen.

Answer: D. Krashen
Cummins' work concerns the benefits of bilingualism and identity eradication. Vygotsky theorized about the importance social context in language learning. Tompkins identified five levels of scaffolding. Krashen believes that ELLs learn only when input is meaningful. Therefore, the correct answer is D Krashen.

40. **Which one of the following is the best way to provide constructive feedback?**
(Rigorous) (Skill 8.2)

A. Give specific information on what is wrong.
B. Give feedback on papers returned a week later.
C. Mark the errors without comments on a written paper.
D. Give feedback during an evaluation.

Answer: A. Give specific information on what is wrong.
Feedback should be separate from an evaluation, so Answer D is incorrect. Feedback should be immediate, so Answer B is incorrect also. Marking errors without information on what the ELL did wrong is of no value, so Answer C is incorrect. Answer A is correct because it states the teacher should give specific information on what was incorrect so that the ELL can notice the error and make an attempt to avoid it in the future.

41. Which one of the following is an example of "integrative motivation" in learning a new language?
(Rigorous) (Skill 9.1)

    A. A State Department officer who will travel to a foreign country.
    B. Foreign university students who plan to return to their country.
    C. Translators.
    D. Children who are new to a culture.

Answer: D. Children who are new to a culture.
Answers A, B, and C are all examples of instrumental motivation—acquiring language for a specific reason, frequently a job. Answer D is correct because it is an example of integrative motivation—the desire to communicate with those of a different culture.

42. The term "affective domain" includes all of the following except?
(Average) (Skill 9.1)

    A. Inhibition.
    B. Reflection.
    C. Teacher expectations.
    D. Classroom culture.

Answer: B. Reflection.
Answer B Reflection is a personality trait and a method of cementing what one has learned. It is not an element of the affective domain, but a learning strategy.

43. Which one of the following is NOT an acceptable way to give feedback in the language classroom?
(Average) (Skill 9.2)

    A. Saying, "I don't understand."
    B. Writing, "Explain this in more detail" on a paper.
    C. Writing, "Good job" on a paper.
    D. Saying, "What on earth were you thinking?"

Answer: D. Saying, "What on earth were you thinking?"
Answers A, B, and C are all acceptable ways of commenting on a student's performance whether written or oral. Answer D is not. It shows exasperation and a lack of professionalism.

44. Inter-language is best described as:
(Easy) (Skill 9.2)

   A. A language characterized by overgeneralization.
   B. Bilingualism.
   C. A language learning strategy.
   D. A strategy characterized by poor grammar.

Answer: C. A language learning strategy.
Inter-language occurs when the second language learner lacks proficiency in L2 and tries to compensate for his or her lack of fluency in the new language. Three components are overgeneralization, simplification, and L1 interference or language transfer. Answer A is only one component of inter-language, making option C the correct answer.

45. According to the acculturation theory, which event occurs with new immigrants arriving in the United States?
(Rigorous) (Skill 10.1)

   A. Two cultures collide; both are displaced
   B. The dominant culture replaces the weaker culture
   C. Biculturalism occurs.
   D. Transculturation occurs.

Answer: B. The dominant culture replaces the weaker culture
Answer A is incorrect because the U.S. culture remains in place. Answer C is incorrect because only in rare cases does biculturalism occur, the U.S. culture does not encourage biculturalism. Transculturation refers to an individual only and is incorrect. Answer B is the correct answer since the minority culture is replaced by the dominant U.S. culture.

46. Which of the following statements is NOT a tenet of Ong's (1982) theory of culture? Oral cultures were:
(Rigorous) (Skill 10.1)

   A. highly socialized.
   B. subordinate.
   C. closer to the real world.
   D. more situational.

Answer: B. subordinate
According to Ong, oral cultures were highly socialized (A), more situational (D), and closer to the real world (B). Answer B is the incorrect characteristic of oral societies.

47. Which of the following concepts by the ELL may reflect the negative feelings of the ELL's family and friends?
(Average) (Skill 10.1)

A. Ignoring time rules and constraints.
B. Acting out in class.
C. Shouting out answers.
D. Failing to sit quietly when requested to do desk work.

Answer: B. Acting out in class.
Answers A, C, and D are all characteristics of many school cultures and run contrary to U.S. classroom norms. Answer B, however, may reflect the stress an ELLs is experiencing when pressured by friends and family.

48. Which one of the following statements about culture and its manifestation is most likely to cause learning difficulties for the ELL?
(Average) (Skill 10.2)

A. Lengthening wait time.
B. ELLs may not understand the new culture and its differences.
C. Teachers may offend the ELLs when they are unaware of cultural differences.
D. Involving parents and guardians in the educational process.

Answer: C. Teachers may offend the ELLs when they are unaware of cultural differences.
Answer A is incorrect because lengthening the time a teacher waits for a response usually gives the ELL needed time to assemble his/her thoughts and respond adequately to a question. Answer B is incorrect because ELLs may not understand the culture and its differences (see Question 47 on classroom norms), but these are not learning problems. Answer D is incorrect because involving parents and guardians in the educational process is a positive action in most cases. However, when teachers offend ELLs, even unwittingly, it takes longer for the ELLs to overcome their aversion to the new society and its culture (if this is the case) or to overcome their resentment of a teacher who has transgressed in the ELL's culture. These feelings may cause temporary or even long term learning problems in a new culture. Answer C is the correct response.

49. Which of the following is NOT an acceptable strategy for involving parents in the educational process?
(Easy) (Skill 10.2)

A. A newsletter in the L1 when possible.
B. Group meeting with parents.
C. Criticizing the ELL's performance during social events.
D. Calling the ELL's home.

Answer: C. Criticizing the ELL's performance during social events.
Answers A, B, and D are all acceptable methods for communicating with parents and keeping the lines of communication open. Answer C is incorrect because any criticism of a student should be in a formal session with only the student, parents or guardians, and possibly other school officials present. The meeting should be documented for future reference.

50. Which of the following statements does NOT illustrate Collier & Thomas's (1999-2000) principles for high academic standards?
(Easy) (Skill 10.2)

A. Set high goals for all students.
B. Including relevant life experiences in classroom content.
C. Appealing to parents for help raising ELL's low results in academics.
D. Talking with students.

Answer: C. Appealing to parents for help in raising ELL's low results in academics.
Answers A, B, and D are three principles of Collier & Thomas's principles of high academic standards for all students. (The others are challenging students toward cognitive complexity and developing students' language competencies. Answer C is the correct response. Appealing to parents will probably not result in better academic results in any student. Many students resent a teacher's attempts to get the parent's involved in their learning.

51. How are California's ELA Standards supported by the ELD standards? (Average) (Skill 11.1)

A. By using videos games designed for academic learning.
B. Through meaningful and comprehensible activities.
C. Activities designed to support language study through cultural studies.
D. By using L1

Answer: B. Through meaningful and comprehensible activities.
Answer A is incorrect because video games are not the only method a teacher would use to provide instruction to ELLs. Answer C is incorrect because culture is part of every activity and not a separate skill to be learned. While students may be instructed in L1, it would not be the only instructional method, so Answer D is incorrect. The correct answer is B. All instructional opportunities in ELD designed by the teacher should support the overall goals of ELA standards.

52. When employing group work on projects, accurate assessments for ELLs may be achieved using _____.
(Rigorous) (Skill 11.2)

A. individual assessment and assessment as a part of the group
B. assessment as a part of the group
C. assessment of the process only
D. individual assessment only

Answer: A. individual assessment and assessment as a part of the group
Answer B is incorrect because when assessing the group, there is no variation for individual performance. Everyone receives the same grade. Answer C is incorrect because it too does not assess individual performance. Answer D is incorrect because the ELL may know far more than he/she is able to convey on/during an evaluation.

Answer A is the correct answer. Assessing ELLs can be a challenging task. Sometimes, teachers are not really sure what the ELL knows. Therefore, it is better to obtain two more than one assessment to arrive at a more accurate evaluation. The individual grade may not reveal what the learner actually knows. For this reason, group grades, where the ELL has participated and contributed to the final outcome of a project, are often used to compensate for the ELL's inadequate expression or knowledge of testing procedures and questions.

53. What technique is being applied in the following situation? (Rigorous) (Skill 11.2)

> Ms. Jones has decided each ELL must know the planets in the solar system in order of their relationship to the sun. She decides that the acceptable standard will be 6 out of 8. Next, she assigns each of the ELL's to a group to investigate the planets and report back to the other members of the class. After the reports a skill will be given to the parents. A final evaluation will be given after all the activities

A. Curriculum mapping.
B. Curriculum calibration.
C. Backwards lesson planning.
D. Differentiated instruction.

Answer: C. Backwards lesson planning.
Answer A may be discarded as there is no mention of the teacher's schematic unit or course outline. Answer B is incorrect since no mention is made of the teacher's research into content standards across grade levels. Answer D is incorrect because the teacher has stated all students must learn at least 6 out of 8 of the planets and their relative order to the sun. Only answer C begins with the outcomes desired, and then a lesson is planned around the outcomes desired. This is backward lesson planning.

54. All of the following are criteria to be considered when reclassifying ELLs except _____. (Average) (Skill 12.1)

A. CELDT
B. parent or guardian opinion
C. Teacher evaluation
D. IQ exams

Answer: D. IQ exams
Answers A, B, and C are part of the criteria to be considered for reclassification of ELLs. The fourth one is a student's performance on basic skills, not IQ exams. Answer D is the correct response to the question.

55. Which of the following statements about tests is NOT accurate? (Average) (Skill 12.2)

A. Language proficiency tests are fairly accurate.
B. Unit tests and final exams are examples of language achievement tests.
C. Language tests test all areas of language learning.
D. The TOEFL is widely used by college admission officers for evaluating foreign candidates.

Answer: C. Language tests test all areas of language learning.

Responses A, B, and D are accurate statements about language tests. The correct answer is C. Language tests test only a small percentage of the possible items that can be tested in language. Most tests test only 12 items out of a possible 200.

56. Translation bias affects which testing criteria? (Rigorous) (Skill 12.3)

A. Validity
B. Reliability.
C. Practicality.
D. None of the above.

Answer: A. Validity

Answer B is incorrect because reliability is the construct concerning the similar results when the test is taken a second time. Answer C is incorrect since a test may be both reliable and valid yet not practical because of costs or time constraints. Avalos claims that translation bias is one of four biases which affect validity as the essence of a test may be lost in translation because of the difficulty of translating cultural concepts. A is the correct response.

57. To eliminate linguistic bias in tests, ELLs may be tested _____.
(Rigorous) (Skill 12.4)

    A. in English only
    B. in their first language
    C. in both their first language and in English
    D. using a translator

Answer: C. in both their first language and in English
Should ELLs be evaluated in English only (A), there is no way to know if the test is a true representation of the ELL's knowledge. If ELLs are tested in their first language (B), English learning is not evaluated. When ELLs are evaluated using a translator (D), translation bias and validity are lost. Only by testing the ELL in both their first language and in English is linguistic bias eliminated. C is the correct response.

58. Identify the most appropriate test for the employment of a court translator.
(Rigorous) (Skill 12.5)

    A. An achievement test.
    B. A placement test.
    C. A proficiency test.
    D. A diagnostic test.

Answer: C. A proficiency test.
Answer A is incorrect because achievement test are designed to test the mastery of course materials—what has been achieved. A placement test (B) tries to place a student in an appropriate place within a certain program based on abilities. Diagnostic tests (D) are used to determine a student's strengths and weaknesses so that additional instruction can be provided if needed. Only proficiency tests are used to evaluate candidates regardless of what or where prior training was received.

59. Teachers with heavy class loads who wish to assess their ELLs writing abilities may decide to use which of the following testing formats because of practicality?
(Average) (Skill 12.5)

    A. Research papers.
    B. One-page essays.
    C. Journals.
    D. Quick writes.

Answer: B. One-page essays.
Research papers (A) may be too long and complex for an overburden teacher to correct with frequency. Journals (C) can also be rambling, disjointed, and casual for evaluation purposes. Quick writes (D) may demonstrate what the ELL has captured of a lesson yet not allow enough time for studious, careful writing. Only B, one-page essays, combines the studious, careful writing aspect in a manageable length for the busy teacher.

60. District benchmarks are valuable to teachers because _____ .
(Easy) (Skill 12.6)

    A. Schools can be compared to each other.
    B. Students can be compared with grade level standards.
    C. Low performing schools can be compared with high performing schools in the district.
    D. One ELL's performance can be compared with other ELLs.

Answer: B. Students can be compared with grade level standards.
Since benchmarks are established to provide the standard by which all others are compared, it would be inappropriate to compare different schools using benchmarks (A) and (C). The benchmarks should not be used to compare different students with each other (D). The correct answer is B; students can be compared with grade level standards.

61. The following are all alternative assessments except _____.
(Easy) (Skill 13.1)

A. portfolios
B. teacher assessments
C. interviews with students
D. seeking parents' opinions

Answer: D. seeking parents' opinions
The correct answer is D. Seeking parent's opinions is valuable as it offers insight into the ELL, his/her community, and his/her family context. However, this would be an unacceptable form of alternative assessment.

62. An ELL's progress may be documented by all of the following except _____.
(Average) (Skill 13.1)

A. achievement tests
B. story or text retelling
C. diagnostic tests
D. language placement tests

Answer: C. diagnostic tests
Answers A, B, and D are acceptable forms of documenting student progress. The correct response is C. Diagnostic tests are used to determine a student's strengths and weaknesses so that additional instruction can be provided if needed.

63. To be eligible for the GATE program, a student must _____.
(Average) (Skill 13.1)

A. demonstrate English fluency
B. score high on standardized tests
C. be referred by his/her teacher
D. have an IQ $\geq$ 132

Answer: A. demonstrate English fluency
The correct response is A, a demonstrated fluency in English.

64. Which one of the follow is NOT a criterion for recommending students to Special Education?
(Easy) (Skill 13.2)

    A. have one of 13 recognized disabilities
    B. already have an IEP from another school
    C. have limitations related to language learning
    D. be at least 4 years old.

Answer: C. have limitations related to language learning
ELLs with one of the 13 recognized disabilities covered under Special Education mandates are just as eligible for Special Education Programs as and other student. C is the correct answer.

65. Which one of the following is NOT a reason for reteaching a skill?
(Rigorous) (Skill 13.3)

    A. the material was too complex
    B. the skill will be recycled in later units
    C. background knowledge was lacking
    D. the student has failed several standards

Answer: D. the student has failed several standards
Answer D is the correct response. When the student has failed to meet several standards, the teacher should consider whether the student needs to be considered for intervention.

66. The Civil Rights Act of 1964 established that _____ could not discriminate against English Language Learners.
(Easy) (Skill 14.1)

    A. Any program receiving federal financial assistance.
    B. Any landlord or restaurant owner.
    C. Any public or private school.
    D. Any employer operating under government regulations.

Answer: A. Any program receiving federal financial assistance.
The act established that schools, as recipients of federal funds, must provide equal educational opportunities for ELLS. "No person in the United States shall, on the grounds of race, color, or national origin, ...be denied the benefits of, or be subjected to discrimination under any program...receiving federal financial assistance."

67. The May 25 Memorandum of 1970 established that school districts with English Language Learners who were excluded from effective participation must:
(Average) (Skill 14.1)

A. Provide special education classes for those students.
B. Provide curriculum in the primary language.
C. Take affirmative steps to rectify the language deficiency.
D. Provide teachers familiar with the primary language and culture.

Answer: C. Take affirmative steps to rectify the language deficiency.
The memorandum does not require or specify what "affirmative steps" should be taken. Special education classes, primary language curriculum, or teachers familiar with the primary language and culture are not specified, so responses A, B, and D are incorrect.

68. A Language Assessment Committee and program criteria for ELL student assessment and monitoring became requirements for schools under:
(Rigorous) (Skill 14.1)

A. *Castaneda v. Pickard.*
B. *Lau v. Nichols.*
C. *Williams v. State of California.*
D. Proposition 227.

Answer: B. *Lau v. Nichols.*
Castaneda v. Pickard established the criteria schools must use to determine the effectiveness of their bilingual education programs. *Williams v. State of California* established that schools must provide equal access to instructional materials, safe and decent school facilities, and qualified teachers. Proposition 227 mandated sheltered English immersion for a temporary transitional period not to exceed one year. *Lau v. Nichols* came first, and established the schools' responsibility to assess and determine the effectiveness of their programs.

69. The Valenzuela Settlement requires that schools receiving funding for intensive instruction take what action to ensure that parents and guardians are aware of the procedure for alleging lack of opportunity if their student has not passed the high school exit exam by the end of 12th grade?
(Easy) (Skill 14.11)

A. Send a letter home.
B. Post a notice in the classroom.
C. Conduct administrative home visits.
D. Ensure personal contact by telephone.

Answer: B. Post a notice in the classroom.
The settlement does not require the school to send letters home, conduct home visits, or make telephone contact, so A,C, and D are incorrect responses.

70. Under the Williams verdict, low performing schools must provide students with what three things?
(Rigorous) (Skill 14.11)

A. Textbooks in the primary language, trained teachers, and after-school tutoring.
B. Trained teachers, safe facilities, and adequate textbooks for home and school.
C. Bilingual aides, bilingual teachers, and textbooks in the primary language.
D. Safe facilities, bilingual teachers, and textbooks for home and school.

Answer: B. Trained teachers, safe facilities, and adequate textbooks for home and school.
A. is not correct, because after-school tutoring is not required under *Williams*. Neither bilingual aides nor bilingual teachers are required, so responses C and D are incorrect.

71. Under the Williams Act, a complaint from parents cannot be turned away if it is:
(Average) (Skill 14.11)

A. Legitimate.
B. Expressed in English.
C. Written.
D. Delivered to the school board.

Answer: C. Written.
Legitimacy, language used, or the recipient of the complaint are not requirements for a complaint to be considered, so A, B, and D are incorrect responses.

72. **When must the CELDT test be administered to English Language Learners?**
(Average) (Skill 14.9)

A. At the conclusion of each school year.
B. Within 30 days of enrollment and annually until redesignation.
C. Within 90 days of enrollment.
D. Immediately upon enrollment.

Answer: B. Within 30 days of enrollment and annually until redesignation.

73. **State law mandates how many minutes of daily instruction in English for students who test below proficiency on CELDT?**
(Rigorous) (Skill 14.8)

A. 10-15.
B. 20-30.
C. 30-45.
D. 45-60.

Answer: C. Thirty to forty-five minutes.

74. **Which has been the most common program option for English Learners in California public schools?**
(Average) (Skill 14.7)

A. Mainstream programs with additional support.
B. Dual-language immersion programs.
C. Structured English Immersion classes.
D. Newcomer Centers.

Answer: A. Mainstream programs with additional support.

75. What is instrumental motivation for learning a second language?
(Rigorous) (Skill 15.2)

    A. A specific goal, such as a job.
    B. A wish to communicate within the culture.
    C. A permanent, culturally acquired motivation.
    D. A permanent motivation based on rewards and penalties.

Answer: A. A specific goal, such as a job.
A general wish to communicate is called integrative motivation, so B is incorrect. C is a personal, internal motivation. D is the closest to being correct, but instrumental motivation is temporary, not permanent, so A is the best response.

76. What defining instructional goal is shared by both ELD and SDAIE instruction?
(Rigorous) (Skill 14.10)

    A. Achieving English mastery as rapidly as possible.
    B. Providing ESL instruction during the regular school day.
    C. Accurately assessing student proficiency levels.
    D. Providing access to the core curriculum for all students.

Answer: D. Providing access to the core curriculum for all students.
The defining difference between ELD and SDAIE classrooms and other kinds of instructional designs is the objective of making core curriculum available to ELL students at all stages of English ability, so C is the correct response. A, Achieving English mastery rapidly, is the goal of ESL instruction and mainstream programs with support. B, Providing ESL instruction during the day, is mandated by most programs, but is not the defining goal of ELD or SDAIE, and D, accurate assessment, is also mandated by all programs, so is not a goal that differentiates ELD and SDAIE.

77. How are students grouped in ELD classrooms?
(Rigorous) (Skill 14.8)

    A. In heterogeneous groups to benefit less proficient students.
    B. In mixed groups of all CELDT levels.
    C. In groups separated into each CELDT level.
    D. In groups that span no more than two CELDT levels.

Answer: D. In groups that span no more than two CELDT levels.

78. Why was California's 2010 application for Race to the Top funding unsuccessful?
(Rigorous) (Skill 14.7)

A. The plan failed to establish a need for additional funding.
B. The plan failed to show an adequate population of English Language Learners.
C. The plan failed to show measures for individual achievement.
D. The plan failed to show measures for assessing the training of teachers.

Answer: C. The plan failed to show measures for individual achievement.
A persistent problem in assessment of ELL students has been the measurement of achievement among students who are progressing, but remain so far below grade level that that progress does not result in passing test scores. California has no difficulty demonstrating A, the need for additional funding, B, an adequate population of ELL students, or D, measures for assessing teacher training, so C is the only correct response.

79. What is SARC?
(Easy) (Skill 14.1)

A. School Acceleration Rate Credit.
B. Standard Area Recognition Cooperative.
C. School Accountability Report Card.
D. Standards Accelerated Rate Credit.

Answer: C. School Accountability Report Card.

80. Under Proposition 227, parents may sign a waiver if they want their student to receive:
(Rigorous) (Skill 14.2)

A. Total Immersion Language Instruction
B. Sheltered English Instruction
C. Bilingual Education
D. Special Education Designation

Answer: C. Bilingual Education.
A, Total Immersion, is offered at the discretion of the school district, as is B, Sheltered English Instruction. D, Special Education Designation, requires a parental waiver, but was not established under Proposition 227. C, Bilingual Education, is the only listed alternative for which parents must sign a waiver under Proposition 227.

81. According to CDOC figures, what is the likelihood of an EL student reclassifying to English proficient status after 10 years in California schools?
(Average) (Skill 14.2)

A. More than 90%.
B. More than 50%.
C. Less than 70%.
D. Less than 40%.

Answer: D. Less than 40%.

82. What challenge is common to a two-way immersion school?
(Average) (Skill 14.3)

A. Cultural and economic differences among the students.
B. Differences in ability levels among the students.
C. Differences in motivation among the students.
D. Differences in skill levels among the teachers.

Answer: A. Cultural and economic differences among the students.
Two-way immersion schools attract parents at a higher socioeconomic level who wish their children to become bilingual. Typically, those children are not from the same neighborhood as the ELL students, and the cultural and economic differences make social relationships difficult. Differences in B, ability levels, C, motivation, and D, skill levels, are no different than in any school setting, so A is the correct response.

83. Why are there no centralized government records for heritage language schools?
(Rigorous) (Skill 14.3)

A. They are private schools, and not required to keep government records.
B. They are after-school programs, and not required to keep government records.
C. Their records are in other languages.
D. They have been discouraged by the Department of Education.

Answer: A. They are private schools, and not required to keep government records.

84. **What did the 5-year CDOE study of California schools show about the effectiveness of various instructional methods for ELL students? (Rigorous) (Skill 14.5)**

   A. Students in Newcomer Centers for a year do significantly better over time.
   B. Students in pull-out programs do significantly better over time.
   C. Students in SDAIE classrooms do significantly better over time.
   D. No method was shown to be better than the others.

Answer: D. No method was shown to be better than the others.

85. **What three elements make a teacher "highly qualified?" (Average) (Skill 14.5)**

   A. B.A. degree, state credential, demonstrated subject matter mastery.
   B. M.A. degree, state credential, demonstrated subject matter mastery.
   C. State credential or waiver, B.A. degree, completion of student teaching.
   D. 160 completed credits, state credential or waiver, completion of student teaching.

Answer: A. B.A. degree, state credential, demonstrated subject matter mastery.
An M.A. degree is not required, so B is not correct. Completion of student teaching does not constitute being highly qualified, so C and D are not correct. A is the only correct response.

86. **What is the result of legislative language such as "overwhelmingly in English" and "appropriate additional support?" (Rigorous) (Skill 14.6)**

   A. Districts have wide latitude in interpretation.
   B. Best practices are difficult to identify and disseminate.
   C. There is a wide variance in the quality of services statewide.
   D. All of the above.

Answer: D. All of the above.
Because the language of the legislation is not specific, districts have a wide latitude in how they interpret the requirements of the law. Best practices have therefore been difficult to identify and share, and there is a wide variance in the quality of services around the state. D is the correct response.

87. **If a student is bilingual and biliterate by third grade, he is likely to be attending:**
(Average) (Skill 14.7)

A. A heritage language school.
B. A dual language school.
C. A Structured English Immersion school.
D. A newcomer center.

Answer: B. A dual language school.
A heritage language school aims to teach literacy only in the heritage language, so A is incorrect. A Structured English Immersion design and newcomer centers share the goal of English mastery, not maintenance or extension of the heritage language, so C and D are not correct. B is the correct response.

88. **If the teacher is speaking only English, but uses pantomime, cartooning, and acting to make his meaning comprehensible, the classroom is probably:**
(Average) (Skill 14.8)

A. An ELD class.
B. A SDAIE class.
C. A dual-immersion class.
D. A heritage language class.

Answer: B. A SDAIE class.
B is the best response, because SDAIE methods use every form of communication possible, from gestures to cartooning, to make meaning comprehensible for students. An ELD class simplifies, or shelters, the language used, a dual-immersion class uses both languages, and a heritage language class uses only the primary language, so A, C, and D are not as correct, although SDAIE methodology may be found in any of the others.

89. A Prereading Plan is one method to: (Rigorous) (Skill 15.3)

A. Separate the students into skill levels.
B. Focus attention on a topic.
C. Activate a student's prior knowledge.
D. Record student progress.

Answer: C. Activate a student's prior knowledge.
A prereading plan does not separate students into skill levels or record student progress, so A and D are not appropriate responses. While a prereading plan may focus attention, (B), its purpose is to activate a student's prior knowledge about a topic, so C is the best response.

90. Posters, exhibits, and organized lists are examples of what kind of literacy activities? (Average) (Skill 15.3)

A. Prereading
B. Extended
C. Scaffolded
D. Enriched

Answer: C. Scaffolded.
Posters and exhibits are not usually done before a reading activity, so A is not the best response. Organized lists are not usually done after a reading activity, so B is also incorrect. While posters and exhibits are sometimes enrichment activities, organized lists are not, so D is not the best response. All of the three activities are ways of scaffolding reading, so C is the best answer.

91. A pull-out program that teaches English learners about the language is: (Easy) (Skill 19.1)

A. Grammar-based.
B. Communication-based.
C. Content-based.
D. Needs-based.

Answer: A. Grammar-based.
Communication-based instruction (B) emphasizes using the language in real interactions, with less emphasis on correct usage. Content-based instruction (C) is centered on the material being taught in the communication, and needs-based instruction (C) is built around survival skills. Only grammar-based teaching (A) actually teaches about the language itself.

92. **Mock telephone conversations, student surveys, and student-developed dialogs are examples of:**
   (Average) (Skill 19.2)

   A. Structured English immersion.
   B. Content-based ESL.
   C. Communicative language activities.
   D. Grammar-based language instruction.

Answer: C. Communicative language activities.
Structured English immersion programs and content-based ESL (A and B) have the objective of introducing the student to core academic curriculum and grammar-based instruction (D) teaches about the language. Communicative language activities include such projects as real conversations, surveys, and invented dialogs which promote active, authentic communication.

93. **Imperfect language structures that are occasional results of carelessness or memory laps and should not be corrected by the instructor are:**
   (Easy) (Skill 19.3)

   A. Mistakes.
   B. Errors.
   C. Developmental.
   D. Implicit.

Answer: A. Mistakes.
Errors (B) are repeated and indicate a misunderstanding that needs to be addressed. Developmental imperfections (C) are a natural part of the learning process and will be addressed, and there is no such thing as implicit imperfections, so (D) cannot be correct. Mistakes are caused by carelessness or slipups, and are not repeated over time, so they do not need to be addressed by the instructor. A is the best response.

94. Key words and phrases such as "In the first place," "Until," or "Therefore," that help students make sense of text are called:
(Average) (Skill 20.2)

    A. Idioms.
    B. Verbal responses.
    C. Details.
    D. Discourse markers.

Answer: D. Discourse markers.
An idiom is a word or phrase with a meaning other than its literal definition, so A is incorrect. The words and phrases listed are not necessarily verbal, so B is also incorrect. They are not details, so C cannot be the answer. Discourse markers help students divide a text into manageable chunks and increase comprehension. D is the correct answer.

95. The main purpose of brainstorming is to:
(Easy) (Skill 20.3)

    A. Assess students' prior knowledge.
    B. Activate students' prior knowledge.
    C. Increase students' prior knowledge.
    D. Compare students' prior knowledge.

Answer: B. Activate students' prior knowledge.
Brainstorming is a preliminary activity, not designed to assess (A), teach (C) or compare (D). B is the correct response.

96. The main purpose of role plays and creative drama activities are to:
(Easy) (Skill 20.3)

    A. Facilitate receptive language skills.
    B. Facilitate productive language skills.
    C. Facilitate both productive and receptive language skills.
    D. Facilitate neither productive nor receptive language skills.

Answer: C. Facilitate both productive and receptive language skills.
Role plays and creative drama activities provide practice in listening, understanding, and speaking, so C is the best response.

97. ELD language standards are designed to:
(Rigorous) (Skill 21.1)

    A. Take the place of ELA standards for ELL students.
    B. Bring ELA standards into line with ELL students' language abilities.
    C. Provide more realistic standards for ELL students.
    D. Provide a scaffolding for ELL students to achieve ELA standards.

Answer: D. Provide a scaffolding for ELL students to achieve ELA standards.
ELD standards are not intended to replace ELA standards (A), lower them to students' language abilities (B), or provide a more realistic measure (C). ELD standards are intended to provide a means for ELL students to reach and meet ELA standards.

98. Duet reading and choral reading are methods for improving:
(Average) (Skill 21.2)

    A. Confidence.
    B. Comprehension.
    C. Fluency.
    D. Word recognition.

Answer: C. Fluency.
Duet reading and choral reading provide opportunities for students to compare their own pronunciation, intonation, pitch, and stress with that of native speakers. Such activities do not always increase confidence (A), comprehension (B), or word recognition (D). They are intended to increase fluency, which is the ability to speak easily and smoothly.

99. Multicultural texts are most helpful if they:
(Rigorous) (Skill 21.4)

    A. Present a positive picture of a minority culture.
    B. Present a realistic picture of a minority culture.
    C. Present an idealistic picture of a minority culture.
    D. Present a negative picture of a minority culture.

Answer: B. Present a realistic picture of a minority culture.
Research has shown that positive (A), idealistic (C) and negative (D) portrayals of a minority culture can negatively impact members of that culture. The best texts present realistic pictures of minority people grappling with real-life problems, so B is the best response.

100. ELL students' written language will typically lag behind their oral language by:
(Rigorous) (Skill 21.5)

    A. A full year.
    B. One-two years.
    C. Five years.
    D. More than five years.

B. One-two years.

101. The most successful teaching of language conventions such as spelling, grammar, and punctuation is done by:
(Rigorous) (Skill 21.5)

    A. Direct instruction.
    B. Practice drills.
    C. The presentation of well-written materials.
    D. The presentation of poorly written materials.

Answer: C. The presentation of well-written materials.
Direct instruction (A) and drills (B) have been found to have little positive impact on the successful recognition and adoption of language conventions. The presentation of poorly-written materials (D) could have a negative effect. Presenting well-written materials has been found to most directly improve the use of language conventions, so C is the best response.

102. Front-loading vocabulary by creating a word bank before confronting a text is one way to:
(Easy) (Skill 22.1)

    A. Create background knowledge.
    B. Provide cognitively engaging input.
    C. Assess students' prior knowledge.
    D. Clarify objectives.

Answer: A. Create background knowledge.
Familiarizing students with vocabulary before they approach a text may be cognitively engaging or not, so B is not correct. Presenting vocabulary in advance is not an assessment process, and does not clarify objectives, so C and D are incorrect. The purpose is to create background knowledge for use in addressing the new text, so A is the correct response.

103. Scaffolded interactions typically follow which pattern of progression?
(Rigorous) (Skill 22.1)

 A. Student-text, student-student, student-teacher.
 B. Student-teacher, student-text, student-student.
 C. Student-student, student-teacher, student-text.
 D. Student-teacher, student-student, student-text.

Answer: D. Student-teacher, student-student, student-text.
In a typical scaffolded lesson, the teacher will give instruction, the student will practice with another student or students, and the text will come last.

104. Resources such as realia, posters, films, and primary-source guests can all
be used to:
(Rigorous) (Skill 22.2)

 A. Analyze a text.
 B. Extend a text.
 C. Contextualize a text.
 D. Take the place of a text.

Answer: C. Contextualize a text.
Such resources will not analyze the text (A), extend the text (B), or take the place of the text (D). They will contextualize the text for the student, so C is the best response.

105. Understanding one's own learning patterns is part of:
(Easy) (Skill 22.2)

 A. Cognition.
 B. Metacognition.
 C. Recognition.
 D. Ignition.

Answer: B. Metacognition.
Cognition (A) is thinking. Recognition (C) is realizing or comprehending, and ignition (D) is simply starting. Metacognition is the process of thinking about thinking – analyzing and understanding one's own mental processes for the purpose of learning more efficiently, so B is the best response.

106. **In building vocabulary, visuals, manipulatives, and realia are examples of:**
(Average) (Skill 22.1)

A. Contextual support.
B. Metacognitive support.
C. The affective filter.
D. Distractions.

Answer: A. Contextual support.
Metacognitive support helps students think about thought processes, so B is incorrect. The affective filter and distractions work against learning vocabulary, so C and D cannot be right. Visuals, manipulatives, and realia help embed new vocabulary in a context so that it can be recalled. A is the best response.

107. **What activity is rated by many teachers as the single easiest way to learn new vocabulary?**
(Average) (Skill 22.1)

A. Learned dialogs.
B. Invented role plays.
C. Singing.
D. Playing games.

Answer: C. Singing
While the other listed activities are helpful, putting new words with familiar tunes makes them not only easy to remember, but virtually impossible to forget. C is the best answer.

108. **Asking students to demonstrate mastery of language objectives by writing a single sentence on an index card as they leave class is an example of:**
(Rigorous) (Skill 22.1)

A. Informal assessment.
B. Standardized assessment.
C. Formative assessment.
D. Formal assessment.

Answer: A. Informal assessment.
Standardized assessments are not developed by the teacher, so B cannot be correct. Formative assessments are given as class proceeds to determine whether understanding is taking place, not at the end, so C is incorrect, and a formal assessment would provide a student with time to study and prepare. A is the best response.

115. Which one of the following is NOT an example of discrimination? (Average) (Skill 23.4)

A. Attacking a woman because she is wearing a burka.
B. Stating that the custom of not looking someone in the eye is devious.
C. Native born immigrant children feeling superior to non-native born immigrants.
D. Minority teachers who are not well trained teaching in remote regions.

Answer: B. Stating that the custom of not looking someone in the eye is devious.
Answers A, C, and D are all examples of cultural discrimination—actual behavior towards another person or group. Cultural bias is interpreting and judging other cultures by one's culture. The correct answer is B.

116. Which of the following illustrates the hardships of immigrants? (Average) (Skill 23.5)

A. long waiting periods to receive basic medical services.
B. difficulty adjusting to climate changes
C. retraining to secure professional status
D. All of the above.

Answer: D. All of the above.

117. When Ms. Jones notices that Yuki is NOT participating in group discussions, she believes that Yuki sees her as _____. (Average) (Skill 23.6)

A. an enemy.
B. someone not giving her sufficient time to answer.
C. silly, for asking stupid questions.
D. an authority figure who has not asked her a question.

Answer: D. an authority figure who has not asked her a question.
It is doubtful that an ELL would see the teacher as an enemy (A). It is also unlikely that Yuki sees the teacher as (C) silly for leading a group discussion where teachers encourage many different responses. Since this is a group discussion, there is little pressure to formulate quick responses (B). Thus, Answer D is the correct response.

118. **Which of the following terms is the correct one for the situation below? (Rigorous) (Skill 24.1)**

> Ursula has lived in the U.S. for nearly five years. She rarely talks about her homeland and tries to imitate her classmates' speech and behavior. She is striving to be accepted by the culture surrounding her.

    A. Acculturation.
    B. Assimilation.
    C. Accommodation.
    D. Transculturation.

Answer: B. Assimilation.
Ursula is making an effort to be like those around her. Her willingness to imitate her classmates' speech and behavior shows her desire to be accepted by her peers. Given her willingness to act like her classmates, Ursula seems to be highly motivated to "fit in" or assimilate.

119. **Which of the following items would cause culture shock to newly arrived immigrants? (Rigorous) (Skill 24.2)**

    A. kissing in public
    B. using a drive-in bank teller
    C. bathing daily with hot, running water
    D. All of the above

Answer: D. All of the above.

120. Based on the example below, in which stage of assimilation is Pierre? (Average) (Skill 24.3)

> Pierre arrived in the U. S. in 2003 at the age of 12. He has been living with his uncle and aunt, who are well assimilated into the U.S. culture. Pierre misses his parents and brothers. He finds his high school studies fairly easy and his classmates lazy. He is worried about his goal of becoming a professional soccer player and doesn't understand why he can't have wine with his meals

    A. Honeymoon stage.
    B. Hostility stage.
    C. Humor stage.
    D. Home stage.

Answer: B. Hostility stage.
While Pierre is probably adapting, he still finds his culture superior ("His classmates are lazy" and "why he can't have wine with his meal') and the new culture deficient ("worried about his goal of becoming a professional soccer player").

121. When faced with cultural habits or beliefs that are completely different from the teacher's beliefs, what is the best way for the teacher to address this issue in the classroom?
(Rigorous) (Skill 24.4)

    A. Politely correct the ELL in private.
    B. Address the issue with the ELL's parents.
    C. Ask for administrative assistance in resolving the issue.
    D. Agree to disagree.

Answer: D. Agree to disagree.
When teachers encounter irreconcilable differences with an ELL's beliefs and culture, the teacher should not try to 'correct' (A, B, and C) the beliefs or values of ELLs but respect them. However, she can present new and differing points of view to permit growth, learning, and understanding of others and the new culture. When these differences cannot be resolved, she must respectfully D. Agree to disagree.

122. How can teachers resolve the issue of students who see her as an authority figure and disdain group work?
(Rigorous) (Skill 24.5)

   A. Accept their feelings and permit them to work alone.
   B. Give lectures on the content and assign individual work.
   C. Balance group work with individual work.
   D. Assign group work and use teacher-directed instruction when necessary

Answer: D. Assign group work and use teacher-directed instruction when necessary
The positive aspects of group work are numerous. Once individuals learn to work in a group, the results are generally positive. However, in some cultures, the teacher is the only authority and 'learning' is considered impossible unless the teacher gives direct instruction. Competition may be fierce and individuals accustom to working alone. Therefore, the best response, to accommodate these different beliefs about education, is D.

123. Which of the following types of reading materials should be avoided?
(Average) (Skill 24.6)

   A. Culturally inclusive.
   B. Culturally sensitive.
   C. Inaccurate gender roles.
   D. Distinct genres.

Answer: C. Inaccurate gender roles.
Reading materials should be culturally inclusive (A), culturally sensitive (B), and of distinct genres (D). Inaccurate gender roles (C) should be avoided. Answer C is the best option.

124. The second most spoken language in California is:
(Easy) (Skill 25.1)

   A. Chinese
   B. Japanese
   C. Spanish
   D. Vietnamese

Answer: C. Spanish

125. **Which event led to the Freedom Flights from Cuba?**
(Rigorous) (Skill 25.2)

    A. the Bay of Pigs invasion
    B. death of Che Guevara
    C. overthrow of Fulgencio Batista
    D. release of Guantanamo Bay detainees

Answer: C. overthrow of Fulgencio Batista
The Freedom Flights from Cuba to the United States began after the 1959 Cuban Revolution that overthrew Batista. They refer in particular the wave of Cuban American refugees who fled to the U.S. during the years 1960 and 1979. Answer C is the best response.

126. **_____ is the term used when a father leaves his native country, comes to the U.S., gets a job, and sends for his wife.**
(Easy) (Skill 25.2)

    A. Assimilation
    B. Socioeconomic improvement
    C. Secondary migration
    D. Accommodation

Answer: C. Secondary migration
The correct term is secondary migration and Answer C is the correct answer.

127. **When children arriving in the U.S. begin using English in a natural way, what cultural phenomenon occurs?**
(Rigorous) (Skill 25.3)

    A. additive bilingualism
    B. subtractive bilingualism
    C. cultural loss
    D. Transculturation

Answer: C. cultural loss
Transculturation (D) is defined as acculturation by an individual, not a group. Some immigrants may become bilingual, but most do not. Additive bilingualism (A) occurs when a second language is acquired without the loss of the first language. Subtractive bilingualism (B) occurs when the child is not provided with the opportunity to fully develop his first language. The correct answer is C culture loss since in most cases the child will not become a fully functioning bilingual, and therefore, loose a significant part of his cultural heritage.

128. **When newcomers and U. S. born members from the same culture group become opposed, this is referred to as _____ .**
(Easy) (Skill 25.3)

   A. polarization
   B. discrimination
   C. intra-cultural division
   D. acculturation

Answer: A. polarization

129. **Identify the way in which oral cultures differ from the U. S. culture.**
(Rigorous) (Skill 26.2)

   A. Use of linear, single topic stories when narrating
   B. Assume shared knowledge of their audience.
   C. Interrupt and challenge teacher's authority.
   D. Use silence as a power tool.

Answer: B. Assume shared knowledge of their audience
The use of linear, single topic stories when narrating (A) is common in U.S. culture and is not the correct choice. Option C is a rude behavior from students and is not associated with only oral cultures. Option D is a tool power of Native Americans (and other cultures). Option B is the correct response because oral cultures feel they are part of the narrative and assume others are too.

130. **To teach non-native speakers of English, the cultural differences in communication styles, _____ is appropriate.**
(Rigorous) (Skill 26.3)

   A. the use of role-plays
   B. debating
   C. holding classroom discussions
   D. extra wait time

Answer: A. the use of role-plays
Answer B debating is a difficult task for beginning ELLs and is a formalized speech pattern. Holding classroom discussions (C) is valuable for encouraging participation in activating prior knowledge and increasing learning, but will do little to demonstrate communication differences between cultures. Providing extra wait time (D) gives the ELL time to formulate his/her answers, but does not necessarily improve communicative competence. The best option is A where students' have the opportunity to act out situations in different contexts. Using this type of activity, ELLs can observe and internalize different communication styles and cement their learning.

131. An open dialogue with parents helps teachers to:
(Average) (Skill 27.1)

A. Explain their standards.
B. Discipline their students.
C. Understand cultural differences.
D. Teach parents as well as students.

Answer: C. Understand cultural differences.
Disciplining students, teaching parents, and explaining classrooms standards are all important objectives, but understanding cultural differences is essential to the development of culturally inclusive instruction, so C is the correct response.

132. A student who assists others, is sensitive to others' feelings, and seeks guidance is:
(Rigorous) (Skill 27.2)

A. Field independent.
B. Field sensitive.
C. Field dependent.
D. Field insensitive.

Answer: B. Field sensitive.
A field independent person thinks independently, and a field dependent person is overly dependent on others' responses and reactions. A field insensitive person is oblivious to others, so B correctly describes one who is helpful, sensitive, and seeks guidance.

133. Teachers reared in North America are typically:
(Rigorous) (Skill 27.2)

A. Field independent.
B. Field sensitive.
C. Field dependent.
D. Field insensitive.

Answer: A. Field independent.

134. Home visits, interviews, and oral histories are ways for a teacher to: (Easy) (Skill 27.3)

   A. Learn about students' home cultures.
   B. Teach about the students' new culture.
   C. Learn about debilitating or abusive conditions.
   D. Change the way students think.

Answer: A. Learn about students' home cultures.
Interviews and oral histories are opportunities to learn, not teach, so B and C are incorrect. Such experiences are not intended to change the way students think, so D cannot be the answer. A is the correct response.

135. A student who believes the teacher is shirking his duty by assigning group work instead of lecturing is probably: (Average) (Skill 28.1)

   A. Uneducated.
   B. Rude.
   C. Lazy.
   D. From a different cultural background.

Answer: D. From a different cultural background.
Students may be uneducated, rude, or lazy, but believing that the teacher should lecture does not indicate any of those deficiencies. Students from other countries have often been taught to believe that what the teacher has to say is more important than what any student could contribute, so group work wastes time. D is the appropriate response.

136. No Child Left Behind encourages schools to raise expectations for all students by: (Rigorous) (Skill 28.2)

   A. Penalizing low scores.
   B. Rewarding high scores.
   C. Disaggregating data.
   D. Allocating funds based on improvement.

Answer: C. Disaggregating data.
Formerly, schools could aggregate the low scores of their English Language Learners with their native speakers to get a better-looking testing result. NCLB specifically forbids the practice, so C is the best answer.

137. **Open discussion of sensitive topics such as racism and discrimination is part of:**
(Average) (Skill 28.2)

A. A reactive approach.
B. An inactive approach.
C. An active approach.
D. A proactive approach.

Answer: D. A proactive approach.
An inactive response means to do nothing; a reactive approach responds to trouble after it occurs, and an active approach simply means to address the problem. A proactive approach is best because it addresses any conflicts before they occur by starting and maintaining open communication. D is the best answer.

138. **Zero tolerance for culturally insensitive behavior requires:**
(Average) (Skill 28.2)

A. Keen awareness of potential conflicts.
B. In-depth study of world history.
C. Constant questioning of students.
D. Strict control of conversations.

Answer: A. Keen awareness of potential conflicts.
Strict control of conversations would be counter-productive to a culturally inclusive environment, as would the constant questioning of students. An in-depth study of history may or may not lead to an understanding of current attitudes. A, a keen awareness of potential conflicts, is the best response.

139. **An advantage of strong community involvement in school activities is:**
(Easy) (Skill 28.2)

A. Parents learn along with their students.
B. Teachers can share the work load.
C. The community becomes a resource if problems occur.
D. Classroom utility is maximized.

Answer: C. The community becomes a resource if problems occur.
Strong community involvement means that community members are more likely to understand and support school policies. That support may not affect parent learning, teacher workload, or use of the classroom facilities, so C is the best response.

140. Encouraging parents to continue speaking the first language at home is:
(Rigorous) (Skill 28.3)

    A. Counterproductive.
    B. Harmful.
    C. Useless.
    D. Advantageous.

Answer: D. Advantageous.
It was believed, and taught, in earlier times, that parents of ELLs should encourage the use of English in the home to facilitate children's assimilation into the new culture. Now research has shown that maintaining the first language is an advantage to the social, emotional, and linguistic development of the child, so D is the correct response.

141. The most frequent statement of concern made by adults about their children's schooling is:
(Average) (Skill 29.1)

    A. I wish I had had these opportunities.
    B. They don't do things the way they used to.
    C. Kids today have it too easy.
    D. Kids today have it too hard.

Answer: B. They don't do things the way they used to.
Each of the mentioned concerns has been expressed by parents, but "They don't do things the way they used to," is the most frequently stated, so B is the correct response.

142. Open communication with parents can help teachers understand:
(Rigorous) (Skill 29.1)

    A. Why students perform poorly.
    B. Why students perform well.
    C. Elements of native culture parents want to preserve.
    D. Elements of native culture parents want to eliminate.

Answer: C Elements of native culture parents want to preserve.
Open communication with parents can reveal any of these items, but the teacher's objective is to learn what elements of native culture are considered essential by parents, so C is the appropriate response.

143. Mentoring and tutoring are ways to get involved for:
(Easy) (Skill 29.2)

    A. Teachers.
    B. Peers.
    C. Parents and grandparents.
    D. Administrators.

Answer: C Parents and grandparents.
Teachers, peers, and administrators are already involved, so C is the correct answer.

144. Teachers have a legal obligation to inform parents about their opportunity to participate in:
(Average) (Skill 29.4)

    A. Classroom visits.
    B. Tutoring.
    C. After-school activities.
    D. Policy-making committees.

Answer: D. Policy-making committees.
Classroom visits, tutoring, and after-school activities are all important for parents to know about, but the law mandates that they be informed of their right to participate in policy-making committees, so D is the best response.

145. Bias-motivated injustice and violence can be reduced by:
(Average) (Skill 29.5)

    A. School security guards.
    B. Police visits.
    C. Anti-racist education.
    D. Stronger punishments.

Answer: C. Anti-racist education.
Stronger enforcement measures have not been shown to be effective in reducing bias-motivated injustice and violence. C, anti-racist education, is the correct answer.

146. Adding ethnic content to the curriculum without restructuring is:
(Rigorous) (Skill 30.1)

   A. The transformative approach.
   B. The additive approach.
   C. The reductive approach.
   D. The simplest approach.

Answer: B. The additive approach.
The transformative approach changes curriculum. Adding ethnic content is neither reductive nor simplest, so B, the additive approach is correct.

147. Extending student understanding of the complexity of U.S. society is a goal of:
(Easy) (Skill 30.1)

   A. The transformative approach.
   B. The additive approach.
   C. The reductive approach.
   D. The simplest approach.

Answer: A. The transformative approach.

148. Service learning projects and personal reflection are part of:
(Average) (Skill 30.2)

   A. Additive curriculum.
   B. Transformative curriculum.
   C. Bilingual curriculum.
   D. Cross-cultural curriculum.

Answer: B Transformative curriculum.
Transformative curriculum aims to change the way students think by providing opportunities for experiences that require activity and reflection. B is the best answer.

149. The learning style of Hispanic students is more likely to be:
(Rigorous) (Skill 30.4)

    A. Auditory.
    B. Visual.
    C. Kinesthetic.
    D. Any of these.

Answer: A. Auditory.
Research indicates that most Hispanic students are auditory learners.

150. American Indians and Asians are more likely to succeed in an environment that is:
(Rigorous) (Skill 30.4)

    A. Cooperative.
    B. Competitive.
    C. Individualized.
    D. Rigidly structured.

Answer: A. Cooperative.
Competitive, individualized, and rigidly structured curricula are less effective for these ethnic groups than cooperative group activities, so A is the correct response.

Sample Essays

Essay #1

Authentic use of language, where students need to use English to give or receive information, is important in the language acquisition process.

1. Why is the use of meaningful, authentic communication essential in second language acquisition?

2. What activities would you select to promote meaningful and real communication among ELL students and others in your classroom? Justify your choices by telling how those activities facilitate language acquisition.

Sample Response

Research tells us that meaningful communication in the second language serves several useful purposes. As students focus on getting or giving real messages, their affective shield is lowered and they are less likely to refuse to speak for fear of making errors. Also, such situations provide students with the opportunity to actually communicate something they know, which increases confidence. Students get chances to rehearse real-life situations and prepare for them. Students are more likely to focus attention, realizing that they will be able to use what they are learning in the real world. Prior knowledge and existing skills can come into play, which increases confidence and comfort.

To promote listening comprehension, I would have students collect information from taped telephone messages, such as movie times, library hours, or hospital visiting hours. The students can listen as many times as necessary without embarrassment, and the skill will be useful in real life. To promote speaking facility, I would have students improvise dialogs for situations such as eating in the cafeteria or shopping for clothing. After practicing with classmates, we could invite a cafeteria worker to come into the classroom and have the students ask her for the various items they want to eat, or bring in a rack of clothing and have someone take the role of a salesgirl, giving students the opportunity to measure their own comprehensibility. For reading and writing, students can do such activities as writing notes in English to one another – an activity that they enjoy. Such activities are high in interest and empower students to express themselves and work to understand others using the new language.

Essay #2:

The ability to use alternative forms of assessment is necessary to fully authenticate an English Language Learner's (ELL's) progress in English Language Development (ELD).

- Why is the use of alternative assessments essential to fully evaluate an ELL's progress in ELD?

- Name one form of alternative assessment. Explain how this form of assessment contributes to a fuller understanding of the progress being made by an ELL.

Sample Response

Alternative assessments are essential to fully understand an ELL's progress in ELD because all too often an ELL cannot fully express himself or herself in the new language. Alternative assessments are criterion-referenced because they are based on actual classroom work and performance. The ELL may have the knowledge to understand the classroom work and function well yet lack the language skills to convey this information to the classroom teacher.

An alternative to the typical classroom tests used for assessment are portfolios. By maintaining a portfolio of the ELL's work over a period of time, the classroom teacher can get a clearer view of the work being done by the ELL and where instruction needs to be provided. By selecting a variety of documents to include in the portfolio, a clearer picture of the performance may be obtained. Some of the documents I would include in a portfolio would be samples of the ELL's work such as writing samples, mathematics problems, social studies reports and science papers that show growth over a period of time. Follow-ups to regular classroom work such as art projects or poetry can be included to demonstrate the creativity of the ELL. The way in which an ELL expresses himself or herself through a creative outlet provides powerful insights into the ELL's personality and reasoning powers.

The ELL's self-assessment can be included. Frequently, the ELL's are harsher on themselves than the teacher. The ELL's insights into his or her own problems can provide guidelines for the teacher. They may indicate where the ELL feels additional instruction is needed or where it is not. Self-assessment is a powerful motivator, because the ELL feels that what he or she thinks is important to the teacher.

Essay #3

California schools have implemented a variety of instructional designs for English Language Learners.

1. Compare and contrast the advantages and disadvantages of any two of the common instructional modes: two-way immersion (dual language) programs, newcomer centers, structured (sheltered) English programs, mainstream programs with appropriate support, ELD, or SDAIE classrooms.

2. If you were starting a new program for English Language Learners, which design would you select? Explain your decision.

Sample Response

Two-way immersion programs have the advantage of leveling the playing field for English speakers and those with limited English, since all students are equally involved in learning a new language. Bilingualism is an advantage for everyone, and two-way immersion prevents the loss of the heritage language. The disadvantages come from mixing students from different socioeconomic backgrounds and unequal advantages, such as home computers and parental support. Also, qualified bilingual teachers can be hard to find.

Mainstream programs with appropriate support have the advantage of keeping the English Language Learner in the classroom with his English-speaking peers, which maximizes the opportunity for student-student interaction and provides some access to core curriculum – especially in P.E., art, music, science, and math, where language proficiency is less important. The disadvantages come in the interpretation of "appropriate support," which can mean anything from a bilingual aide who translates teacher instructions, to peer tutoring, to pull-out ESL sessions during the regular day. The effectiveness of these supports varies widely, and some – such as a translating peer or aide – have been shown to actually retard language acquisition.

The CDOE five-year study of programs throughout California indicated that there is no significant difference in the effectiveness of the various programs as reflected in CELDT scores. If I were starting a new program, I would select the dual language immersion model, in spite of the difficulties in implementation. Bilingualism is a great advantage to native speakers as well as limited English speakers, and the process of learning to communicate in a second language promotes understanding of newcomers' difficulties. Moreover, honoring and preserving the heritage language of ELLs can help prevent emotional and familial problems. These advantages seem to me to outweigh the problems of finding qualified teachers and promoting social interaction.

Essay #4:

Use the information below to complete the assignment that follows.

The process of culture shock can be difficult for most English Language Learning students.

- Describe one strategy an ESOL instructor can use to support the ELL in the process of culture shock.

- Explain why the strategy would be related to better academic achievement.

Sample Response

One strategy an ESOL teacher can use to support English Language Learners suffering from culture shock would be to assign another student of the same language background to be the buddy of the newly arrived student. Since each school has its own rules about how to line up, how to ask for food, or how and where to sit, it is intimidating for newcomers to face these obstacles alone.

This strategy would be effective in supporting a newly arrived English Language Learner and promoting feelings of safety and security. By helping the new student to overcome the anxieties of the first days in the new school, the ESOL teacher is helping the English Language Learner work through the hostility stage of culture shock. As the student develops more coping mechanisms by reducing his or her anxiety, the student will be able to focus more on learning.